Linda E. Olds, Ph.D., is an associate professor and department head
of psychology at Linfield College, McMinnsville, Oregon.

FULLY HUMAN

DISCARDED

HUMAN

*How Everyone Can Integrate the Benefits
of Masculine and Feminine Sex Roles*

LINDA E. OLDS

A SPECTRUM BOOK

Prentice-Hall, Inc., *Englewood Cliffs, New Jersey 07632*

Library of Congress Cataloging in Publication Data

Olds, Linda E.
    Fully human.

    (A Spectrum Book)
    Bibliography: p.
    Includes index.
        1. Sex role.   2. Androgyny (Psychology)
I. Title.
HQ1075.04   305.3   81-10630
                             AACR2

ISBN 0-13-332213-0

ISBN 0-13-332205-X {PBK.}

This Spectrum Book is available to business and organizations
at a special discount when ordered in large quantities. For
information, contact Prentice-Hall, Inc., General Book Marketing,
Special Sales Division, Englewood Cliffs, N.J. 07632.

10 9 8 7 6 5 4 3 2 1

Editorial / production supervision
and interior design by Kimberly Mazur
Cover design by Jeannette Jacobs
Manufacturing buyer: Cathie Lenard

Prentice-Hall International, Inc., *London*
Prentice-Hall of Australia Pty. Limited, *Sydney*
Prentice-Hall of Canada, Ltd., *Toronto*
Prentice-Hall of India Private Limited, *New Delhi*
Prentice-Hall of Japan, Inc., *Tokyo*
Prentice-Hall of Southeast Asia Pte. Ltd., *Singapore*
Whitehall Books Limited, *Wellington, New Zealand*

To my mother and father

CONTENTS

PREFACE

This book is dedicated to the exploration of the image of human wholeness: how we can become more fully human as men and women, how we can move beyond the stereotypic traits narrowly defined for each sex and embrace our full human potential, how we can take the best of both worlds of traditional masculinity and femininity and create a new and dynamic balance in our individual lives. Much has been written on the subject of changing sex roles, both in terms of external issues in the world (how women can move ahead in the work force, how men can become more involved in child-rearing) and internal issues of personality development (how women can become more assertive, how men can become more aware and expressive of their feelings). Often, however, these two directions of exploration have remained inaccessible to each other.

Social psychologists have addressed themselves to the questions of what men and women typically can or cannot do in the world and how flexible their behaviors are in the face of a variety of sex role related tasks.

This research gives much insight into what sex role flexibility might look like, and it leaves us with the observation that people who have developed both the traditionally masculine and feminine traits in themselves are *more* adaptive and flexible in meeting a whole range of life situations than people who have specialized in only one set of sex role traits. However, it offers few clues or hints about how to evolve in the direction of fuller human development.

In contrast, the research of clinical psychologists is rich in insights about the process of human development, but those clinicians who have directed their attention to the subject of sex roles have been either unduly abstract and metaphysical or overly pragmatic, lacking a grounding in theory. The Jungian tradition in particular has remained relatively inaccessible to the non-clinician, despite its special relevance to the topic of human wholeness, and it has remained largely within the realm of myth and metaphor. Since one of the major problems of this age has been the loss of access to the world of living myth and metaphor, the Jungian approach often remains untranslated and alien to a contemporary world very much in need of its insights.

This book, therefore, is written at the edge of this boundary between the insights of social psychology and of clinical psychology. We will explore what each field has to offer to the basic question of how we can become more fully human by developing the entire range of personality characteristics in ourselves, rather than rationing them out by sex. This book is dedicated to the creation of a dialogue about external and internal sex role development: external development refers to new behaviors and actions in the world, and internal development refers to the broadening of those inner values, orientations, and modes of consciousness that affect personality development.

In recent years the concept of androgyny has been revived from its ancient groundings in myth and has been proposed by both social psychologists and clinicians as a new norm for sex role and personality development. *Androgyny,* coming from the Greek words for man and woman, refers to the relatively equal development and flexible integration of both the traditionally-labeled masculine and traditionally-labeled feminine characteristics in one individual of either sex. This book will explore the concept of androgyny from both an external (social psychological) and an internal (clinical, philosophical) dimension. While I will use the word androgyny as a complex symbol for the fully integrated human personality, I have no objection to going beyond this word to speak instead of total humanness. New words often alienate and, while they are effective in refocusing attention on a crucial aspect of human development, they often will be outgrown as the concept they represent gains in cultural acceptance. Androgyny is not a new concept, but it is only recently returning to our cultural consciousness as an idea that holds great potential for personality and social development. It is my hope that this book will make this concept accessible to those struggling for new options to the traditional sex role dichotomies and polarities in which we often feel cut off from our full potential. It is a book dedicated, however, to the preservation of *both* the metaphorically masculine and feminine realms of behaviors, values, and inner orientations. The contemporary person in our world cannot afford to lose touch with either side of our human possibilities. This book is, therefore, intended as a partial critique of the vast array of sex-role literature written at the height of the women's movement in the 60's and early 70's, much of which came dangerously close to extolling only traditional masculine values. In the excitement of this movement, women were urged to gain access to the male world with little concern for the potential loss of feminine values which such a whole-hearted and eager endorsement of the masculine might create.

This book is both practical and theoretical. It is concerned not only with developing a conception of what androgyny or total humanness might look like and does look like in real lives in the external world, but it also provides suggestions on how to move psychologically in the direction of greater wholeness. The book discusses psychologists' research that is relevant to androgyny, but also suggests exercises and life experiences which would help one become a more androgynous human being. In addition, this book introduces and offers the riches of metaphorical understandings of androgyny, drawing from the insights of Jungian approaches to the masculine and feminine. The relevance of androgyny both to individual personality and total cultural development will also be explored. Finally, in a time when the majority of work in the sex role area has been devoted mostly to female development, it is my hope that this book will offer insights to both women and men who are asking questions about the traditional sex roles and seeking more satisfying solutions to becoming fully themselves.

ACKNOWLEDGMENTS

I wish to thank all the family, friends, teachers, students, and acquaintances who have nourished my interest in the integration of polarity and from whom I have learned so much. I am especially indebted to the men and women who gave so generously of their time and energy as participant-collaborators in my research on androgyny. Special thanks go to Dr. Selma Hyman, Dr. June Singer, and Betty Smith who have encouraged and inspired my Jungian studies and work on androgyny and from whom I have been privileged to learn. Additional thanks are extended to Drs. Leonard Goodstein, Leonard Lansky, and Elizabeth Wales whose support and insightful critique of my original research encouraged me in the writing of this book. I feel deep gratitude for the insights of my friends and colleagues throughout the country with whom I have shared and wrestled with so many of the issues discussed in this book. I also extend a special thanks to the many students who have encouraged my work in this area and whose questions and ideas continue to stimulate my thinking. In particular I want to thank Ann Johnson and Jill McGavin for their generous and long hours typing the manuscript and for their support and encouragement in the long period of writing. Many thanks go also to the editors of Prentice-Hall for their guidance and help in preparing this manuscript for print.

1

EITHER/OR—
AND/ALSO

Human beings seem to have a penchant for conceptualizing the world in terms of sets of opposites or polarities. Thus, we divide the world into light and darkness, good and evil, outside and inside, self and other, birth and death, past and future, matter and energy, reason and emotion. Philosophies vie with one another in their emphasis on one side of the polarity or the other, or on the extent to which they introduce an integrative viewpoint that allows for some coexistence of these polar opposites. Human history, at times, appears to recycle in pendulum-like swings between the poles of these core dichotomies, only pausing at times in perspectives of integration.

Despite this widespread use of polarity in human functioning, psychologists have rarely directed their attention to the role of polarity in cognitive and personality development. The use of polarity, however, may serve both cognitive and emotional functions that are vital to understanding the nature of human development. As cognitive psychologist George Kelly (1963) points out, the process of human thinking appears to depend on the articulation of contrast, on sharpening concepts by differentiating them from opposites. In this analysis, polarity is built into the very process of reasoning and construing events. Polar constructs may serve the vital cultural function of highlighting and carving out the boundaries or guidelines for that culture's particular interpretation of reality. Polarities then mark the major intellectual landmarks for how a culture views its world. Not only does this tendency simplify the mental landscape, calling attention to those key concepts which are thought and felt to be vitally important, but it lends our vision an emotional security, a stable set of structures to cling to in the midst of competing alternatives and potentially overwhelming complexity.

It should probably not be surprising that among the wide-ranging polarities that characterize human culture, the male-female polarity stands out almost as a paradigm of all dichotomies. So deep and pervasive is the perceived difference of male and female sex and gender in human experience, that the concepts of masculinity and femininity have taken on a kind of status as symbolic carriers of all polarity. Thus in their metaphorical representation as Yang and Yin energies and experience, masculinity and femininity have come to stand for and subsume the dichotomies of mind-body, rational-emotional, analytic-holistic, objective-subjective, active-passive, becoming-being, transcendent-immanent, independent-dependent, dominant-submissive, and external-internal ways of being in the world. Men and masculinity have come to be seen in terms of the qualities of assertiveness, intelligence, and strength, while women and femininity have come to be associated with the qualities of receptiveness, nurturance, and emotional sensitivity. Not only are men and women perceived as opposites in gender, but the qualities and personality characteristics judged to be appropriate to each sex are also conceived of as opposites, unsuitable in the other sex. Although we are taught that these qualities are complementary to each other, the stress remains on their oppositeness, reinforcing the sense of difference and the potential gulf of alien experience between the two sexes.

It is a striking fact that in the realm of human experience there is a variety of ways to approach the world; there is a range of personality characteristics which represent different skills and qualities available to human use. Thus, a map of human potentiality, given our tendency toward polarity, might indeed begin to cluster together certain polar ways of acting/being in the world. If these ways of relating to the world appeared to be associated with such an obvious biological difference as male and female gender and body, one might expect concepts like "masculinity" and "femininity" to emerge as a way of describing those more general orientations, whether or not there was any intrinsic, genetic relationship between the body and psychological traits. There is, of course, no way of tracing back the cultural and biological origin of such concepts as masculinity and femininity, but it seems valid to speak of their playing a role as ostensible sex-linked carriers or symbols of two very important ways of being in the world. Two complex, subtle, and differing modes of behavior and consciousness have become crystalized around a gender core, linking these concepts linguistically and hence inextricably with our mental imagery of maleness and femaleness, or what it is to be a man or a woman.

The traditional approach to these crystalized concepts of masculinity and femininity has been to treat them as literal translations or inevitable correlates of gender identity. Men were intrinsically, genetically, and biologically "masculine," that is, assertive, strong, and active. Women were intrinsically, genetically, and biologically "feminine," that is, harmonizing, nurturant, and passive. If biology shapes personality development inevitably and inexorably, channeling men and women into totally different ways of being in the world, then these recurrent dichotomies of masculinity and femininity represent firm guidelines and patterns for ways of being male and female in the world. They restate conceptually the obvious and the existent; they are reiterations of reality. If, however, biology does not dictate personality or merely serves as a point of departure or predisposition to the possibility of certain personality characteristics, then these very same dichotomies of masculinity and femininity, when hooked to the behavior of individual men and women, become ways of coercing or restricting the potential variation of ways of being human. The dichotomies then become social norms that are not merely descriptions of reality, but powerful prescriptions.

A BIOLOGICAL-CULTURAL ASIDE

I am aware that some may wish to argue this point further and reach a more definite judgment as to the possible role of biological factors in sex role development, before moving on to a more thorough critique of dichotomous views of sex roles. Such an argument is entirely legitimate and I would refer the reader to such excellent treatments of this topic as are provided by Maccoby (1966), Maccoby and Jacklin (1974), Money and Ehrhardt (1972), Sherman, (1971), and Tavris and Offir (1977). It is only possible here to briefly summarize the state of research on sex differences.

The vast majority of research on sex differences has suffered from methodological shortcomings. The difficulty of designing culture-free studies, even at the primate level, posed a constant challenge; research bias has affected the questions asked and the operational definitions and methodologies used. Maccoby and Jacklin (1974), in their comprehensive compendium of the research in this area, found only four areas of significant sex differences, three of which appear only in the preadolescent years, suggesting ample time for the intervention of cultural socialization. Those sex differences found in the research are small average differences, affording no predictive ability in the individual case, and witnessing that the variation among men and among women is typically greater than the average differences between the sexes.

The issue of the biological origin of sex differences has always been very vulnerable to projection of cultural ideology and *ex post facto* reasoning, readily confused for intuitive validity. We can easily look to biology to back up value judgments already formed. Thus, Freud points to the existence of widespread penis envy among women, and Karen Horney (1967), hypothesizing on the basis of the same differences in anatomy, can point to the existence of repressed womb envy among men. The anatomy is the same; the differences in interpretation of the implications of this anatomy reflect the different perspectives of the theorists. Consider, too, Theodora Wells' clever fantasy of reverse sex role discrimination based on a purportedly biological rationale: the need to protect men because of their dangerously vulnerable external genitalia (Cox, 1976). The idea that a logical and plausible rationale for reverse discrimination can be so readily constructed on an appeal to anatomy and biology must surely caution us to the dangers of an *ex post facto* biological appeal in arguing issues of sex role superiority or inferiority. As Hillman (1972) points out, even the differences between egg and sperm and other aspects of reproductive anatomy formerly served as ready targets for projected assumptions of female inferiority. (Semen, for example, was seen as whitened and purified menstrual blood.) We further see ample readiness in history to link female menstruation and childbearing capacities to presumably universal female emotionality and maternal nurturance, as well as male testosterone and greater physical size to greater aggressiveness in males, the latter of which does appear to be the core area where research continues to find a small male-female difference even at early ages (Maccoby and Jacklin, 1974). Erik Erikson (1963) may have improved on Freud by no longer rendering women permanently insecure and destined to feelings of inferiority and passivity because of their lack of a penis, but he still relegated women to an inextricable tie to their anatomy by emphasizing their tendency to embrace "inner space," an orientation to the world supposedly reflecting the interior mysteries of their hidden genitalia. Even the new current of feminism which extols women's connection to the earth and nature appears to be reaffirming the importance of dichotomous definitions of masculinity and femininity and their hypothesized tie to biology.

It is too early to predict whether the new interest in biological bases to behavior that is currently popular in psychology will result in any more definitive findings than the sketchy hypotheses now entertained. Thus far the evidence for cultural shaping, behavioral reinforcement, and cognitive identification, imitation, and generalization of dichotomous sex role patterns appears to most psychologists much stronger than a strict biological explanation for their existence. Numerous studies underscore the importance of early sex role training and differential learning of sex role expectations for the two sexes. Among these are studies like Lewis (1972) or Goldberg and Lewis (1969) on the differential touching of boy and girl infants by their mothers, with implications for the socialization of independence and dependence on boys vs. girls, and such research findings as Money and Ehrhardt's (1972) discovery that the culturally assigned sex of sex-ambiguous children is far more important in determining their later sex role identity and comfort than their genetically determined sex. Cross-cultural studies like Margaret Mead's (1969) famous work on the varieties of human temperament suggest the potential variability of sex role training, while other comparative studies like that of Barry, Bacon, and Child (1957) stress instead the widespread similarities across cultures in socialization pressures on boys for achievement and self-reliance and on girls for nurturance, obedience, and responsibility. Although these anthropological findings might appear contradictory at first, the overwhelming emphasis in both is on the importance of cultural variables in shaping what a culture means by masculinity and femininity.

Given that women are necessarily the child-bearers in all cultures (thus far), it seems plausible to speculate that women in very disparate cultures might find themselves restricted by pregnancy to a very different pattern of living than the men, staying closer to a home base and perhaps inheriting by association the task of early child-rearing, so crucial in the human species. If such a division of labor did develop very early in which women were the child-rearers and men the farther-roaming hunters, then personality traits that reflect these different orientations to the world might indeed have developed in dichotomous ways (deBeauvoir, 1953). However, although this argument might appear plausible, it risks being as vulnerable to *ex post facto* reasoning as the biological arguments for sex roles given earlier. Although women may have been the chief child-rearers, they might also have been engaged in early hunter-gatherer societies as equals to men, and according to recent anthropological speculation, may have had ample opportunities to develop the more self-transcendent, agentic parts of their personalities through inventions in pottery, agriculture, and language (Borun et al., 1971; Dinnerstein, 1976). Perhaps it is as dangerous to hypothesize about the origin of dichotomous thinking from a cultural perspective as it is to speculate from a biological one.

No matter what the origins, the phenomenon of dichotomous descriptions of male and female roles is a major characteristic of traditional culture in this country. Even if the cultural origin of sex role characteristics is *not* the only explanation for their origin, and even if there *are* biological underpinnings, this would not obviate the need to take a critical look at dichotomous assumptions. Just because we are born with certain characteristics or tendencies does not mean that those characteristics are sufficient for human development. It appears to be part of human experience, as de Beauvoir (1953) and Dinnerstein (1976) reiterate so well, to transcend the "natural;" one might say that, for our species, it is natural to go beyond the biological givens. Even a biological trait like tallness does not mean that, on occasion, a human will not attempt to develop or approximate its opposite trait, smallness, by stooping for example to enter a small enclosure. Likewise, genetic arguments even in strictly biological situations always allow for environmental interactions. Pure genetic expressions in external behavior would be a rare phenomenon. Individuals are unique, even in the playing out of strict biological destinies—how much more so in the realm of personality and behavior.

DICHOTOMOUS APPROACHES
TO THE SEX ROLE POLARITY

The problem of polarity does not rest in the polarity itself, which actually can serve some useful functions in highlighting important dimensions, but lies instead in a particular use of polarity, the dichotomous approach. In dichotomous approaches to polarity, the two ends of the conceptual pole are treated in an either/or fashion as mutually exclusive opposites. In the dichotomous view of the male-female polarity, masculinity and femininity are conceptualized as polar opposites rather than qualities that can exist in different balances within each individual. Dichotomous sex role norms convey the message that traditional masculine traits are intrinsic and appropriate in men exclusively, whereas traditional feminine traits are intrinsic and appropriate only in women.

In western society these norms translate into two different socialization blueprints for boys and girls, men and women. Men are to be independent, rational, achieving, competitive, success-oriented, tough, self-reliant, and aggressive. Women are to be emotional, nurturant, interpersonally-oriented, dependent, caring, and intuitive. Men are urged to be "the big wheel," "the breadwinner," "John Wayne," or "Give-'em-Hell-Harry," as David and Brannon (1976) describe these categories, or in Farrell's (1974) words, "success objects" who are "upwardly mobile" in work and sex. Women are urged to be wives, mothers, lovers, sex objects, caretakers, and muses for the inspiration of male creations. Bakan (1966) labels this cluster of self-assertive, self-extensive qualities encouraged in males as "agentic" and the cluster of qualities encouraged in females as "communal" (the latter quality summing up such traits as the expression of feelings, interpersonal sensitivity, empathy, and the capacity for intimacy). Block (1973), following up on this terminology, points out how men and women in our culture have indeed been taught to specialize in one end of Bakan's agentic-communal dichotomy.

The dichotomous assignment of personality characteristics to male and female sex roles represents a deeply ingrained social norm in our culture and, as such, influences not only our individual behavior but also our sense of self-esteem and self-evaluation of our adequacy as men, women, and persons. Our assumptions of what constitutes masculinity and femininity affect what we accept and reject in personality development, as well as what is socially reinforced by the environment and socializing agents, teachers, peers, and the media.

The greatest danger of dichotomous approaches to sex roles, however, stems not from what we do develop in our personalities as we endorse one end of the sex role duality but in what we irrevocably relinquish of our potential in excluding the other end of the polarity. The most destructive aspect of dichotomous sex role training consists of the message that one must not only take on the traits advocated for one's own sex but one must stringently avoid any of the characteristics of the other sex. This is especially true for men, for whom the very definition of masculinity is often: being "not feminine." Farrell (1974) and Hartley (1959) emphasize how training in masculinity is typically accompanied by an equal emphasis for little boys on avoiding anything that could be considered feminine. Thus the expression of feelings is to be avoided at all costs by a man or he risks being labeled a "sissy" or having his "masculinity" questioned. Even hand gestures or facial expressions that might be construed as effeminate are studiously avoided. As one person in a study of this area[1] described his earlier concern about not looking feminine: "Maybe this is going to sound dumb, but [when I was younger I would sometimes] stand in front of the mirror and try to respond to things and look with my face in what I thought was a very masculine way. I would find myself in there scowling a lot of times, and this sort of thing."

The typical dichotomous approach to masculinity and femininity describes these concepts as "complete opposites," "almost the opposite," or as referring to differences that "should" exist between men and women. Feminine characteristics especially are taboo in men. This conviction does not imply a denigration of the traditional feminine traits, however. More accurately it might be argued in this viewpoint that all aspects of femininity are positive in the context of female behavior and negative in the context of male behavior. For example, to be "mealy-mouthed" or "sissy" are negative qualities when applying to men and, despite their possible negative ring to some ears, are perceived as likeable qualities when found in women. Dichotomous assumptions are reflected in such comments as, "A female is a very special separate person to me, with very special traits" or, "Well, I don't think men *should* be like women . . . It bothers me more to see a man acting like a woman than anything. I just think it's ridiculous."

Although men seem to be given an especially strong introduction to the dichotomization of masculinity and femininity, women reflect these dichotomous assumptions as well. This is particularly true when women are attracted to and therefore reinforce the dichotomous tendency that is so strongly reflected in the male's self image, the idea that male desirability is characterized by having exclusively masculine traits. Women, thus, have reported: "There are men that I see very feminine tendencies to, and I guess that kind of bothers me . . . To me, if a guy is masculine . . . he doesn't have any feminine characteristics at all;" or "a weak-appearing . . . man never appealed to me . . . very very small, slight . . . I don't think of him as very masculine . . . I did date men who loved poetry and were very philosophical and all, and that's not the kind of man I wanted to marry, for some reason. Now maybe inside a man that's very very emotional and very very philosophical . . . suggests a weakness to me." Even women claiming the right to broaden their image of femininity by developing more of the traditional masculine traits often stop short of endorsing the same broadening process for men, disapproving of or feeling unattracted to more sensitive, emotional, or less career-oriented men, for example. This subtle double standard may, in fact, turn out to be one of the chief reinforcers of dichotomous sex roles and certainly suggests the ways in which the male sex role may turn out to be more rigidly enforced than the female sex role in our culture.

The parallel dichotomous message, that women should guard against the expression of traditional masculine, striving, assertive characteristics, is perhaps less extreme currently than the corresponding taboo for men. Since the dominant value system in the United States extols the masculine traits in its citizens, it is perhaps not surprising that deviation from the norm in the masculine direction would be more tolerated than deviation in the feminine direction. The women's movement, too, has done much to widen the range of acceptable behavior for women, at least at the more overt level, by allowing women more access to the world of masculine-dominated behavior and institutions. If the dichotomous message is softened for women in contemporary American society, however, it would still be a mistake to think that the message is absent. Its presence has become more subtle and can be seen in the still frequent risk of being labeled "castrating bitch," "ball-breaker," "controlling woman," or "overly-intellectualized woman" if the woman publicly and consistently expresses the more assertive side of her personality. If these labels are used now in the spirit of teasing, this does not lessen the socialization message but makes it instead more subtle and difficult to confront.

Psychologists make frequent use of the word "deviance" to represent behavior differing from that advocated by social norms. In that context, the word often does not carry the sense of abnormality, bizarreness, or violation that is often evoked in the more popular use of the word. However, in the case of sex roles, the emotional power of the word deviance in its popular usage is probably closer to the experienced reality of not fitting into conventional sex roles. Because sex role identity is such a major part of our self-concept in this society, the sense of not fitting the traditionally appropriate sex role norms, of differing from them even in minor ways can be devastating for a person. Furthermore, since no one fits exactly into any pure stereotypic image, this experience of insecurity and self-doubt at one's adequacy as a man or woman is destined to be the subjective experience of many people in this culture, if not all of them. Tremendous personal energy in this culture goes into maintaining a facade of adherence to one's appropriate sex role and trying to camouflage those personality aspects that do not fit the dominant image.

This phenomenon of repression is especially true in a culture which has ready-made negative labels to throw at the person who differs in some way from the social norm. In a very perceptive argument, Elizabeth Janeway (1971) calls attention to the ways in which our dualistic social myths maintain the status quo during periods of social unrest by creating negative shadow roles to project onto any person who deviates from the prescribed roles. These shadow roles are polar opposites of the socially prescribed role and, therefore, do not represent real alternatives to the role but merely a reversal of basically the same pattern. For example, myth creates the picture of the ideal pleasing submissive woman, and then creates a "negative caricature," the shrew. The deviant assertive woman is then seen in terms of this negative shadow role (shrew), which maintains the status quo with little threat since it robs the new action (assertiveness) of any status as a real behavioral alternative. The old role survives by innuendo in its newly reversed form, and alternative strategies for living get driven out of a legitimate cultural existence. So, too, the array of labels for homosexuality lurks at the edge of sex role exploration and can be used, externally and internally for those who feel vulnerable, as a way of scaring people back into conformity to traditional roles.

A CRITIQUE OF DICHOTOMOUS
SEX ROLES

Although one might expect that the field of clinical psychology would be among the first to note and raise concern about the ways in which dichotomous sex roles encourage repression of the full range of human living in men and women, the earliest and strongest critiques of dichotomous sex role assumptions in the psychological literature (apart from the tradition of research begun by the inspiration of the Broverman et al. study, 1970, on double standards of mental health) tended to be voiced by psychologists concerned about the methodological issues at stake in measuring concepts like masculinity and femininity and conducting research in this area. The issue they addressed is, of course, at heart a critique of all dichotomous and unidimensional scales of personality measurement. In many instruments to measure personality characteristics, polar qualities are set up as two end-points of the scale and little attention is given to the dynamics of the possible interplay between the poles. As Rae Carlson (1972) observed, this tendency often yields an either/or understanding of personality characteristics based on the presence or absence of a trait rather than a more complex understanding of the ways the polar qualities may coexist in varying balances within every individual. Thus we are concerned with measuring typically how independent or dependent someone is, whereas if we considered both dimensions at once we might arrive at a new, useful, and psychologically profound construct like the capacity for interdependence, which combines the qualities of independence and dependence in new and creative ways and may, in fact, be more predictive to success in interpersonal situations.

Historically, most psychological measures of masculinity and femininity have also consisted of unidimensional, bipolar scales in which the endorsement of masculine traits precludes endorsement of feminine traits and vice versa. Subjects in experiments receive single scores and, therefore, must inevitably appear less feminine if they come out higher on the masculine end of the scale, or less masculine if they score high on the feminine end. In 1970, Cottle, Edwards and Pleck raised some critical questions about the dichotomous assumptions behind these M-F scales, and in addition Bem (1974), Carlson (1972), and Gonen and Lansky

(1968) have argued that masculinity and femininity may be independent, unipolar dimensions and that new measures must be developed to allow for this potential independence. It might be perfectly possible for someone to score high in both masculinity and femininity, if the dichotomous assumptions are abandoned. What we call masculinity and femininity may, in fact, be categories which we have imposed on a range of human personality traits, artificially dividing up these characteristics into male and female groupings.

This is, in fact, the direction Constantinople (1973) has taken in her insightful challenge to the continued use of masculinity and femininity as valid personality variables. After reviewing cumulative research, she suggests that "masculinity" and "femininity" have little more than the status of summary words or rubrics for a wide range of subtraits that have been differentially socialized in the two sexes. A measure of "masculinity," for example, would be better conceptualized as a measure for the general endorsement of a cluster of human personality characteristics traditionally esteemed only for men, for example, assertiveness and logical or analytic thinking; femininity would be reconceptualized to refer to a cluster of personality traits traditionally esteemed only in women. It seems plausible that men and women might each develop, within their personalities, traits from each of these two broader clusters, although given our current cultural norms people might have felt pressure to specialize. However, these possibilities cannot be reflected in psychological research which depends on sex role classification systems or instruments with only two dichotomous alternatives, masculine or feminine. Without new instruments and conceptualizations for studying masculinity and femininity, psychologists run the risk of great oversimplification and distortion in the understanding of each individual's unique personality functioning.

It is probably important to note at this point that if the words masculinity and femininity begin to be perceived more as summary categories, continuing to call them by these names as if they had an intrinsic relationship to the male and female gender might be very misleading. There has, in fact, been considerable debate over what to re-label these two polar concepts to free them from exclusive reference to one sex. Bakan's (1966) suggestion of agency vs. communion has received some attention, as has the sociological terminology from Talcott Parsons of instrumental vs. expressive (see Lynda Glennon's [1979] recent analysis). Bezdek and Strodtbeck (1970) suggest the concepts task-pragmatic vs. person-idealistic as ways of summarizing these two different value orientations. This issue of re-labeling these two categories of value and orientation is a lively one with tremendous implications that I hope the reader will keep in mind. For the present I will continue to use the words masculinity and femininity in their general and metaphorical sense as labels given to broad categories or ways of being in the world. I am not committed to using these concepts indefinitely, as they do keep us dangerously close to assuming they bear some intrinsic relationship to maleness or femaleness. I will run the risk a little longer, however, because of the ability of these words to provoke fruitful speculation about the organization of personality and cultural values.

There are other cognitive and psychological dangers of dichotomous treatment of sex roles that deserve examination if our critique of these norms is not to be based only on the concerns of research psychologists. One of the significant problems with dichotomous thinking of all kinds is its particular tendency to shape and distort perception in line with the dualistic assumptions of the perceiver. This danger can be seen most immediately and comprehensively in the risk of carrying dualistic assumptions along as the blinders of any classification system. As Castaneda (1968, 1971, 1972), Laing (1967), Pearce (1971), and Watts (1966) so well articulate, the concepts with which we approach the world affect our perceptions of that world and often trap us into presuppositions that do not match very well with the full concreteness of existence. In this analysis, dualistic constructs and dichotomies become habit patterns which curtail our vision about possible alternative interpretations of reality. Dualistic concepts shield us from the possibility of fresh insights into the nature of reality ''in itself'' by eliminating the jarring of assumptions that comes from the juxtaposition of opposites. Polarities, like all linguistic forms, function as organizers and distorters of experience, and because of the heavy weight that our polar constructs carry within a culture, they are especially powerful shapers of expectations. The danger always exists that the polarities we learn may not represent reality very adequately, and that the dualistic constructs take on a kind of Aristotelian ''essence'' that resists any kind of empirical test (Lewin, 1931).

Dichotomous thinking leads, furthermore, to a tendency documented in the person perception literature of social psychology, for one's perception and attributions of another person's characteristics to be often more dependent on the categories one holds than the actual characteristics of the person one is perceiving. In other words, in person perception, what I notice in you may say more about me and my expectations than about your traits. Thus, those personally or culturally salient polar constructs which a person holds may be more predictive of what he or she perceives than the more immediate data provided by a perceived object. If we hold strong dualistic concepts of male and female characteristics and have different conceptual categories in mind when we look at men vs. women, the way we describe or perceive any individual man or woman may say more about those categories than about the individual person seen. We may label the same behavior differently depending on whether it occurs in a man or a woman. For example, if emotionality is a construct particularly salient in looking at women but not men, a calm behavior on the part of an individual woman might be labeled "cold," whereas the same behavior in a man might not even be noteworthy (that is, call out an emotionality construct). The same phenomenon might be at work when a man's passive behavior is labeled "weak, soft, gay" whereas an assertiveness construct might not even be evoked for the same behavior in a woman, and her passive behavior might be seen as "normal" and hence often unlabeled. This type of thinking leads to a reinforcement of stereotypes and a distortion of behavior much along the line of the frequently observed judgments made about the behavior of businesswomen vs. businessmen: he is called intense, she is hysterical, when both are dealing with emotional crisis; he is efficient, she is robotlike, when both are displaying perseverance and competence in their work.

   The either/or quality of thinking fostered by dualistic concepts interferes with psychological functioning, in addition, by blocking the individual from exploring real alternatives of action or thought within the middle ground between his or her constructs. As Kelly (1963) observed, disturbed people tend to flip back and forth between the poles of their constructs rather than test midrange alternatives, which might provide a more integrated and stable base than cycling between either/or extremes. George Orwell (1949) actually built this tendency of dualistic thinking into the structure of the language he designed to represent the coerciveness of his *1984* regime. Newspeak was created to make all divergent modes of thought unthinkable. By diminishing the range of possible thought through carefully circumscribing a word and severely curtailing its opposite (for example, good—ungood), Newspeak eliminated the range of alternative shades of meaning that might have been unleashed by other words or through a dialectical relationship with a former opposite construct (for example, bad).

   This either/or style of thinking renders people particularly vulnerable to the dangers of what Toffler (1970) called "future shock." Dichotomous thinking thus has the potential of fostering rigidity and extremist thinking in the face of rapid change and impeding the ability to adapt and deal with complexity. For those accustomed to either/or simplicity, the novelty, complexity, and unpredictability of today's environment pose high stress to which the individual often responds with even more exaggerated dichotomous modes of thought, that is, denial, overspecialization, reversion to previously adaptive but now inappropriate action, or super-simplification. In the face of rapid change, issues become readily polarized along simplistic dichotomies. The middle ground becomes an obscenity to both extreme positions, and a complex, difficult resolution that incorporates the assets of both extremes becomes libelized as an "inauthentic middle-of-the road cop-out" or "compromise." The win or lose battle is a dichotomous one, which visualizes no middle ground alternatives where both sides can "win." Dichotomous thinking rarely offers a way out of such dilemmas; more often, it only serves to harden the lines of conflict. Thinking in terms of either/or kinds of concepts seems to be easier than teasing out the subtle gradations of alternative choices, mediating constructs, or midpoints along the range between the extreme poles.

Perhaps the most seductive and subtle danger of dichotomous thinking, however, coincides with a basic tendency in human personality development for people to accept, value, or identify with only part of a whole range of potential human characteristics. This tendency plays an important role in nearly all models of personality development, particularly in Rogerian, Gestalt, and Jungian analyses. Often in learning to accept certain qualities or aspects of the self as good, their opposites are condemned or feared. This fear of the other end of a polarity (for example, the fear of assertiveness in someone raised to only value gentleness and acquiescence) decreases the extent to which persons explore their own living spaces and traps them into lopsided development in different dimensions of their personalities. That which is disowned, however, continues to exert pressure and tension in the system. The repressed and denied impulse repossesses what we isolate as good (Laing, 1967); the dissociated daimonic pulls with it the sources of love and will (May, 1969).

The process of identifying with only those parts of the self which one considers acceptable is closely related to the psychological process of projection. Projection is a self-defensive process in which one attributes to other persons or to the environment those characteristics in oneself which one is unable to own or accept (Perls, 1969). Dichotomous thinking can be seen to foster the psychological process of projection by reinforcing a tendency to understand oneself in terms of polar opposites, where one end of the polarity is affirmed as typical of oneself and the other end is disowned. It is these disowned, undeveloped dimensions which are most likely to be projected onto others, either in hate or love. The tendency toward polarized thinking and low tolerance of ambiguity may thus serve an ego defensive function, protecting the person from awareness of his or her own ambiguities and undesired traits, and facilitating projection of those onto the environment (Frenkel-Brunswik, 1949).

Those qualities disliked in others are frequently clues to one's disowned "opposites" which lie latent within one's own personality. Thus, in Philip Slater's (1970) insightful analysis of American culture, the intense antipathy of the silent majority toward the hippie and the radical student in the late 60s can be seen as an overreaction against the middle class's own frustrated needs for community and engagement in meaningful activity. The anger we perceive and fear in others may be a ready clue to our own unrecognized anger. Projections can also be positive, as Putney and Putney (1964) so clearly describe. We often project onto those we love the highly esteemed characteristics we cherish but have not developed or do not recognize in ourselves. Whatever the traits projected onto a polar opposite, whether they represent positive or negative qualities, they function essentially as a mechanism for perpetuating a truncated existence in which part of the self is disowned. Dichotomous thinking leaves us with either/or constructs and a breeding ground for projection.

It is not surprising that the danger of projection is especially likely to be present in cultures advocating dichotomous sex role norms. As both Roszak and Roszak (1969) and de Beauvoir (1953) have postulated, our cultural sex role stereotypes and male-female polarities have served as mechanisms for the projection of unacceptable human characteristics for each sex. They speculate that male-oriented cultures have carved up the human characteristics of the entire species and created either/or categories and polarities, projecting onto women those characteristics they could not acknowledge in themselves and yet had to legitimize in some dimension in the world (for example, emotionality, tenderness, intuitiveness). These qualities of nurturance and intuition have been projected onto women, in part, because these qualities have been feared and not legitimized by men.

De Beauvoir (1953) writes further of how man has asked woman to be the mysterious Other onto which he projects all that he dares not be, yet needs to complete himself. In de Beauvoir's analysis, the tremendous ambivalence that has characterized the myths and images of woman throughout history is largely related to this phenomenon of projecting onto women all that man desires and fears, loves and hates, wants and does not attain. De Rham (1965) adds that woman plays the role of a complementary "scapegoat" for negativities that cannot be admitted in men and which fluctuate with the prevailing image and aspirations of the male sex. As Ellmann (1968) writes, this fluctuation in the perceived nature of woman varies often not only from speaker to speaker but from moment to moment.

For women also, as Putney and Putney (1964) speculate, many of the characteristics that are alienated from the self and loved in others are those culture has assigned to the other sex (for example, intelligence, assertiveness). Man can be seen to represent strength, vitality, rational objectivity, and all those characteristics disowned from the feminine archetype. Thus men and women both have been imprisoned by their bondage to artificial dualities and characteristics that are projected at a cultural level and falsely deemed male or female. Rather than developing both ranges of qualities in oneself, men and women trap themselves into a confluent kind of dependency on the other to fulfill their own unmet needs. This interweaving of projection and need is beautifully articulated by Roszak and Roszak (1969) in the introduction to their book *Masculine/ Feminine* and is included in part in the exercises at the end of the chapter.

INTEGRATIVE APPROACHES
TO SEX ROLES

Integrative or dialectical thinking stands in direct contrast to the dichotomous use of polar constructs. Integrative thinking begins with articulating and sharpening opposites but uses these polar constructs as anchor points to generate tension (that is, thesis-antithesis) and to facilitate reaching new integrations of these polar constructs. Polarities are differentiated as a first step toward a new synthesis. The risk with integrative thinking is a premature synthesis which does not reflect the full range of alternatives or a clear exploration of extremes and differences—a watered-down, pablum-like synthesis which avoids the creative tension present in a juxtaposition of polarities. However, the advantages of integrative thinking have been acclaimed as a symbol of full psychological functioning by numerous theorists of personality. The capacity to contain dissonance, to develop the full range of human potential, to integrate diversity within ourselves, would appear to bring with it a sense of wholeness, flexibility, and health.

Maslow (1962, 1970), for example, characterizes peak experiences and self-actualized living in terms of the qualities of wholeness, unity, interconnectedness, and synergy. Polarities dissolve at the highest levels of human functioning, as opposite ends of a straight line meet when they are joined to form a circle. Self-actualizing people appear more tolerant of the simultaneous existence of inconsistencies and their lives are characterized by the process of transcending dichotomies, of integrating polarities, and transforming oppositions into unities. Underscoring Maslow, Shostrum (1968) suggests that self-actualizing persons tend to integrate complementary and opposite qualities (for example, assertion and caring) in their interpersonal styles.

The capacity to integrate polarities appears to characterize persons of high cognitive complexity who have been found in research to hold more differentiated "cognitive maps" for looking at the world (Bieri, 1961), are more capable of comprehending ambiguous information and dealing with the coexistence of incongruous qualities within one person (Tripodi and Bieri, 1966; Halverson, 1970), and are more able to change set (Delia, Crockett, and Gonyea, 1970). Furthermore, in personality theorists ranging from Freud, Jung, Erikson and Loevinger (1966) to polarity theorists like Rank, Angyal, Bakan, and Koestler and humanistic-existential theorists like May, Maslow, and Perls, the importance of reaching integrations between the major polarities or diverse personality traits of human life represents the key developmental task of the fully functioning person.[2] When this goal of flexibility and wholeness is translated into the psychotherapeutic context, therapists work with clients to enlarge the range of their behavioral and emotional alternatives, to allow for the identification, differentiation, and development of ignored or repressed parts of the self, and to create new and vital integration of these qualities in a dynamic dialogue. In Gestalt therapy in particular, the aim is a new composition of the capacities within each individual. The new unity of the individual is based on inclusion, not specialization, and the goal of the therapist is to help the person replace a "dictatorship" of favored characteristics with the inclusion of a full range of his or her potential characteristics (Polster and Polster, 1973). Whether the goals of the integrated personality are echoed in the language of Gestalt, of Jungian analytic psychology (Singer, 1973), or of psychosynthesis (Assagioli, 1965), the emphasis on the healing and creative power of integrative thinking is clear.

The value of transcending polarities as a means of access to a more accurate view of the world is a time-honored theme in philosophy and religion as well, although it is far more frequent in Oriental approaches. In this view, dichotomous thinking is a trap, an illusion, a limited way of perceiving. The logical construct "A or not A," the basis of Western logic, is viewed in the East as a limitation on the possibilities of reality. The ultimates in life transcend all those polarities we learn to hold on to in everyday: reality good-evil, being-nonbeing, life-death, beginning-ending. The way out of illusion lies in abandoning attachment to these either/or ways of conceptualizing. Often the mode of liberation comes precisely through the heightening of tension between two incompatible modes of thought or concepts. The leverage point for new alternatives of thought or action lies in the posing of paradox and the simultaneous existence of two incompatible thoughts or commands. This is the method of Zen (Suzuki, 1964) and of the Yaqui sorcerer in Castaneda's (1968, 1971) writings who helps him break through the interpretive webs he confuses with reality by flowing back and forth between discrepant, alternative world views and learning to "see." Thus wholeness, synthesis, and the transcending of polarity seem to characterize the human ideal in philosophic speculation as well as in psychological health.

In this context, the recent interest expressed by psychologists in integrative alternatives to dichotomous treatment of the male-female polarity seems long overdue. The proposed integrative conceptualization of sex role characteristics and behavior has been given the name *androgyny,* in what turns out to be a fascinating revival in modern form of an age-old philosophical principle or ideal. Derived from the Greek *andros,* meaning man, and *gyne,* meaning woman, androgyny has represented in history a mythological construct referring to the "Two in One," the potential unity of all polarity within the individual as symbolized by the masculine and feminine principles harmonized within one person. The word and concept have a long history, traced so poignantly by June Singer (1976) and illustrated as a theme in literature by Heilbrun (1973). Both these authors treat androgyny from a conceptual, literary, and mythological point of view, and Singer proceeds to portray androgyny as a powerful metaphor for our time, a rediscovered archetype and inner guide toward increasing wholeness in psychological development. This theme will be developed at great length in the second half of this book, in order to gain additional insights into the perspectives of mythical and symbolic thinking and the richness of treating androgyny as an internal, metaphorical process as well as a literal, external expression of sex role equality.

Sandra Bem's research on androgyny (1972, 1974, 1975b) represents, in contrast to the approach taken by Singer and Heilbrun, a social-psychological approach and has served as a stimulus to much of the empirical research on androgyny which is now being pursued. Bem's definition of androgyny can thus be taken as a major point of reference in our exploration of the construct. Androgyny refers to the relatively equal development within one person of the personality characteristics traditionally associated with men as well as women. Androgyny, as a personality and behavioral characteristic, represents the flexible integration of the traditional "masculine" and "feminine" polarities within an individual of either sex. Based on this definition of androgyny, we can also speak of an androgynous social norm or value which would reinforce the development of the full range of human characteristics within individuals of both sexes. Androgynous norms thus contrast directly with dichotomous norms which designate certain characteristics as appropriate to one sex exclusively.

For many years, psychological research had suggested that the fully-functioning individual was characterized by what we might today call androgyny. Maslow (1942) found that self-actualizing men and women tend to resemble each other through the process of developing their full range of potential and thereby transcending the traditional truncated male-female repertoires of behavior and characteristics. Several investigators (Barron, 1957; MacKinnon, 1962; Oetzel, 1966) found that the most creative and brightest men and boys had developed many traditionally labeled "feminine" qualities whereas the most creative and brightest girls and women had developed their "masculine" side. Other researchers point to greater maturity (Block, 1973), greater social adjustment (Cohen, 1966; Heilbrun, 1963, 1968), greater intelligence (Sontag, Baker, and Nelson, 1958), and fuller enjoyment of sexuality (Maslow, 1942) in women who develop cross-sex characteristics in addition to more traditional feminine characteristics. Gump (1972) found that college women who want to integrate both career and home life had the highest measures of ego strength.

Mussen (1962) found that adult men who had displayed high-masculine interests as adolescents differed from adult men who had displayed low-masculine interests as adolescents; the former were rated by interviewers as less self-confident, less self-accepting, and relatively lacking in qualities of leadership in adulthood. These findings were even more noteworthy in that these same men as adolescents had seemed to be better adjusted than the low-masculine boys. Mussen suggested that the lower degree of emotional-expressive interests and skills among high-masculine men as compared to low-masculine men may have become increasingly a handicap in achieving satisfactory interpersonal relationships and occupational success in adulthood. Harford, Willis, and Deabler (1967) also found high masculinity in adult men to be positively correlated with proneness to guilt, anxiety, and neurotic tendencies, whereas low masculinity was correlated with emotional stability, warmth, and sensitivity. Worell and Worell (1977) found that college males and females who supported feminist values differed from opposing men and women in being more independent, self-reliant, flexible, and less authoritarian. Dempewolff (1972) also found college student supporters of feminism to score higher than opposers on several measures of autonomy.

Androgynous alternatives to the dichotomous treatment of sex role characteristics also would be expected to lessen the likelihood of projections of disowned traits onto the other sex. The process of reowning projections, and developing one's own masculine or feminine half instead of seeking those qualities in others, is a first step to healing and wholeness. The growing popularity and virtual rediscovery of Jungian analytic therapy is perhaps a sign of the relevance of integrative approaches to the dichotomies of our time and the necessity of developing the full range of human potential for both women and men. The rebalancing of agentic and communal traits within each person raises the possibility of nourishing our fullest creativity.

The construct of androgyny, however, has only begun to be explored in psychological research. Earlier dichotomous methods fo measuring masculinity and femininity did not even allow for the possibility that a person could evidence both masculine and feminine characteristics to a highly developed degree. Bem's (1974) development of a sex role scale capable of measuring the construct of androgyny provided a key stimulus to research in this area. The Bem Sex Role Inventory (BSRI) contains two independent scales, a masculinity and a femininity scale, which allow separate scores for a person's endorsement of each set of characteristics. Thus the degree to which a person describes himself or herself in terms of masculine and feminine attributes can be compared and a measure of androgyny obtained. If the masculinity and femininity scores are not significantly different from each other, the person is said to be androgynous. If one score is significantly higher than the other, the person is said to be masculine-identified or feminine-identified. Although the BSRI has received a variety of criticisms and discussion in the literature (Strahan, 1975; Spence, Helmreich, and Stapp, 1975; Bem, 1977), it remains perhaps the key heuristic contribution to ongoing research in the area of androgyny and establishment of its construct validity.

Using this scale to identify androgynous vs. sex-typed college students, Bem (1975a) found that androgynous individuals show more sex role adaptability than sex-typed individuals, flexibly expressing behavior according to its situational appropriateness. Sex-typed individuals showed behavioral deficits in two situations calling for typically cross-sex behavior, that is, in showing independence from pressure to conform ("masculine") and in playing with a kitten ("feminine"). In similar studies, Bem (1975b) reported other behavioral deficits from feminine sex-typed individuals in experimental situations involving assertively refusing an unreasonable request ("masculine"). Bem, Martyna and Watson (1976) found that masculine sex-typed individuals also showed behavioral deficits in interacting with a baby and showing empathy and concern for a person with problems, two traditionally "feminine" behaviors. In all these studies, androgynous persons showed flexible behaviors appropriate to the situation. Bem and Lenney (1976) also reported an experiment in which persons were given a choice between acting out a typical masculine or feminine behavior, each with some monetary payoff. Compared with androgynous students, sex-typed students avoided activity inappropriate for their sex, even though it paid more. In these studies, Bem finds support for the hypothesis that traditional sex role concepts restrict behavior in significant ways.

More recent experimental work on androgyny has focused on exploring the hypothesis that androgynous people are more effective and healthier than persons identified with one sex role. Many studies are in process; the results are equivocal and it would be premature to make any definitive conclusions on the basis of studies which largely correlate BSRI scores and measures of self-esteem or self-actualization through paper-and-pencil tests (Allen 1977; Ginn, 1975; Hjelle, 1977; Spence, Helmreich, and Stapp, 1975). In one sense these experiments can be considered only a beginning in establishing the validity of the construct of androgyny. Further research also must move beyond single-item tests toward more complex situations for assessing attitudinal or behavioral correlates of androgyny.

FEARS, CONCERNS, AND POSSIBILITIES

Despite its promise for fuller psychological development, there has been considerable public fear generated around the possible implications for human behavior proposed in this new integrative concept of androgyny. Sometimes this fear has been exacerbated by the way this concept has been misrepresented or distorted in the media or even perhaps by authors themselves; at other times the distortions have followed, in all likelihood, from the tendency in our culture to confuse issues of sex role behavior with issues of sexuality. Although sexuality has often been a target for sex role definitions of appropriate behavior, sexuality represents only one dimension of human behavior that has been affected by dichotomous interpretations of masculinity and femininity. Likewise, integrated alternatives for sex role behavior affect a far more wide-ranging set of human activities and personality characteristics than are represented by sexuality alone.

I will be arguing in this book that androgyny is a concept that offers the possibility of expanding our range of permissible behaviors and expanding the opportunities for being fully human. Androgyny is in every way the antithesis of the popularly-feared concept "unisex." One could, of course, argue that androgynous persons, in developing their whole selves, would come to resemble each other in that they were all flexible, fully functioning human beings, but this similarity is a long way from the concept of unisex. Far from increasing homogeneity among men and women, androgyny would unleash far greater uniqueness and heterogeneity for each person. We would be likely to see far greater diversity rather than the two major sex role patterns that tend to characterize our human choices now.

To return to the issue of sexuality, I will also be arguing in this book that androgyny is primarily a concept with relevance for the whole human spectrum of personality traits. To focus in on sexuality, however important an issue, is a distortion of the potential implications of androgyny for our time. I have been recurrently distressed by the repeated visual representations in the media of androgyny, which lead to easy distortions of its implications. Our society is so cut off from our heritage of alchemical symbolism and mythical or metaphorical thinking that any attempt to represent androgyny through the fused torsos of a man and woman will send modern Americans running for cover before they will even take the time to open a book and attempt to understand the imagery. The metaphorical rendering of the psychological union of masculine and feminine principles is far better rendered in our sexually anxious time by the traditional Yin-Yang symbol of the Orient than by our own Western medieval and alchemical images of the divine marriage, the king and queen, soror and adept, man and woman.

One of the great misfortunes of recent writing on androgyny has been not in the power and articulation of the concept itself, but in the possibilities for misrepresentation which have been caused by the way in which these ideas have been packaged. June Singer's beautiful exploration of androgyny has been affected in its circulation not only by the above-mentioned metaphorical rendering of a half male-half female body on the book jacket, but in the display on the cover of the paperback edition of her book of a woman dressed in what appears to be a typical businessman's hat and suit, sending unintended messages that androgyny implies possible masculinization of women, and also that androgyny is a woman's issue without relevance to men. I do not believe that I am overreacting in my fear that the unintended association of androgyny with hermaphrodism or homosexuality is enough, in this culture, to discourage many men and women from acquaintance with this very important concept.

Androgyny may, in its fullest implications, open up alternative behaviors to such an extent that some persons will explore varieties of sexual lifestyles and consider this an expression of their androgyny. However, androgyny is not likely of any necessity to alter choice of sexual partner or one's identification with one's bodily gender or sex; in fact, it is every bit as likely to free men and women up to enjoy their own conventional sexual identity as a man or a woman because of the concurrent opportunity to explore the full range of possible human characteristics in their personalities. It will be important to reiterate that androgynous men and women like being men and women and, though they are more typically tolerant of a wide range of human lifestyles for human beings, they may not personally explore or advocate sexual alternatives to traditional heterosexual relationships. I dislike placing undue emphasis on this issue which seems to tear apart our culture and dramatize the worst of human mutual intolerance, but I have found that over and over again resistance to learning more about the concept of androgyny veils fears that this concept necessitates sexual explorations into homosexuality or bisexuality. Though I might wish these recurrent fears were not so strong, they bear witness to the depth of feeling associated with sexual and sex role choice. It is my hope that by stressing the differentiation of the two areas, we might more fully explore the implications of androgyny for broadening our range of personality characteristics. June Singer has made an admirable effort to trace out the possible implications of androgyny for the sexual dimension, although it is important to remind the reader that she is introducing us to the metaphorical dimensions and one must beware becoming overly literal in one's interpretation. Although I will touch on issues of sexuality and, most definitely, on issues of relationship in this book, I will be primarily interested in tracing out the implications of androgyny for personality development in general. Sexual choice is a personal choice that, in my opinion, bears no necessary relation to sex role orientation or advocacy. Obviously those world views that promote flexibility will be more supportive of a variety of lifestyles; they do not, however, necessarily create them. I do not believe that androgyny, any more than feminism, necessitates any political expression of sexual preference.

I have two remaining and overlapping concerns related to the issue of androgyny, and they are related not to the possibility that the concept will not receive the attention it deserves, but are paradoxically related to the possibility that androgyny may indeed become a new norm to guide sex role behavior. In other words, I am concerned that in making androgyny a new norm for personality development, we do not set up a new coercion by which we then analyze ourselves and others to find out how meritoriously androgynous we are. In a world only too familiar with the dangers of sex role conformity, I would consider it a great and discouraging irony if we were to set up the androgynous person as a kind of new age ideal. It is certainly reassuring that the very nature of androgyny bespeaks individuality, and that androgynous persons appear to be more tolerant and understanding of persons in traditional sex role orientations than the feminism of the late 60s and early 70s was often prone to be. However, we must consciously guard against the tendency to create a new idolatry, complete with a new vocabulary, even though it seems to be extremely important to explore the concept of androgyny in our individual lives.

Androgyny is a process, a lifelong pursuit, and it has many starting points. In one sense there is not even a need for a new word, especially one that takes so long to become familiar to our eyes and ears. However, words carry power; they open up psychological and cognitive space, and this is precisely the challenge that must be met by integrative alternatives to well-established and conventionally-empowered dichotomous sex role norms. Were we to really allow ourselves and others the flexibility and range of behavior implied by the word androgyny, then we might not need a new vocabulary. But such is not the case, and though we may grow beyond the words and concepts that fill this book, they will prove useful in stretching the boundaries of our current explorations and providing guidelines for the next transitions.

I see this book as an invitation to a journey: a psychological journey, a metaphorical and cognitive and emotional journey into ourselves and our culture. Where I advocate, it is in the interest of opening our eyes to the very real varieties and possibilities that lie in being human and of calling attention to the very real destructiveness and inflexibility we occasion in ourselves and others by cutting ourselves off from this potential. In some ways one might say that we are all androgynous; we all weave together a unique blend of personality characteristics into our identities, but we have not been encouraged to honor that androgyny. The psychological tragedy against which a concept like androgyny protests is the stifling and truncating that occurs in the name of being conventional men and women. Clinical psychologists witness over and over again the insecurity that people in our culture carry inside due to their fears that they are not totally masculine or totally feminine in the traditional sense. It is in answer to this need and the self-doubts, aspirations, and questions of many people that I write this book. It is my hope that it will open new questions and explorations, and not leave you with a reified new coercion against which to judge yourself.

My second major concern about the implications of the renewed interest in androgyny stems also from my more clinical and philosophical interests. I am delighted to see the abundance of research, judged on a relative scale, on androgyny in the social-psychological literature. However, I am concerned that very little work of a more clinical nature is occurring. Androgyny risks becoming an abstract, cognitive construct, operationally defined in a number of ways but linked inevitably to the psychological laboratory, and destined to a premature retirement after this initial wave of experimental enthusiasm. It has been my concern for some time that we deepen the experiential roots and construct validity for androgyny by anchoring this concept more adequately in the real lives of men and women. We need a far deeper appreciation and understanding of what androgyny actually looks like in everyday life. We need to find out what types of life experiences seem relevant to the development of androgyny; what struggles or issues or even lack of struggles have characterized the lives of androgynous persons. Do androgynous men and women have different life patterns and challenges?

This type of research represents a different approach to understanding phenomena than that more typically characterizing the psychological literature. In fact, it illustrates the very dilemma of expressing androgynous alternatives in the face of dichotomous cultural norms. The traditional modes of inquiry most honored in contemporary psychology have been what might be called the more agentic or metaphorically masculine modes of inquiry, involving manipulation, quantification, and control. In a very important article calling attention to this tendency, Carlson (1972) pointed specifically to the need for developing complementary research styles to these more agentic styles currently in use. She suggested, for example, the need to legitimize more communal (metaphorically feminine) research styles with an emphasis on naturalistic and qualitative studies developed by other disciplines or represented within psychology itself by the case study or applied psychology approach. This need for more exploratory research on naturalistic changes through a case-study approach was also beginning to be advocated by such researchers as Bergin and Strupp (1970). Koestenbaum (1963), too, argued that science needs to investigate more thoroughly the existential and phenomenological experience of sex roles and sex role change. With more legitimization for these more process-oriented studies, it seemed increasingly possible to imagine designing research which might combine both the quantitative and qualitative methods of inquiry with sufficient rigor to arrive at findings of significance. This is the direction I have tried to take with my own exploratory research on the concept of androgyny, from which I will be drawing partially in this book, and it is also a direction of research which I hope will receive increasing attention and legitimization in the future by other psychologists.

Typically, psychologists also shy away from moving too far from their data to speculate about the implications of the phenomena they are studying. Although I believe this is an important caution, and speculation or generalization can lead to many distortions, I am concerned that psychology has allowed itself to stay so far away from the kinds of cultural and philosophical discussions that interweave with our discipline in so many demanding ways. In the case of androgyny, there are many implications that need to be developed at the cultural level, and so, in this book, I will also move beyond the psychological level of analysis to suggest that Western culture, not just the individual person within that culture, is in need of rebalancing in androgynous directions. Highly "masculine" in its values and norms, Western culture has been characterized by rational, individualistic, competitive, technological modes. Slater (1974) has suggested that the needed values and norms for rebalancing a society lie latent within its oppressed groups and that, today, women—with their own internal values of community and interrelatedness—hold the key for humanizing our overly "masculine" society. This is the concern, too, of writers and therapists like Irene Claremont de Castillejo (1973) who fear that instead of increasing wholeness in personality development, women will develop their masculine side and neglect their feminine side which is undervalued in our society. The development of true androgyny in both sexes and in our culture at large must thus proceed hand in hand.

ANDROGYNY: EXTERNAL AND INTERNAL

The movement toward integrative ways of dealing with sex roles that is represented by the concept androgyny occurs at the level of external behavior and cognitive attitudes, as well as at the more subtle level of internal values, modes of consciousness, and orientation to the world. To facilitate an understanding of these two overlapping approaches to androgyny, I have separated their discussion to some extent in the plan of this book. In the first part of the book, I will attempt to ground the concept of androgyny in real life developmental issues, attitudes, and behaviors that illustrate what androgyny appears to look like in day-to-day living. I will also be providing exercises, sometimes at the ends of chapters, sometimes interspersed with the text, to highlight or facilitate an exploration of the concepts or areas of behavior that I will be discussing.

Much of the data and discussion of this first part of the book will be based on my own extensive, in-depth research on androgyny. In this research, I was interested in exploring the phenomenological constructs androgynous persons hold of sex roles and words like masculinity and femininity. I was looking, in addition, for clues to the development of androgyny and was interested in finding whether androgynous persons differed from people highly identified with one sex role in their life history, in critical shaping events, models, or reinforcers, and in factors they considered important in any changes of their sex role attitudes in the direction of greater equality and androgyny.

The research involved extensive, in-depth clinical interviews, structured to direct questions toward all these areas of interest. The participant-collaborators were recruited from various formal or natural groups and forty-eight men and women were chosen on the basis of the Bem Sex Role Inventory and an independent rating scale filled out by two of their nominated friends. The latter measure was designed to approximate a more behavioral measure of sex-typing than that measured by the self-report data of the BSRI. Attempts were made to obtain diversity of age, marital status, occupation, and religion among participants where possible, although a priority was placed on indentifying persons with at least a high school educational background.[3] The final forty-eight individuals chosen for the study were those persons judged on a combination of all the foregoing criteria to best represent the four groups of twelve persons, each of which constituted the comparative groups for the study: Androgynous Men (AM), Masculine-Identified Men (MIM), Androgynous Women (AW), and Feminine-Identified Women (FIW).

In discussing the data from this study in following chapters, I will be drawing from an extensive content analysis of the transcribed interviews. Where possible I will draw for illustration directly from the qualitative data, including quotes and comments by the participants to enrich the area I will be discussing. I will be guided, however, in my use of qualitative material by statistical comparisons which were also made and report as findings only those differences between androgynous and same-sex-identified persons which, even in this small sample, reached statistical significance at least at the .05 level. Other qualitatively important findings will be presented as trends, or used merely as illustration outside the context of any intended conclusion of difference between any of the groups.

I feel that this data is very important to share, not only because it is based on the openness and generosity of people talking about their own lives relating to sex roles, but because direct quotes take us more deeply into the experiential detail and visual elaboration so crucial to really exploring change in this area. I am deeply grateful for the participation of all the wonderful people who spent on the average two hours with me in their homes responding to a vast array of questions and sharing so much of themselves. There is perhaps no way of thanking persons who are so helpful in the articulation of new knowledge other than to hope to accurately portray their views of the world in the richness with which they were shared with me. I will always be grateful, too, that not only did I learn and grow a great deal from this process, but that the persons with whom I talked also seemed to find the process helpful, interesting, and meaningful to participate in. It is my deep wish as a researcher that this mutual enrichment process could follow from all research exploring new terrain, not only because the findings might thereby be much more valid reflections of real beliefs and behavior, but because this collaborative atmosphere seems the highest reflection of mutual respect.

In the second part of this book, however, we will be shifting gears to a very different level of exploration of androgyny. I will begin this section with an introduction to the nature of mythic and metaphorical thinking, crucial to an appreciation of the possible broader interpretations of masculinity, femininity, and androgyny as metaphors for different ways of looking at and interacting with the world. I will also be introducing Jungian analytic psychology as a very helpful schema for understanding personality development in the context of androgynous goals and images, and I will be very interested in making this profound and difficult approach to personality more accessible to those without background in this area. With these tools from mythological and Jungian research in mind, we will then explore the realms of the metaphorical masculine and feminine and the task of developing those parts of our personality within ourselves. We will be moving toward an exploration of internal androgyny, the nourishment and reunion of the "inner man" and the "inner woman." This section of the book will draw not only from my own Jungian studies but from my background in comparative religion and my continued interest in comparative mythology and the psychology of religion and consciousness. The final chapter will address itself to issues in understanding the cultural expressions of androgyny, and will provide a critique of the dangers of oscillating toward extremes in our cultural efforts to move toward a real integration of the metaphorically masculine and feminine modes of consciousness in our culture.

It is, finally, my hope that this book will introduce the reader to alternatives to "either/or" modes of thinking about sex roles and encourage some explorations of "and/also" ways of integrating the traditionally masculine and feminine realms of behavior and value. It has always been a philosophical conviction of mine that truth can be more closely approximated by inclusion rather than exclusion, and androgyny offers a way of exploring this possibility in actual behavior. It is my hope that this book offers in its own structure, too, an integrative format, offering not only a social psychological viewpoint but a clinical one, not only a psychological perspective but a philosophical, mythological and cultural one. The integration of the masculine and feminine is both a compelling personal and cultural challenge and I hope this book will draw us closer to both its literal and symbolic implications for human and cultural wholeness.

EXERCISES

Breaking Through Dichotomous Imagery
and Freeing Vision

Our language holds many traps for sexism and has built-in assumptions about differences between men and women. So often the female of the species is left out of our awareness by being lumped into the expressions of "mankind," the "evolution of man," and the "nature of man" or by being displaced by the use of the male pronoun "he" to stand for any ambiguous or neutral situation. These issues are not idle complaints of feminists trying to elbow into the language as into other realms of male-dominated power. Language is a crucial source of the constructs by which we think and act; what we have been trained to think and speak is often what we see. The following exercises are opportunities to stretch our language system, to see an image in a new way. They are invitations to take a second look.

1. Consider for a moment the image you have of the evolution of homo sapiens, the earliest human beings. When you conjure up the image of an early human being, is it male or female? What activities is this human being engaged in? What is it doing? How does it spend its time?

Typically anthropologists and others who have studied human evolution have tended to take the concept of early "man" literally, following the images laid down by our language which uses man to stand for all human beings. Thus, we have been taught by this tradition to visualize the early human being as the male of the species, a Tarzan-like figure and mighty hunter, running upright onto the savannah, learning to hold tools and hunt. This is the tradition represented by such popular writers as Desmond Morris (1967) who traces the evolution of the "naked ape" with a nearly exclusive emphasis on male evolution, arguing that humans lost their hair to avoid overheating during the exertions of the hunt. Again with his eye on the male, he argues that the female of the species had to become, along with the male, inordinately "sexy" in order to cement a pair bond with her mate which would endure the long separations while he was away on the hunt and she confined at home base. The increase in erogenous zones, face-to-face sex, fleshy breasts, and red lips, all shifted interest to the front of the female, presumably for the benefit of the male.

In contrast, consider more recent anthropological emphasis on the importance in human evolution of sharing and community survival (Leakey and Lewin, 1977) and of the possible role played by women in the development of pottery, agriculture, and the use of fire. These perspectives emerge much more easily by a simple, yet radical, shift to focusing on the female of the species rather than, or at least simultaneously with, the male. As Elaine Morgan asks in her startlingly fresh discussion, *The Descent of Woman* (1972), what does human evolution look like if we talk about the early human as "she"? We have to focus on totally different variables, including pregnancy. We must explain how the female can survive during evolution from her perspective. If the male is away at the hunt, what is she doing? How might early humans have evolved if we do not make such male-oriented assumptions that life was focused on the hunt?

Morgan's new questions open up an entirely new theory on human evolution through an aquatic phase during which humans sought shelter from animals by wading into water, developing the subcutaneous fat, "pendulous breasts," and tendency to weep when emotionally upset, common to aquatic mammals. Hair on the head remained as a protection for the scalp from sun rays and as a tool for young swimming children to hang onto as they played in the water. The internalizing, protecting, and moving-forward of the vagina, requiring the concommitant lengthening of the male penis, may have evolved in this analysis in order to give greater protection to the body orifices against the exposure of sitting on rocky, pebbly beaches. Whatever the merits of this argument, the contribution of

Morgan and others rests surely in the capacity to broaden our vision and generate a whole new set of questions and images.

2. Theodora Wells offers another provocative opportunity to break through to new visions of the supposedly intrinsic connection between biology and behavior (Cox, 1976). She asks us to envision a world in which the word "woman" is used to include generically both women and men and female pronouns and female voices dominate the media and government. Women play the roles of leaders in the world, for their tight and well-protected genitals give them a freedom and confidence enduring an entire lifetime. Little boys grow up with the embarrassment and vulnerability of dangling external genitalia and need protection from the external environment. Men, therefore, are naturally more passive and fulfill themselves in the role of homemaker and father. While the fantasy represents an exaggerated and still unequal role reversal, its internal logic allows for a totally new perspective on the question of "anatomy as destiny."

Take the time to fantasize this scenerio with your eyes closed, noting your feeling reactions. Share the fantasy with a friend of the same sex, of the other sex. Discuss the differences in your reactions if there are any. What can you learn from their perspective? What is new or different in this view of the world? What do you like about it? What is objectionable?

3. This exercise involves exploring the double standards of person perception: the images and behaviors we allow for men but not for women, or for women but not for men. Although we may feel we are free of such stereotypes, when we visually imagine a person or see someone in real life doing something atypical of their sex we often become uncomfortable or notice that behavior more than usual. These are clues for our hidden assumptions and visual stereotypes.

Consider, for example, an angry man and an angry woman. Picture them fully in your mind, one at a time. Do they look different in your own mental picture? If so, how? Examine them carefully; notice any subtle differences in your perception, and what this may suggest to you about the feelings and behaviors you differentially allow or expect from men versus women.

Repeat this experience with a variety of adjectives: funny, loud, sensitive, frustrated, quiet, intelligent, and so on. Experience your imagery world which carries so many of our hidden assumptions about sex roles.

Stretching Lifespace Nonverbally

Sex role issues are built into the very way we move our bodies or allow them to act. These experiences are intended to stretch your awareness of how you limit your behavior and action by your male and female stereotypes. They are designed to confront us with some of our social stereotypes about appropriate male and female power, with nonverbal signals of power. You will get the most out of these exercises if you really exaggerate them, stretching yourself into the polarities, finding out where you need to stretch the most, where you are uncomfortable, what feels right at home. It may help to have others participate in the exercises with you, if you can agree to suspend your self-consciousness. This will allow you to discuss your experiences with others.

1. Androgyny has to do with expanding the boundaries of what I consider "me," allowing into myself more of my own polarities. Take some time now to experiment with polarities nonverbally. Walk around the room exaggerating the following sets of polarities: tall-short, happy-sad, sophisticated-awkward, fast-slow, crazy-sane, interesting-boring, whimsical-serious, relaxed-stiff. Think up other polarities to explore. Watch people in the street and experience their behaviors and their potential opposites. Experiment with moving to various kinds of music.

2. This exercise focuses on some of our stereotypic nonverbal behavior as men and women. Take some time now to exaggerate and alternate nonverbally how men and women walk. Start with the other sex and walk in exaggerated fashion. Now switch to your own sex and walk in an exaggerated manner. Do not walk in your typical mode yet. Exaggerate the stereotypes. Which feels more comfortable? Which is awkward, embarrassing for you? Which leaves more freedom? Alternate back and forth rapidly. How do you feel in each?

Now walk in your typical fashion. Notice whether you allow yourself the full range of alternatives you may have discovered in the "male" versus "female" walks. Is there any more range of motion you could allow yourself? Why or why not?

Repeat this exercise with the experience of sitting down in a chair. Notice your everyday behavior, how you enter a room, walk, sit. Notice other people's behaviors in similar situations. Experiment with new behaviors. Keep your awareness heightened; it is in our habit patterns that most of our unexamined assumptions about male and female roles are carried.

3. This exercise experiments with the role of height as a signal of sex roles and power. With a partner, take turns talking while one of you stands on a chair above the other. Alternate turns. What does this experience feel like? Compare the sensations and feelings associated with the two positions. Which is the most comfortable, the least comfortable for you? Was this a new experience for you? Can you generalize anything to other everyday behaviors from your experience with this exercise?

Recognizing Projections

Projections involve the attributions to others of what is really your own undeveloped or unacceptable side. Androgyny involves the confrontation with one's own projections and the reowning of one's own unaccepted polarities. Exploring projections is neither easy nor comfortable. It is a long slow process of becoming increasingly aware of what we notice in others, both negatives and positives, as clues to our own preoccupations and possible projections. The hardest part of dealing with projections lies in the fact that they represent our areas of blindness. As the Russian proverb argues, the fish will be the last to discover water.

1. One of the most insightful introductions to the concept of projection in the context of sex roles comes from Betty and Theodore Roszak (1969, pp. vii-viii). Read their words slowly and carefully, allowing the intricacies of the whole projective process to filter through to your feelings so that you can sense the convolutions involved in the process of projection. Note too the defensive function projections play, and at what price.

He is playing masculine. She is playing feminine.

He is playing masculine *because* she is playing feminine. She is playing feminine *because* he is playing masculine.

He is playing the kind of man that she thinks the kind of woman she is playing ought to admire. She is playing the kind of woman that he thinks the kind of man he is playing ought to desire.

If he were not playing masculine, he might well be more feminine than she is—except when she is playing very feminine. If she were not playing feminine, she might well be more masculine than he is—except when he is playing very masculine.

So he plays harder. And she plays . . . softer.

He wants to make sure that she could never be more masculine than he. She wants to make sure that he could never be more feminine than she. He therefore seeks to destroy the femininity in himself. She therefore seeks to destroy the masculinity in herself.

She is supposed to admire him for the masculinity in him that she fears in herself. He is supposed to desire her for the femininity in her that he despises in himself.

He desires her for her femininity which is *his* femininity, but which he can never lay claim to. She admires him for his masculinity which is *her* masculinity, but which she can never lay claim to. Since he may only love his own femininity in her, he envies her her femininity. Since she may only love her own masculinity in him, she envies him his masculinity.

The envy poisons their love.

He, coveting her unattainable femininity, decides to punish her. She, coveting his unattainable masculinity, decides to punish him. He denigrates her femininity—which he is supposed to desire and which he really envies—and becomes more aggressively masculine. She feigns disgust at his masculinity—which she is supposed to admire and which she really envies—and becomes more fastidiously feminine. He is becoming less and less what he wants to be. She is becoming less and less what she wants to be. But now he is more manly than ever, and she is more womanly than ever . . .

2. Make a list of the qualities you most like in your best friends; the qualities you most dislike. Try on the possibility that these qualities might be projections of your own qualities: those which you value but have left undeveloped in yourself, and those which you devalue and have left hidden in your personality. Ask yourself, for every trait you dislike in the other person, how have I shown that same quality on a different scale, perhaps, in my own life. Search hard; catching a glimpse of projections may be painful, humbling. Sometimes awarenesses come while you are doing something else and you notice yourself doing something you have just complained of recently in someone else. Becoming aware of projections is a little bit like being haunted by your own self.

3. Take a long look at all those qualities which you most dislike in others, characteristics that drive you to anger and irritation or disgust.

Strong emotions are good clues to possible projections for they are loaded issues for your self-concept. After making a list of these qualities, go through the list slowly. Try to come up with some of the possible valuable qualities that lie submerged within these disliked traits. This will be very hard to do, since they are objectionable to you largely because you find them to have no redeeming values. Look again. There may be qualities embedded in the disliked traits which you are depriving yourself of by insistence on excluding them from your personality. For example, obnoxious, loud people often also have great vitality, power, and assertiveness as part of that constellation. Each of these qualities might have some merit in certain situations in enriching the range of your repertoire. Passive, dependent people may have developed skills in really listening and hearing what is going on in their environment. They may allow themselves to ask for help when they need it and be able to surrender their egoistic preoccupations in times when others need attention.

ENDNOTES

[1]The following quote and all succeeding ones in the text not cited from an identified author represent transcriptions of data from a major research study on androgyny undertaken by the present writer. This research will be described in the final section of Chapter 1.

[2]Despite the poverty of experimental research on the use of polarities in conceptualizing and the historical disrepute in which the dialetical mode of theorizing has been held in scientific circles (Rychlak, 1968), numerous personality theorists use polar constructs. Among these theorists, least well known are Angyal (1941; 1965), Bakan (1966), Koestler (1967), and Rank (1929). These theorists use a variety of terminology to portray human development as a struggle to integrate two fundamental and opposite life tendencies: the need for increased separation, individuation, and differentiation of self, and the need for increased integration and union with aspects of the environment. Optimal functioning demands the simultaneous development of both tendencies toward increasingly sophisticated forms of resolution.

[3]The participants in the study were most similar in religious background, tending to come most often from Protestant backgrounds, although more women than men in the sample come from Roman Catholic backgrounds. The male participants resembled each other in being somewhat more likely to not have a current religious affiliation; the female participants

were somewhat more likely than the men to claim current religious affiliations, the feminine-identified women to a slightly greater extent.

Androgynous participants in this sample tended to be somewhat younger than sex-typed participants, with age ranging in the total group from twenty-one to fifty-one. Compared to androgynous participants, same-sex-identified participants were more likely to be married and less likely to have pursued graduate education. Three androgynous participants were currently divorced, whereas none of the sex-typed participants were currently divorced. The participants also seemed to show differences in current or intended occupations, although these differences probably reflected, in good part, the nature of the groups from which the participants were recruited. Thus, the modal occupation for androgynous men consisted of some form of counseling, although college teaching, law, psychology, theology, and chemistry were represented as professional fields. The modal occupation for masculine-identified men was industrial management, with counseling, engineering, college teaching, or administration also represented. The modal occupation for androgynous women was also some field of counseling, with lawyer, research assistant, educational consultant, and college professor or administrator mentioned as current or intended professions. Feminine-identified women were most likely to mention housewife, homemaker, and/or mother as their current occupation, although two feminine-identified women mentioned secretarial and editorial work. Post occupations of feminine-identified women included preschool and kindergarten teacher, secretary, bank clerk, telephone operator, and counselor. All of these differences need to be taken into consideration in generalizing from the study.

2

RESTRUCTURING COGNITIVE MAPS

In light of the strong dichotomous norms and taboos which have governed sex role behavior until recently, it is important to ask whether people will be willing to experiment overtly wiith new, more flexible, androgynous behavior without some prior working through of the issues at the inner, cognitive level. The concepts we hold and the way we organize them function as permission-giving systems for our potential behavior. We will rarely have the courage to step out of the bounds of what we commonly know and value, without some internal justification for our intended behavior. Of course, some of us jump into new actions and are forced into behavioral changes by new situations, and the attitude change process then works with the opposite dynamics. The behavior change then forces us to confront the values and internal judgments we hold and revise them toward greater consistency with what we are doing. It is probably not profitable in the context of sex role behavior to argue which direction of influence typically takes precedence. Some androgynous persons find themselves experimenting and struggling to reconceptualize important sex role related issues, and then begin to incorporate more cross-sex behaviors into their repertoires. Other androgynous persons find themselves having cross-sex characteristics in their personalities and behavior, and struggle to rework their thinking about masculinity and femininity to fit their own experience.

Whether sex role change begins at the behavioral or cognitive level, it would appear that the cognitive level is involved at some point in the process, and it is this dimension which will be the focus of this chapter. We will be attempting to map out the concepts, attitudes, and values which characterize androgynous thinking, contrasting these maps with those held by people highly identified with only one sex. How do masculine-identified men and feminine-identified women differ from androgynous men and women in their views of sex role areas and their impressions of masculinity and femininity? What kinds of images, feelings, thoughts, and attitudes do these differing groups of people hold when they focus their attention on sex roles? This chapter also will offer an opportunity to you, as reader, to interact in a sense with these groups, to try on their opinions and contrast them with your own, to sketch out your own cognitive maps, and to wrestle at the borderline between ideas and viewpoints. With this goal in mind, I have organized this chapter into a series of questions and topic areas which will allow you to explore the terrain of your mental sex role assumptions and beliefs.

DEFINING SEX ROLE IDEALS

Pause a moment to consider what your sex role ideals are. How would you like to see men and women relating to the areas of work and home? What do you want in your own life with respect to your own sex role behavior and those close to you?

It is probably not surprising that androgynous men and women are much more nontraditional in their views of male and female roles at work and in the home than attitudes of masculine-identified men and feminine-identified women. Androgynous men and women place emphasis on the desired equality of men and women in these roles, including the sharing of home and work responsibilities and, in fact, will often stress the undesirability of traditional and perhaps any role distinctions based on sex. They argue for the development of human characteristics for each sex rather than differentiation of tasks or personality traits on the basis of sex alone, and they are more likely to stress that the similarities between men and women are more numerous than the differences. They lean toward a view that currently-observed differences between the sexes are culturally learned rather than biologically innate. In other words, they echo the arguments outlined in chapter one regarding integrative approaches to sex roles.

Although the arguments of masculine-identified men and feminine-identified women differ significantly from the above in the direction of dichotomous assumptions that male and female role behavior are mutually exclusive opposites, it is very interesting to note that these arguments may not be stated as blatantly and unequivocally in today's society. In a culture which has been sensitized to sex role issues by an active women's movement and affirmative action guidelines, the open assertion of strong dichotomous assumptions has become muted at times. Attitudes toward the sex role area become more subtle not only through intentional caution but because they reflect realities and blurrings and contradictions that accompany social and personal change in these areas. It is almost impossible in our media-satiated nation, to avoid dealing at some level with the issues of changing sex roles, even if the impact may often only serve to rigidify dichotomous assumptions. I am suggesting, then, that more and more people who are highly identified with one sex are nonetheless verbalizing questions about sex roles and beginning to create a complex borderline of opinion, value, and feeling which may indeed be a kind of incipient androgyny. This is particularly true among women who, despite voicing dichotomous distinctions between male and female roles or personality characteristics, may on occasion make side comments suggesting a questioning of these very dichotomies. Thus, it was a feminine-identified woman who said, almost in parentheses, "I think a fellow can be masculine in a kind of . . . quiet manner," and another shared, "I'm happy with my husband as the head of the family but he isn't that way through shouting, yelling, and aggressiveness." One feminine-identified woman confided, "I'm teaching my [son] to fight because he's picked on, and I never thought I'd do that . . . I'd rather have gentle men and loving men . . . but if they can't survive that way, I don't want them to lose their feelings about themselves because everybody else . . . is a toughy and they can't hold up to that"; another added, "I wish there was a . . . medium between [men and women] where they could both be at ease in a certain way, because I just feel that my husband and my father could find life so much easier if they could just relax a little and show those emotions."

In the area of home responsibilities, most feminine-identified women subscribe to the dichotomous assumptions that it is part of a wife's responsibilities to clean the house, have a meal ready, and create a quiet and peaceful atmosphere for the return of her husband at the end of the day, perhaps even to bear "the brunt of her husband's anger and what-not when he comes home from work." However, some feminine-identified women hinted that they wished their husbands would help more around the house, although generally they did not openly request that he help:

> He doesn't demand that I go in there and make dinner but I automatically go in and start dinner and he automatically gets the paper, and I think sometimes I should go in and sit down and read too and then say 'Let's go make dinner,' but patterns . . .

> To wash the dishes, he doesn't even know that you have to do such a thing . . . I get tired of it but everybody gets tired of doing the same things all the time. But he was never forced into doing it, and doesn't like to do it, and therefore doesn't do it.

Several feminine-identified women felt that if both husband and wife work, they should share household responsibilities. Some of the feminine identified women also mentioned disliking the tendency for men to treat women as inferiors or to feel that women "should not have any mind of their own":

> I'm very plain that the man should be the dominant one in the family . . . but I do feel that a woman has a life of her own and she should be able to carry on a life outside the home, to feel equal with the man. She shouldn't feel like she's less than him because her part is just as great as his. It's just a different kind of position that she has.

It is not rare, then, for same-sex-identified people to lean in the direction of greater equality between men and women, and this is true especially in the area of work. "Equal pay for equal work" is rarely a point of contention. It is not uncommon for masculine-identified men, therefore, to express support for more equality in one dimension of public life, or to allow that right for others, but to express a preference for dichotomous role divisions within their own homes. The ratio between publicly-advocated and privately-practiced behavior becomes a subtle clue to understanding the extent of one's own dichotomous assumptions. Examples of the tension between these two viewpoints are illustrated in the following quotes from masculine-identified men:

> I'm pretty liberal as far as the woman's role outside the home, as far as my working relationship goes. However, my wife, that's another thing. I prefer to have her home.

> If I had my druthers, if I could set it up the way I thought it ought to be, women would not work outside the home.

> In terms of having children . . . then I would probably have a few more stronger feelings . . . here I would probably see a clearer need to have some separation of roles, to have the male figure seen as the provider, to seem as the stabilizing force, as opposed to the female.

> Our roles are really defined in our house and that . . . has developed out of the necessity to move one of the two of us in an occupational or professional direction in terms of our . . . work . . . We made the decision early that it would be me that would pursue the career and not my wife.

The purpose of emphasizing the subtleties in current expressions of dichotomous roles is not to create an androgynous vigilante eager to spot discrepancies in other people's behavior, but rather to call attention to the dynamics of sex role conceptual change in current society. We are all, in a sense, masculine-identified or feminine-identified in that we are influenced by the sexism and dichotomous assumptions of our culture. We could all be more fully human; androgyny is not an arrival point. Therefore, in understanding the differences between androgynous persons and same-sex-identified persons who may be also struggling to be more flexible in sex role change, we are in an exciting position to gather some clues to our own potential resistances to change. In other words, no matter how androgynous one may see oneself, it is possible to ask the additional question, how am I like this feminine-identified woman or this masculine-identified man? We might make guesses that those areas where androgynous persons differ from same-sex-identified persons will offer clues to our trigger points, resistances, and lingering dichotomous identifications. As we explore the next set of questions, be alert to the subtleties that seem to differentiate androgynous from same-sex-identified persons.

The Female Role

Ask yourself first, what is your view of the female sex role? What do you feel women should or should not do in the worlds of work and home? In particular, what is your view toward the working mother?

Although androgynous persons are far more flexible in the range of behaviors they consider appropriate to women, it is not uncommon, as mentioned above, for feminine-identified women and masculine-identified men to believe in the concept of "equal pay for equal work" and to be at least partially supportive of more equality between men and women in some work areas. One aspect of the traditional female role, however, remains inviolate for most same-sex-identified persons: the importance of a mother not working when her children are young. This issue serves as a key differentiator of androgynous and same-sex-identified persons and is one of those trigger areas which may be more resistant to attitude change than many others.

The negative reactions to working mothers held by masculine-identified men dealt mostly with the harmful effects on children of not having parental guidance in the home, as well as negative comments toward women who worked chiefly to increase their standard of living beyond what was judged necessary. For example:

> I think that once children are born into that marriage, that a woman has no business being out of the home. She has a business that's more important than that and that's home taking care of the children . . . I know a lot of different women that are working . . . that I personally believe ought to be home . . . I see their families going down the tube, or their kids are in deep trouble, or they're working and buying their kids all sorts of expensive little goodies and they're just spoiling their kids rotten . . . I'm very negative about that.
> Well I know one couple, they both work, both have careers, and their kids are all screwed up and I think that's partly the reason. I think that's a *big* part of the reason.

Feminine-identified women are also much more likely than androgynous women to stress the importance of a mother being in the home while children were young:

In my own belief I think a mother should be home when her children are very small, until they're in school, I definitely believe that.

I think it's important to be home when my kids are home . . .My mother always worked and my grandmother . . . mainly took care of us and when I look back, I can remember that when really important and exciting things happened, I would run to my grandma before I would run to my mother and I don't want my kids to be that way. I want my kids, I want when something happens and they're really excited, I want to be here when they come home so that they can tell Mom about it, so that when they get older they have . . . a home life to remember.

As a mother and a woman, I see the woman in the home as a mother. I have a very strong belief that that is their job and their responsibility.

Well, [working and raising children] wouldn't work out for me [laugh]. I guess it's because I read too much and worry too much about my own child, and I feel that a babysitter has so much influence on your child, if you would leave her, it would be a very tricky situation.

In considering the issue of working mothers, feminine-identified women were concerned chiefly with the welfare of the child: "I feel sorry for the child . . . when they're very small I think they need all the attention they can get." It is interesting, however, that unlike masculine-identified men, many feminine-identified women also expressed an understanding and tolerance, despite their own personal preference for staying in the home, that some women "are just not meant to be a motherly, housewife type person, some women have to get out and they have to work, they're just career-oriented." Several women speculated that in such cases the children might be better off with the mother working:

I'm sure some women have to keep working 'cause that's really what they're cut out for. I mean it would really hurt them not to be working, they need that outside stimulation.

[A friend] went back to work right after each kid was born, but for her, that's what she had to do or she would probably have climbed the walls [laugh].

I do understand the woman who stands in the doorway and says I cannot stand to stay home with these children and is working for that reason. She's far better off and so are the children.

Satisfactions and Dissatisfactions
with the Female Role

If you are female, you might ask yourself at this point, how would you rate yourself on a seven point scale of satisfaction with the traditional female role where one equals highly dissatisfied and seven equals highly satisfied? In addition, what satisfactions and dissatisfactions with the female role have been most noteworthy in your life?

The answers androgynous and feminine-identifed women give to these types of questions vary significantly. Androgynous women are far more dissatisfied with the traditional female role than are feminine-identified women. It is important to note, however, that this does not imply that they are unhappy being women. On the contrary, androgynous women are very affirmative in their enjoyment of being women; it is the restrictive female role as traditionally defined that they are rejecting or questioning.

It is interesting, too, that feminine-identified women report almost twice as many satisfactions as dissatisfactions with the female role, whereas the ratio is about 1.5 to 1 in favor of dissatisfactions for androgynous women. You can get a sense of your own ratio of satisfactions to dissatisfactions by comparing the length of your two lists. The two groups of women appear to differ also in the kinds of examples given in each category, suggesting a different mapping out of these dimensions in their cognitive structure and internal experience. In the imagery and choices made by these two groups of women, we will be seeking clues to differences in their existential and phenomenological experience of the female role and clues to the parameters of our own inner worlds.

Feminine-identified women most often described the satisfaction of giving birth to a child or being a mother:

> I think one of my biggest thrills of being a woman was having a baby . . . that is the ultimate in experiences, I think.
>
> I guess having a baby is one of the most wonderful things of being a woman, of being feminine, it's just about the most important thing and . . . besides giving birth to a child, having the rapport that a mother has with the child, rather than a man, is really nice.

Feminine-identified women also mentioned most often such satisfactions as being a wife or having one's husband proud of you and being creative in the home; dressing up in beautiful long dresses; dating and becoming engaged; being able to "smooth over conflict" or act as a "go-between, . . . a sounding board," and being treated by men with a kind of respect, "awe," or greater care and tenderness: "I could get hurt if a man treated me just like he treated another man . . . like if they told me to go to hell and the next day they're buddies. Well, if they did that to me, I would be crushed and I would never forget it."

Androgynous women, in contrast, most often stressed the satisfaction of being warm, loving, supportive, and expressive of feelings. They also mentioned being associated with the women's movement and feelings of sisterhood and increasing opportunities (for example, "It's a nice time to be a woman, it really is.") and described appreciation for not having had the conditioning men are exposed to with regard to being invulnerable and unable to express feelings: "I think it's easier for a woman to keep the nurturant type qualities, the openness, the sensitivity and to add on a repertoire of career-orientation, verbal skills, etc. than it is for a man to . . . gain that same type of sensitivity . . . It seems like it's easier for a woman to become a person than a man." However, several androgynous women expressed that they could not think of many satisfactions specifically related to being female as distinct from being a person, and several others stated that most of their satisfactions in terms of competence, professional activities, or being a woman had been associated with deviating from traditional female roles.

Dissatisfactions with the female role also differed between feminine-identified women and androgynous women and suggest clues to their different senses of the female role and related constructs. For the most part, differences between these women in their dissatisfactions at least partially reflect differences in the context of their lives, the emphasis being on home life for feminine-identified women and on career environments for the androgynous women. Dissatisfactions mentioned by feminine-identified women thus centered around the relatively greater responsibilities that fell to women as the ever-present person at home, and occasional feelings of being burdened or lacking certain freedoms their husbands had:

> Having to remind him of things dissatisfies me, you know, keeping track of a calendar, what events we have . . . his relatives' birthdays . . . Now that we're married it's my responsibility to do all that

and sometimes I kind of wish that he'd be a little more thoughtful and remember some things too.

If your husband wants to sleep late in the morning he can, but you still get up and take care of the kids on Saturday morning. You're more in demand. When you're on vacation, the woman is still working. When you're having a party, the woman is still working and the man's entertaining himself.

I think that sometimes men can take so much for granted and my husband has done this. He'll call up and say, 'I'm going hunting Saturday morning,' and you know he doesn't say, 'Do you have anything else planned.' I mean if I would protest it, fine, he'd say if it's that important or so on and so forth, but it's just the idea that they just don't quite have the responsibility. They're a little more carefree. Like I said, if he's an hour late from work, he's an hour late from work. Well I can't do that. I just can't pick up and leave for an hour, because I've got two kids at home.

An additional concern and regret present in a small number of feminine-identified women concerned their avocations and life plans, expressed in such comments as, "Sometimes I think that I'm probably not doing all that I should for myself as far as getting out and doing something" or "Sometimes I had to wait too long between opportunities [to do art work]."

In contrast to these concerns, dissatisfactions expressed by androgynous women, who are more likely than feminine-identified women to work, centered around pressure to conform to traditional female role expectations, being treated as inferior, "presumed to be less likely . . . to succeed" professionally, and not taken seriously in their career efforts:

The way it is now, females have to shut up too much, have to know their place too much, have to take orders from men too much, have to be victims of the male world too much. I don't like that at all.

[Another] dissatisfaction is with the educational system and the way they treat the female role . . . we had a boys' and girls' water fountain . . . and one time I drank from the boys' water fountain . . . and someone reported me and . . . I really became belligerent to the teacher about it and . . . I was just stifled. All of a sudden my assertiveness was just stifled and that is one of the reasons why I became really afraid of different [things]. All of a sudden I just got in line, and you know, that dissatisfies me that that happened.

That's to me . . . the whole crux of everything . . . that men simply don't take you seriously. You have to keep proving yourself over and over again and it gets to be so oppressive to have to prove to every-body that you're really serious . . . pretty soon you don't care any-more, and I really think if a lot of women 'fail,' in quotes, that's why, because they don't think it's worth it anymore, to have to prove . . . everything constantly and . . . never arrive at [the] position where you really are considered totally serious and totally equal.

Androgynous women also stressed dissatisfactions related to job situations:

The paranoia in other people . . . who were threatened by any sort of assertiveness on my part.

The occupational hazard that a woman [in a leadership position] falls into . . . that they burn themselves out [in conflicts around the] fine line between [exercising the power and authority of your job] and looking like you're a woman who doesn't know her place to too many people who want a woman to know her place.

Being restricted as to what kind of jobs I could get and lower pay scales, because I'm a woman, regardless of the fact that I'm a head of a household . . .You know, they asked me what was my experi-ence . . . I'd tell them that I have a B.A., and they'd ask me if I could type.

There just weren't any role models . . . like when I was in seventh grade, I decided I wanted to be a lawyer but it seemed like looking around to be sort of an outrageous kind of idea . . . so that was dis-satisfying.

Androgynous women were also dissatisfied with past feelings of inferiority about their appearance and with past worries about being pretty, having to "put on this big show to appeal to . . . boys especially," and not fitting the media image (for example, "I couldn't be . . . happy with my body, I always should be something else. I should be thinner or heavier here, I hate all that. That hurts so much, and so often as I was growing up."). They also mentioned dissatisfactions with not being encouraged to enjoy athletics or exercising their bodies and with having such a hard time and so little support in becoming confident of themselves as a nontraditional woman.

Tracing out the differences between the satisfactions and dissatis-factions between androgynous and feminine-identified women suggests that the groups relate quite different images and pictures to their views of the female role, reflecting their different life experiences perhaps. Since imagery is such a crucial part of one's existential stance and of one's mental and emotional maps, the contrasts in imagery may heighten the difficulty of communication between these two groups. One might note, however, that the trend toward more feminine-identified women working and more androgynous women returning to an affirmation of traditional feminine skills in the home alongside their other work interests (for example, Betty Friedan, 1977) may signal an interesting rapprochement of cognitive maps and experiences which might enhance the androgynous dimension in both groups. Until such a time, however, the key satisfactions and dissatisfactions of each group could alert us to sensitive areas either inhibiting or facilitating movement toward androgynous life styles.

The Male Role

After this lengthy exploration of concepts and cognitive maps of the female sex role, take some time to consider your views of the male sex role. What do you feel men should or should not be doing in the realms of work and home? What changes would you like to see in the male role?

Attitudes toward the male sex role appear to be an even more dramatic differentiator of androgynous and same-sex-identified persons than were attitudes toward the female role. In fact, one of the real signals that someone is changing their cognitive constructs towards greater androgyny appears to be their willingness and indeed enthusiasm for changes in the male role. Unlike feminine-identified women and especially masculine-identified men, androgynous persons are critical of the traditional, dichotomously-portrayed male sex role, rather than focusing exclusively or predominantly on the female role as the locus of sex role change. In other words, androgynous people have gone beyond the media emphasis on the female role and the women's movement and have raised serious questions about the male role as well. Androgynous men in particular argue along the following lines:

> I think that the male should spend at least 50 percent of the time with the children. It shouldn't be just the woman's job, and men ought to learn how to emote and react and feel with their kids . . . I don't want to see the man saddled with the responsibility for providing the sole source of income . . . for the family.
>
> I'm very down on the traditional roles. I think both sexes lose. Women lose lots worse than men, but men lose too . . . I think women should

have careers; I think that couples should share housework and child rearing equally.

Several androgynous men mentioned the ideal living/working arrangement between a man and a woman as a situation where one job would be shared by both. Two even suggested that they would enjoy a role reversal for a period in which they could stay home and care for the house while the woman worked. These types of criticisms of the traditional male role were missing in the comments of masculine-identified men.

Feminine-identifed women differed also from androgynous women in conceptualizing and stressing the male role in the traditional terms of career orientation and being the primary provider for the family. They also were more likely to add that they would not like this role for themselves:

> To me that's a man's job, to support his family, and I've never thought about doing that, I've never had the desire to go out and work all my life supporting myself, a family.
>
> I wouldn't want my husband to stay home and me try to do his job or I wouldn't like to have to go out and have him depend on me earning a living [laugh].
>
> I'm not a career-type person, and so I like to see a man make good, I like to see him get . . . up the ladder, you know, make good money and be happy in his work and his job . . . Sometimes I'd like to work but I don't think I'd ever like to work full-time, so I would definitely like my husband to have a good-paying job and to be happy, so I won't have to [laugh].
>
> [My husband] is the breadwinner and I like it. I expect it . . . I think it's a big responsibility to have to get up every morning and go to work and you are the one who is being depended on for the income and the insurance and the doctor bills, everything . . . I really feel that it's a terrible responsibility, a terrible job. Maybe I'm almost saying that I'd get terribly bored, if I had to. I'd have to love it a lot to get up there and know that this is my job, and I had to put everything into it, that this is my responsibility, my family was my responsibility. I'd have to choose something everyday that is going to bring home X amount of dollars to support this family. I really have a lot of respect for him, and I really admire him.

In none of these comments is there the suggestion that this conception of the male role as full-time provider might have some creative alternatives, such that neither spouse need carry the burden of that total responsibility. The concept of shared employment typically does not appear to be tenable in their cognitive fields.

Satisfactions and Dissatisfactions with the Male Role

If you are male, you might ask yourself at this point, how would you rate yourself on a seven point rating scale of satisfaction with the traditional male role, where one equals highly dissatisfied and seven equals highly satisfied. What satisfactions and dissatisfactions would you point to in particular?

As was the case in comparing satisfactions and dissatisfactions for feminine-identified women and androgynous women above, masculine-identified men and androgynous men also differed significantly on this dimension. Masculine-identified men were clearly more satisfied with the typical male role and reported over twice as many satisfactions as dissatisfactions. Again, it is important to note that the dissatisfactions androgynous men felt for the traditional role did not reflect dissatisfaction with being male.

Androgynous and masculine-identified men tended to resemble each other in the main areas of their satisfactions and dissatisfactions, but the accent and stress on these dimensions varied. Both groups included as major satisfactions the opportunities for success, accomplishment, leadership, competence, and being in control of one's life and the greater freedom and independence in what they could or were allowed to do as men compared to women. Masculine-identified men, however, also placed emphasis on being seen as an authority as a satisfaction of the male role:

> I'm not going to say I . . . feel badly about my wife putting me in the role of having to make decisions. I revel in it.
>
> Even though my wife and I share a lot of the decisions, my kids still look at me as being the authority in the family . . . from the viewpoint of Daddy's the wise old owl.
>
> I've found tremendous satisfaction out of being able to give direction to people and having an authoritarian posture as a by-product in terms of my role as a male.
>
> I suppose in general the people that seemed to come to me and confide things . . . people who are several years my senior . . . gives

me a very warm feeling, to think that . . . evidently I do come across as being rational, as being consistent, as having it together fairly well, which again relates back to what I had said in terms of my idea of a masculine role, having a rational, firm approach to things.

Both groups of men also discussed their dissatisfactions with the male role in terms of the pressures to perform, to provide money for the family, to maintain the male image; relationships with women; and relationships with men; however, their emphasis differed even more. Masculine-identified men tended to discount or underplay their dissatisfactions with responsibilities at work or home, mentioning that they viewed the perceived alternative (that is, the traditional female role) as undesirable:

> Well I get tired some days [laugh] . . . I wouldn't want to reverse the role and stay home; I think I'd go bananas. So even though I get tired sometimes of fighting the crowd, I guess, what are the alternatives, so . . . I don't know of anything I'm really dissatisfied with.
>
> Oh, I think sometimes when I'm having particular problems with the [children] . . . and it's my responsibility to sit down and counsel them, and it's really hairy and hard going, I guess sometimes I think, you know, I'd really like to come back the next time as a dog [laughs] . . . you know, it's a very minor thing and . . . I really have never gotten to a point where I felt seriously about not wanting to be a male.
>
> I've never really thought of my job that way, that, boy, the pressures are getting too tough for me, I'm going to cool it because maybe this is as far as I want to go. I've never gotten to that point.

These men seem to be more likely than androgynous men to perceive the alternative female role as very unattractive:

> If I was a woman, I could look back, none of the life I've had could I have pursued, *none.*
>
> If I had the same thoughts and ideals and I were a woman, I would feel terribly suppressed . . . during my childhood.
>
> What I wouldn't like about being a woman it'd be staying home and not going out working.

A few masculine-identified men mentioned dissatisfactions in male-female relationships (for example, relatively undeveloped social skills in men or lack of depth in men's relationships to women) and in male-male relationships (for example, not liking to settle disputes by fighting, not enjoying feeling pressure from male friends to go hunting and fishing as a male thing to do, and not liking competition between men where each tries to "out-masculinize the other": "You know, 'Well, I watched one football game on Saturday and my wife didn't say anything.' And the next guy said, 'Well I watched two football games on Saturday and she got me a beer everytime I wanted one' ").

Androgynous men were stronger and more articulate in their dis-satisfactions with all these areas: the pressure to achieve in work and life, traditional male-female interactions, and the distance and lack of openness between men. They emphasized in particular their discontent with pres-sures to perform and provide:

> Pressure. Push. Push. Go. Go. Be great, be good, be terrific . . . I'm uncomfortable with that . . . be a good sport . . . go to college, bang, go out, get a job, get married, be a success . . . whew! Too much pressure, too much push.
>
> The pressures that a man has to get a job and be the sole supporter of the family.
>
> Simply not being able to fulfill all those expectations . . . achieving, intellectual, capable.
>
> When you are responsible and you do OK, why that is fine, but when you are not responsible and you fuck up, then you are a failure.
>
> People either expect things of me that I don't want to do or give, or they assume I am a certain way and I am not.
>
> Expectations that I perform, that I do well, that I progress . . . to re-main strong and not let things bother me . . . because I am male.

What is perhaps most striking in this comparison of the cognitive maps and images of the male role held by the masculine-identified men and an-drogynous men is the differential willingness of the two groups to be critical of the male role. While the masculine-identified men perceive similar stres-ses in the male role of provider, they are less willing than androgynous men to consider these stresses as overt negatives or dissatisfactions. In fact, they buttress this tendency by an appeal to what they perceive as an even more dissatisfying alternative, the traditional female role. Recall, too, that feminine-identified women hold an equally rigid conceptualization of the typical male role as career-oriented, full-time provider, and are very reluc-tant to imagine it as a role they might embrace. We begin to get a clue that one of the powerful stabilizers of dichotomous sex roles might be this tendency to hold highly stereotyped conceptions of cross-sex behavior. This prevents an exploration of alternatives which might force a reevaluation of one's own sex role. Same-sex-identified people may have difficulty perceiving that each sex role has both strengths and weaknesses and might be broken down and put together in a more flexible way, if both sex roles were reevaluated together. Instead, such persons may limit their choices in behavior because of undesirabilities in what they perceive as the other side of an inevitable dichotomy. We can speculate that change toward more androgynous, integrative cognitive maps might be facilitated by focusing on changing the rigid definitions of roles for both sexes simultaneously. In the meantime, the way in which the male role is conceptualized and whether it is seen as needing change will remain a trigger point or clue to potential androgyny.

Sexuality

What are your attitudes about male and female roles in the area of sexuality, for example, in terms of such issues as who initiates sex? What are your attitudes toward male and female homosexuality?

It appears that both men and women in general would like to see more equality in the male and female roles around sexuality, particularly in the direction of women being more active sexually than the typical role allowed. Even masculine-identified men and feminine-identified women tended to report a preference for women and men taking equal roles in initiating sex rather than have the male play the more dominant role. The overt view that "the man ought to be the aggressor and . . . the female ought to be passive . . . I can't stand a pushy woman" was a minority opinion among masculine-identified men and only somewhat more common among feminine-identified women, a few of whom mentioned their preference for male dominance of sexual behavior or introduced their statements about their own sexual assertiveness almost apologetically by such prefaces as "it's terrible" or "that's another thing that's funny about me."

A more subtle examination of people's responses, however, suggests that "more equality" in the sexual area can be defined in a great number of ways and may not represent such a consensus of change in this area as may have appeared at first. For example, although masculine-identified men may express a desire for women to be more active sexually, this might mean simply: slightly more active than the traditional totally passive woman. Thus, masculine-identified men were much more likely to qualify their support for increased sexual activity by females through the following types of comments and imagery:

> I don't like a superaggressive girl, not one that's on the prowl and on the make all the time. That turns me off. Again, this is getting back to the idea of the feminine role, a certain degree of dependency but yet, the ability to respond independently and respond without any qualms or any fears.
>
> I don't like a woman to be very passive all the time, sometimes, but not all the time . . . I'm saying sometimes I feel like being aggressive, and I want to be, you know, the man, swoop down on my woman kind of thing.
>
> It doesn't really bother me one way or the other, although if . . . my wife kind of approaches me, I'm probably not as open to her approaches as I expect her to be of mine.
>
> It should be kind of two-way . . . I guess I'd just like to see my wife initiate sex one time [laughs].

In contrast, more androgynous men tended to mention the burdens and "pressure on men *always* to be the initiator" or their personal discomfort with that expectation, and one might infer that androgynous men would be more consistently supportive of women exploring more assertive sexual styles.

Women, in particular, placed emphasis on the difficulty of over-coming earlier "conditioning" in the sexual area and learning to be more assertive. As one feminine-identified woman described: "Once you're married, it's all right and everything's OK, and a woman can be as aggressive as a man, but I can't do it. There's something subconsciously that's stopping me." Androgynous women especially discussed this subtle difficulty of becoming more assertive sexually despite the desirability of doing so, and one gets a sense that sex role change in the sexual area, even where perceived to be desirable, may be proceeding more slowly than in other areas of work and home responsibilities. It would not be surprising if this were so, since sex role change in the sexual area is even more intimately tied to an interpersonal situation than changes in other areas. If one's partner leans toward traditional sex role views of sexuality, even the androgynous woman is going to have difficulty being more assertive in such a subtly interdependent type of situation. Androgynous men, lacking strong social support for their inclinations toward a less dominating sexual role, may have hidden this tendency even from androgynous women and forced themselves into a kind of role playing traditionally thought more common among women. Women may have faked orgasms, but it was not often thought that men may have felt the necessity to "fake" aggressive, dominant sexuality. In addition, the residual tendencies for many women to be less assertive about their sexuality and for some assertive women to feel attracted to a more assertive man, probably feed the difficulty of men becoming open to a more flexible, receptive, sensual style in themselves. In the area of sexuality, possibly more than in all other areas of human experience, the mutually reverberating cycle of role expectations seems to mitigate against rapid sex role change and is a trigger area well worth exploring by those who wish to move in the direction of greater androgyny.

In contrast to the subtlety of attitudes toward sexuality in general, androgynous persons differed far more clearly from masculine-identified men and feminine-identified women in their acceptance or tolerance of homosexuality in society. As mentioned in chapter one, this openness should not be construed as reflecting personal choices of sexual lifestyle; rather it reflects a greater acceptance and respect for the rights of persons to make sexual choices in a variety of directions despite one's own personal stance. Perhaps the noteworthy feature in these findings is not the tendency of androgynous persons to be more accepting of homosexuality, but the same-sex-identified persons' tendency to be unaccepting. This relatively greater intolerance of homosexuality might well be expected as a corollary of the belief that cross-sex behaviors are particularly taboo in persons of either sex and the ingrained fear of homosexuality built into strict adherence to traditional sex roles. In light of this strong attitude difference between androgynous and same-sex-identified persons, one might well examine one's attitudes toward homosexuality and heterosexuality at length to explore the range of feelings elicited by these choices. Some social and feminist critics like Charlotte Perkins Gilman even draw attention to the possibility that emphasis in our society on sexuality per se, whether heterosexuality or homosexuality, may be a sign of sexism, unduly interpreting the relationships of persons in terms of sexual dimensions as opposed to issues of intellect and friendship (Lane, 1979). In any case, issues of Sexuality and homosexuality are trigger points for re-evaluating one's own sex role attitudes and possible movement toward androgyny.

The Women's Movement

Take a moment to ask yourself, what are your attitudes toward the women's movement, the idea of an organized group of feminists working together to raise consciousness of sex roles in our culture and to implement changes toward greater sex role equality in the various institutions which comprise that culture (for example, legal, economic, educational, religious, and other institutions)? What were your attitudes toward the early radical feminist movement of the late 1960s and early 1970s?

Although it is perhaps not surprising that androgynous men and women are more positive than same-sex-identified persons towards the women's movement in general, attitudes in this area are characterized by some interesting trends that may prove helpful in teasing out some subtleties of sex role attitude change. First, feminine-identified women appear to be more positive about the women's movement than masculine-identified men, and more than half mentioned some positive outcomes of the women's movement in such areas as equal pay for working women. However, many of the feminine-identified women made negative qualifying statements about the extreme protests or "squalking" of the movement's advocates and labeled themselves deliberately as "not a woman's libber." This label had a negative value in the cognitive maps of most feminine-identified women.

Even more interesting, perhaps, is the tendency for androgynous women, despite their greater positiveness about the women's movement, to not identify with the radical wing of that movement. Only a small minority of androgynous women defined themselves in radical feminist terms, although several were active in professions where they stressed feminist issues and others were very excited and involved in consciousness-raising groups and courses. Androgynous women tended to define themselves as interested in human liberation and not just women's liberation and, therefore, were not identified typically with the more extreme "radical feminist" emphasis of the late 1960s and early 1970s.

The masculine-identified men expressed the most mixed and negative reactions to the women's movement, tending to criticize either the degree of radicalism and over-reactive tendencies of the women's movement or the political and group nature of the movement:

> I think it's kind of comical . . . if these women want to be liberated, let them go ahead, but why bother everybody else.

Again, it's the individual thing. OK, if a person wants to say 'Hey, I'm going to break down this barrier by myself' and not . . . raise a big cloud about it. OK, that's fine, . . . that's the way it should be done . . . I think that the ones that are really sincere about it don't necessarily go through groups . . . They just go out and do things.

If they'd just . . . be people without having to hide behind some kind of label, I'd be much happier with it.

They're [the spokespersons] there for political ends; if the group was for left-footed soccer kickers, they'd be in that, if they thought they could get some political mileage out of it, I think. People are in there blowing their own horn, they're not there to help people; that's what I find trouble with.

This criticism of the group-oriented nature of the women's movement is a very noteworthy trend, for it suggests a powerful source of resistance to sex role change. Feminists have long argued that women have not been able to effect change toward greater sex role equality in large part because of their lack of group or class consciousness. Since social change requires challenging the power structures of the society, women who remain isolated and reluctant to organize their own power structures will be handicapped, at least in terms of this type of social change strategy. Men who argue against the group nature of the women's movement are perhaps reluctant to face the real power issues at stake in social change and, to some extent, the widespread implications of such change. Although one woman can work on her own to effect change, to emphasize only this approach is to underrate the real group and social pressures maintaining the status quo.

Where androgynous men made criticisms of the women's movement, the stress was more likely to fall on negative attitudes toward men which alienated even those men who were trying to grow in this area themselves: "I think it's a great idea, but if somebody comes up to me and says 'Hey buster, get with it,' I feel like you haven't listened to me, you don't know if I support you or not . . . calling the males names is not going to facilitate communication." As will be seen in a later chapter, androgynous men have been influenced considerably by key women in their lives who have advocated sex role equality, and it is not surprising that they would emphasize the personal context and quality of communication in their concerns about the women's movement. Again, the nuances of these different groups' attitudes toward the women's movement can serve as a comparison and exploration of your own views in this area.

Future Changes

Again, pause for a moment to ask yourself a different kind of question. Do you see your attitudes toward male and female roles or your development as a man or woman changing or moving in any particular direction in the future? Give yourself time to think about the evolution of your views in this area and to speculate on the future.

It is interesting that masculine-identified men tend to be less likely than androgynous men to foresee future changes in their sex role attitudes in the future. Although this may appear as an overly fine point, one might hypothesize that one of the key stabilizers of sex role attitudes may be the tendency even among masculine-identified men who have become less traditional in their sex role attitudes, to level off earlier and reach less intensive levels of awareness compared with changes experienced by androgynous men. In other words, a clue to androgyny may not only be a presently-expressed interest in sex role equality, but a sense of expected evolution in one's life as one encounters even more complex and subtle situations requiring sex role flexibility.

Although the majority of androgynous and feminine-identified women did speculate about some future changes, the kinds of changes each group anticipated appeared to be qualitatively different and the androgynous women could more clearly articulate those changes as part of an ongoing process. Androgynous women focused chiefly on career development and increased personal confidence, independence, and assertiveness, building a picture of increasing balance as their desired goal over time:

> Something I'm working on right now . . . is that I'd like to keep the warmth, softness, caring, loving attitude I have toward life and toward people and yet, I would like to become more forceful and strong and powerful.
>
> I would like to develop more of the . . . skills that have been traditionally female . . . some of the home skills, I guess, like cooking. I've always hated cooking . . . my viewpoint was that it was . . . the negative feminine thing to do because it indicated staying home with the

kids and taking care of the house and all that . . . I think I have been exploring some of the traditional ways of being that I had rejected for a long time, and after I'm finished exploring . . . I'm hoping that I can . . . take the good parts out of those traditional things that I never allowed myself to explore before . . . but then go back a little bit more toward the radical side of things, but feel comfortable in being there and feel comfortable with the things out of the traditional femininity that I'm able to glean, but still be more my own person too, become a little bit more aggressive and . . . active, but with the warmth and with the confidence.

I know that I'm . . . feeling more confident and more competent, and more able to actually define what I want, whereas before, I didn't really know what I wanted. I was just sort of blowing in the wind and pretty much adapted to anything that would really come my way, but I think the direction that I am moving in is that I can sort of define what I want and know how to go after it.

In contrast, feminine-identified women seemed less likely to have clear plans or goals for the future:

> I guess I've never really projected what I'd be doing.
> I'm not sure I really ever know what my direction is until I'm there.
> I wish I did. I talk about looking forward but I don't look way far ahead. If you asked me what I'll be doing ten years from now, I don't know. I guess that's kind of sad in a way, not to have a long range plan.

Many feminine-identified women did speculate about some changes in their lives by some indefinite future point, and these changes chiefly revolved around working:

> I do want to go back to school. I'd like to be able to say that I can do this, that I have a trade, that I have a particular area that I'm good at, because I can do a little bit of everything but I can't do anything really really well, and I'd just like to be able to say, well I have a job and can make good money, if I wanted to. But that I don't think will ever be totally important to me.
>
> Someday I want more education and I want to go back to work again, but I don't want to go back and work for nickel and dime type thing. I'd like to get some kind of training so I could get a job that's worthwhile,

where I'd feel like I was contributing something rather than just putting in my time and bringing home a pay check.

I'm trying to change. I have these ideas that I've wanted to be all my life . . . a housewife and a mother and I'm finding out that that's not necessarily enough because . . . in this time and age, you don't keep as busy as our mothers did when they were rearing their children . . . I'm trying to think . . . maybe that my idea of leaving my child with a babysitter isn't quite so bad . . . and to see whether I could do something outside the home also, but it's hard when you've thought of things one way all your life. It's hard to change and accept them yourself.

I have these . . . two me's and one me is going the career route and one is going the mother route . . . I feel like I'm either going to end up at home, feeling a little bit discontented but feeling it was important for me to be there, or I would try to combine, I mean I definitely want children, the other me would be somehow trying to combine a profession with raising a family and probably feeling guilty because I would always be wondering if I was devoting enough of myself to them.

The tendency among feminine-identified women to have fewer long-range goals and vaguer, more indefinite anticipations of future changes than androgynous women parallels the greater tendency of masculine-identified men to level off earlier in their sex role changes than androgynous men. The tentative future wishes of some feminine-identified women appear even more poignantly against the backdrop of their tendency to not expect much change in their lives in these areas. This tendency to be less future-oriented may serve as a continual brake to exploring life alternatives that demand looking beyond present circumstances and planning, and numerous researchers have pointed to the widespread tendency in women workers to overlook the need for long-range career planning (Hennig and Jardim, 1976). It is possible, too, that same-sex-identified persons may restrict the range of their future speculations about sex roles because for them the traditional roles overshadow other possibilities. If one believes there are only the presently existing alternatives to choose from, one might well be more content to stay within the imaginal framework of the known and restrict one's cognitive map to the familiar. For all these reasons, findings in this area underscore the need to examine not only one's own present cognitive maps, but to question their flexibility through some kind of time dimension.

MASCULINITY AND FEMININITY

The words masculinity and femininity are the key concepts by which societies have generally spoken of sex role related behavior judged to be appropriate to the two sexes. It is helpful to distinguish masculinity and femininity from maleness and femaleness, these latter two concepts referring to the biological states of having a male or a female body or genetic make-up. This separation of concepts allows for the possibility that prescriptions about appropriate masculine and feminine behaviors in a society might not be simple descriptions or translations of biological givens, but might reflect the role of cultural norms in shaping our expectations of sex role behavior. This debate is, of course, central to many of the differences in conceptual schemas of androgynous and same-sex-identified persons.

Take some time to reflect on your own use of the words masculinity and femininity. What do these concepts mean to you when you hear them? Do you use the words yourself and in what context?

As mentioned in the first chapter, the traditional use of the concepts of masculinity and femininity by same-sex-identified persons has been dichotomous. In other words, masculinity and femininity are mutually exclusive opposites thought to be only appropriate for men versus women. In this way of thinking, masculinity conjures up images of strength versus the images of softness and gentleness evoked by the concept of femininity. In contrast, androgynous persons appear to have struggled to use these concepts of masculinity and femininity in new ways and many attempt to avoid their use completely. Androgynous persons might use these concepts in quotes as referring to those sets of traits typically expected of the two sexes, but their feelings may be quite negative toward the continued use of the constructs and their use of these terms often pejorative as a signal of stereotypic behavior in someone. One common tendency among androgynous persons is to describe these concepts as "social fictions," "universal constructs that apply to either sex," or ways to summarize two patterns or ways of looking at and interacting with the world. As such, masculinity and femininity become metaphors for two clusters of human tendencies, each of which might characterize a person of either sex depending on their goals, interests, or upbringing. Masculinity, in this context, might refer to a linear, rational, aggressive way of interacting with the world and femininity might refer to an intuitive, interrelated, receptive way of taking in information, a difference resembling, for example, the two modes of processing information that seem to characterize the two halves of the cerebral hemispheres (Ornstein, 1972). Men and women would both have access to each type of functioning.

It appears that the cognitive maps of androgynous persons for masculinity and femininity may also reflect a struggle to redefine and open up the meaning of these two words. This alternative type of struggle centers on the attempt to allow more range and flexibility in behaviors and characteristics that men and women could include in their self-concepts. The ideal involves opening up the positive qualities of each sex role for both sexes, with a particular concern for not losing the positive qualities traditionally assigned to women (for example, compassion, less competitiveness), but allowing men to assume these characteristics too.

In this process of redefinition, "feminine" comes to describe whatever a woman wants to be or do and "masculine" refers to whatever a man wants to be or do: "I am female, therefore I am feminine . . . regardless of whether I paint the house or fix the faucets . . . and if you are male then, therefore, you are masculine, regardless of whether you play the piano and take care of your children or not." One androgynous woman described at great length, for example, the difficult process for her of changing the "social role definition of femininity" into a "personal role definition": "It was a very big step. It was also a very traumatic period for me . . . but . . . I began to see myself as an individual, so my concept then of what was feminine to me changed. A person who was feminine could be independent, a person who was feminine could do things . . . could go, could do this or that. That had not been possible before in my thinking . . ."

These attempts by androgynous persons to redefine the meaning of masculinity and femininity all have the common effect of defusing the prescriptive, "should-" carrying messages of these words in our culture. This is accomplished either by using these concepts only as summary words for bundles of traditional sex role stereotypes, the words thereby taking on a historical or abstract flavor, or by broadening the meaning of these terms to apply to anything that a man or woman chooses to do, thus dissolving any dichotomous role definitions the terms traditionally carried.

Masculinity

In exploring cognitive maps for masculinity and femininity, it becomes important to sample the range of images and the feelings associated with the abstract concepts as clues to the kind of associations androgynous persons may have about these concepts. Imagery is a very powerful way of storing information and may influence our attitudes and the likelihood of attitude change in significant ways.

What, then, are your associations to the word masculinity? For example, if you had to choose, what would be the key characteristic or quality that you associate with the traditional concept of masculinity? Do you have any images or fantasies that you associate with traditionally-defined masculinity? What feelings does this characteristic evoke, positive, negative, or neutral? What is the opposite of this characteristic to you? What quality or characteristic of traditional masculinity do you consider most negative, do you most dislike? How would you rate yourself in terms of how characteristic this quality or behavior is of you?

—1———	2———	3———	4———	5——	6———	7——
never or almost never true	usually not true	sometimes but infrequently true	occasionally true	often true	usually true	always or almost always true

What quality or characteristic of traditional masculinity do you feel is most positive? Again, how characteristic is this behavior of you? Note that if you are female, you can still rate yourself according to those abstract qualities you have identified.

Androgynous and same-sex-identified persons do not appear to differ so much in their overall associations to the traditional concept of masculinity as in their feelings about those associations and the subtle ways they go on to define the characteristics that make up these associations and images. Thus androgynous and same-sex-identified men and women all tended to associate concepts like strength and dominance or physical and psychological strength with the concept of masculinity. The men chose strength and independence as "most positive" masculine traits, the women mentioned the qualities of assertiveness and self-confidence as "most positive" masculine traits. They also tended to agree on "most negative" masculine traits, with slight differences in emphasis: androgynous men stressed "macho-aggressiveness" and "not showing feelings"; masculine-identified men mentioned "inflexible, bullheaded dominance" and "now showing feelings"; androgynous women stressed "emotional insensitivity," "inability to express feelings," and "macho-aggressiveness"; feminine-identified women stressed "ego-inflation," "bragging," and "feeling superior or infallible." Thus, at their most general level, the cognitive maps of these differing groups refer to many of the same dimensions. We must look at more subtle dimensions to detect important differences.

Androgynous persons, for instance, were much more likely to have more negative or ambivalent feelings towards these core characteristics of traditional masculinity than either masculine-identified men or feminine-identified women. Androgynous men gave much more negatively-toned, stereotypic images about masculinity, sketching such images and metaphors as "the unflinching six foot tall [cowboy] in the white hat that, you know, didn't say much of anything but led the posse out to get the outlaws," "the fraternity brothers, the whole big he-man routine, if they weren't trying to make a girl, they were lifting weights so that they could make a girl," "brick towers" and the "Rock of Gibralter," "Charles Atlas," "the very stocky, almost a football player type image, . . . 6'2", a square jaw, . . . a five o'clock shadow on his face from needing a shave." Masculine-identified men in contrast offered fewer images, among which were a "marine," "businessman," "Superman who works on Wall Street," "old time Western stock," and a "hard manual job."

Androgynous men were also particularly negative about the "lack of feelings" implied in the traditional male role, and mentioned this as one of their key associations to masculinity, whereas other groups tended to mention this feature only when focusing specifically on negative aspects of the traditional image of masculinity. In other words, androgynous men seemed primed to perceive the relative unemotionality of the masculine role as one of its main features and drawbacks, suggesting subtle differences in their cognitive maps in this area.

The most noteworthy clues that androgynous persons have constructed different cognitive maps for masculinity come, however, from an examination of how the varying groups of persons discuss and further define the positive qualities of strength and assertiveness they associate with masculinity. That is, all groups point to the concept of strength as a key ingredient of masculinity; however, androgynous persons and same-sex-identified persons differ considerably in how they proceed to describe strength.

Recurrently, masculine-identified men and feminine-identified women define strength in terms of traditional masculine associations stemming from the world of work or in terms of images rooted in the male role at home. Thus masculine-identified men often used the concepts of aggressiveness, "drive," and "competitiveness," to define strength, words that can be readily assimilated into an all-male stereotype conjuring up images of the traditional world of work and the masculine-dominated marketplace. Feminine-identified women tended to define the strength of masculinity in terms of images rooted in the male role of husband and father:

> My husband with his arms around me.
>
> My husband . . . someone who is . . . bigger than I am and . . . that looks like if I really had a problem, he could really help me out.
>
> My husband . . . being able to face things . . . strong enough to hold up against, strong enough to take care of me, I guess, is a masculine person.

In contrast to these definitions of strength, which carry heavy loadings of mental imagery associated with traditional sex roles, androgynous men and women defined strength in a very different conceptual way. Androgynous men, for example, broke down the concept of strength into a range of different concepts less typically associated with an all-male stereotype. Thus, they spoke of competence, assuredness, initiator, ability to endure hardships, and individuality—all traits that could apply to both men and women in a variety of contexts. It is tempting to speculate that this translation of traditional sex role traits into personality characteristics and human capabilities which both men and women could readily adopt is one of the powerful cognitive processes involved in androgynous thinking. This retranslation process may free these traits of any negative connotations left over from traditional roles and may allow more experimentation with a broader range of behavior. The translation of "masculine" to "human" traits, accompanied by a release from traditional contexts and mental imagery, may thus be crucial to allow everyone, male or female, access to the full range of personality characteristics and hence to androgynous development.

Androgynous women, too, emphasize that strength is a very broad concept that includes both positive characteristics, which need to be made available to women as well as men, and negative characteristics that already are too often overdeveloped in the lives of men in the forms of stoicism and excesses of responsibility and control. Thus, they described strength both positively, in terms of mental fortitude and standing up for what you believe, and negatively, in terms of the "facade of the young executive type . . . who has got it all together, who is very strong, never shows any emotion, never cries, but he's really very empty." Several androgynous women saw the key masculine traits of physical and psychological strength and leadership as important and positive skills for women to develop, but negative in their exaggerated form in most men:

> It puts too much responsibility on half of humanity [men] and kind of leaves the other half [women] unable to express themselves and also not take their share of the responsibility.
>
> In terms of masculinity . . . I feel negative about those things, [but] for myself, a feeling that I should be more competitive and try to be more superior, because in the past I have not been expected to be at all. And I want to be, because if I can be more, then men can be less. And we can end up closer together.
>
> I'm just really beginning to enjoy using my body, being active, having my body be strong and healthy . . . I have very positive images about that, at least in me. I think when they are the exclusive source of an identity for man, that's a negative thing.

Thus, again, the main thrust throughout the definitions of "strength," on the part of androgynous persons, is to defuse the strictly male connotations of these traits and make them more available to both men and women as human characteristics.

Femininity

Cognitive maps for femininity with their associated feelings and imagery can also be investigated in a manner parallel to that described under the section on masculinity. Thus, take the time now to ask yourself: if you had to choose, what, for you, is the key characteristic or quality that you associate with the traditional concept of femininity? Do you have any images that you associate with traditionally defined femininity? What feelings does this characteristic evoke, positive, negative, neutral? What is the opposite of this characteristic to you?

In addition, what quality or characteristic of traditional femininity do you consider most negative, do you most dislike? How would you rate yourself in terms of this characteristic in your own behavior, if you were to use a seven point rating scale where 1 equals never or almost never true and 7 equals always or almost always true? What quality or characteristic of traditional femininity do you feel is most positive? How characteristic is this behavior of you? Note that if you are male, you can still rate yourself in terms of these dimensions as you have described them.

As was the case with cognitive maps for masculinity, androgynous women were clearly more negative or ambivalent in their feelings about the construct of femininity than were feminine-identified women and were more likely to mention as their key association to femininity a cluster of traits including helplessness, dependency, passivity, and submissiveness. Androgynous women gave what they consider largely negative images of femininity:

> Frilly fluffy doll.
>
> A Victorian woman who is just prim and proper and . . . smiling and loving, . . . a weakling person who can only get what she wants by being extremely mild and hoping someone will read her mind and give her what she wants.
>
> The I Love Lucy kind of thing where the woman is totally dependent on the man, not able to do much of anything. That is the way she appears to be but in reality she is in the back room plotting . . . but she can't show the strength that she actually has.
>
> Somebody with long flowing curly hair and dressed in a really frilly negligee that's probably pink and sort of lounging on a couch reading a magazine.

In contrast, feminine-identified women were more positive about the construct of femininity and tended more than androgynous women to stress the qualities of softness, gentleness, and delicateness as their key associations to femininity. Actually, the images of femininity held by all the women were quite similar, but feminine-identified women tended to view these qualities (for example, looking nice, dainty, being soft-spoken, or, ladylike) as positives rather than as negatives:

I've always kind of envied little bitty people . . . that maybe a fellow feels like, well gee, maybe I better open the door for her because maybe she won't be able to handle that big heavy door and that type of thing.

Soft clean bouncy hair, bright eyes, just even tempered . . . a soft person . . . probably frilly things.

It is interesting that in addition to more highly valuing these images, these women were also significantly more likely than androgynous women to mention feelings that they didn't quite measure up in some way to some of their positive feminine images such as the "pretty, real little type lady" or the housewife who sews everything and makes homemade bread. One gets the impression that the traditional ideals around femininity may offer a goal and identity to the feminine-identified women, but leave her often with another source of insecurity if she does not fully live up to the image.

Androgynous men tended to be less positive and more ambivalent than masculine-identified men in their feelings about feminine characteristics, stressing "sensitivity to feelings" but also "subordination/passivity" as key associations to femininity. Their images of traditional femininity also showed this ambivalence: "the blind consumer," "the meek, mild and demure sister-in-law," versus the ability to "let boundaries dissolve" between you and an object—an artistic leaning, and qualities of "understanding." In contrast, masculine-identified men most often mentioned "supportive/sensitive" and "soft/seductive" as key associations to femininity. These qualities were evaluated positively and illustrated in such images as "mothers," "wives," "Doris Day—being polite and graceful to somebody you don't like," "a woman in a pink negligee, weak and innocent," or "powder puff."

Descriptions of "most negative" qualities of femininity were quite similar in all groups: androgynous and feminine-identified women mentioned "submissiveness/dependency"; androgynous men chose "subservience/passivity" and "feeling inferior"; masculine-identified men also mentioned "subservience/passivity" and added "being indirect, cunning, and playing games." In turning to "most positive" qualities of femininity, however, some subtle but suggestive differences emerge. The women tended to mention a composite image of sensitivity, warmth, compassion, and nurturance as the "most positive" femine characteristic, although androgynous women did tend to mention these qualities more often than feminine-identified women. The noteworthy tendency, however, emerged among the men.

Androgynous men significantly more often than masculine-identified men described "the ability to express feelings and emotions" as the "most positive" characteristic of femininity, although they also added the qualities of "understanding and loving" as next in importance. The "ability to express feelings" was described as a general trait, applicable to a wide range of situations. In contrast, the "most positive" feminine characteristics nominated by masculine-identified men centered on loving, supportive qualities expressed in traditional female-role contexts with the male as recipient. Examples help clarify this subtle emphasis:

> Most important I suppose that I look for [in femininity] is a kind of sensitivity, a kind of perception or ability to read between the lines, to . . . kind of help draw feelings out of a man . . . a combination of assuming an independent and dependent role and knowing when to come across as more dependent and when to come across as more independent, . . . knowing how to use the dependent kinds of behaviors in making a man feel good, feel like a man . . . I look for comments, I look at tone of voice, I look at eye contact, I look at body movements . . . things that would indicate I can take care of myself, but it's nice to be able to depend upon *you*, which makes me feel not so much better than, not so much above, but useful, worthwhile, and this kind of thing . . . I guess an ideal woman for me would be let's say, a very very effective, efficient RN who could take control, could work in the clutch, but who when she was giving direct patient care to individuals . . . would come across as very feminine, very caring, very warm, thoughtful.
>
> Compassionate . . . if I come home and have had a particularly bad day, my wife is very soothing and she'll talk with me about it and that kind of thing . . . if I'm willing to talk at all when I come home.
>
> The ability to be comfortable while somebody else is doing all the interacting and doing their whole thing and playing more of a supporting role to them . . . the ability to respond to a person as if that person was the only one consuming any of your time . . . if I come home from work and I'm tired . . . and [my wife] responds in a way that, like, it makes it seem like all she did all day was wait for you to come home and to say something.

The subtle difference in emphasis between androgynous and masculine-identified men in their definitions and examples of the "sensitivity" that they see as central to femininity is highly reminiscent of the differences between androgynous and same-sex-identified persons in their conceptualizations of the "masculine" quality, strength. Here, as in the case of "masculine" strength, the androgynous definition of "feminine" sensitivity is reworded to free the quality from association with traditional sex role images or contexts. No longer does the concept "sensitivity" conjure up only female behavior relative to a male recipient. We might hypothesize that this process likewise frees the androgynous individual to more fully explore those alternative behaviors which, prior to such a reconceptualization, may have been considered appropriate for only the female sex.

Personality and Behavioral Characteristics

If people differ in their cognitive maps for masculinity and femininity, they might also be expected to differ in the permission they give themselves to experiment with cross-sex personality traits. Those with flexible cognitive maps might allow themselves to rate high on cross-sex traits and to acknowledge the existence within themselves of characteristics often traditionally attributed to the other sex. In terms of self-ratings on various characteristics of masculinity and femininity, androgynous persons might be expected to rank themselves more equally on masculine and feminine qualities, and indeed that appears to be the case. Thus, androgynous men attributed to themselves positive feminine and masculine qualities to a significantly more equal extent than masculine-identified men, claiming these traits as about equally typical of their personalities. Androgynous women, too, rated themselves as possessing positive masculine and feminine traits to a more equal extent than feminine-identified women did. In addition, androgynous women ranked themselves higher than feminine-identified women did on those masculine characteristics they considered "most positive," suggesting that they were more likely to see themselves as possessing those masculine traits they saw as desirable. By returning to your self-ratings on those qualities of masculininity and femininity you chose as most positive and negative, you can get some feel for your own tendency to have attributed or developed potential same-sex versus cross-sex traits in yourself.

Another way to explore the relationship of behavioral flexibility and cognitive permission systems is to ask people what traditional masculine and feminine behaviors or characteristics they have wanted and developed in their lives versus those characteristics that they did not want, avoided, or left undeveloped. Such questioning yields a matrix, which allows for an interesting comparison of androgynous and same-sex-identified persons. The questions to ask yourself are the following: (1) What specific behaviors or characteristics have you demonstrated or tried to develop that could be traditionally labeled masculine? (2) What behaviors or characteristics that are traditionally labeled masculine have you not developed or have you tried to avoid? (3) What behaviors or characteristics have you developed or learned that are traditionally labeled feminine? (4) What behaviors or characteristics that are traditionally labeled feminine have you not developed or have you tried to avoid? Describe any critical incidents or vivid images you have related to each of these categories of behavior. You might also rearrange the questions to begin with qualities traditionally more characteristic of your sex, if that is easier.

The ways in which androgynous men (AMs) and androgynous women (AWs) differed from masculine-identified men (MIMs) and feminine-identified women (FIWs), as well as from each other, can be clearly seen in the two matrices for "wanted or developed" versus "unwanted or undeveloped" masculine and feminine characteristics (See Tables 1 and 2). These comparisons not only yield some interesting data about the various groups' behavioral and personality characteristics, but also sketch out patterns of associations that yield further clues to their cognitive maps and feelings regarding masculinity and femininity. In the comments made by these various groups, one gets a sense of some of the hurdles or subtle messages each group felt in carving out their own sex role behaviors in the world. Thus, for example, it is not just the major categories of career orientation and aggressiveness that might be associated with "masculinity," but more subtle, daily, and even apparently insignificant issues come to mind when androgynous persons reflect on this area. Androgynous men were especially skillful at articulating some of the "masculine" behaviors they had developed in their lives, suggesting the pervasiveness of sex role feelings even in seemingly tangential areas:

> Dominating the conversation . . . being initiating a lot, first one who will talk up in class . . . whenever there is a heavy discussion, bango my hand wants to go up first, and I'm not going to do that [now]. I'm going to sit on it for awhile . . . Always be in there with an answer: 'Well you got a problem, . . . you don't know whether to do this or that, well,

Table 1. "MASCULINE" CHARACTERISTICS

WANTED OR DEVELOPED		UNWANTED OR UNDEVELOPED	
AMs: 54* Emotional stoicism Career orientation	MIMs: 73* Aggressiveness Athletics Push to succeed in career	AMs: 46* Aggressiveness and/or domination Spectator or active athletics Money/status jobs	MIMs: 20* Hunting Smoking/drinking
AWs: 60* Assertiveness Ability to handle things, be independent, make decisions Career orientation Competitiveness Goal orientation	FIWs: 37* Athletics Able to fix things, do outside chores around house or car	AWs: 43* Domineering, aggressive, insensitive behavior toward others Cold, self-contained, unemotional attitude Super competitive, dog eat dog success drive	FIWs: 32* Being sole provider and career person in family

why don't you do this,' you know, always doing that . . . always have an answer.

Oh sure, men are better drivers than women, so *I am,* I'm a better driver than most women, I am a better driver than most men, because it is important to be a good driver to be a man, to be masculine . . . I've always felt that gluttony correlates highly with masculinity. Men are allowed to be gluttonous, they can overeat, it's not feminine to overeat, sit around and belch after a great big meal. It's OK for men, overdrinking too. So I think there have been times in my life when I felt I had license to overeat or overdrink or overindulge, period, because, well that's the flip side of having all the responsibilities of the world on your shoulders.

TABLE 2. "FEMININE" CHARACTERISTICS

WANTED OR DEVELOPED		UNWANTED OR UNDEVELOPED	
AMs: 54*	*MIMs: 33**	*AMs: 31**	*MIMs: 43**
Ability to express feelings Household skills (e.g., interest in nutrition, plants, sewing, cooking, caring for apartment or child Aesthetic appreciation (music, arts, theater, writing, poetry, literature major)	Household activities (e.g., "bake a helluva pie," "like things orderly and clean" Caring for people Expressing emotions	Passive or overemotional in reacting to stress, unable to cope Nagging, bitchy	Not appearing feminine in gesture, voice or dress Crying Taking a backseat and being supportive in interactions Doing volunteer work unrelated to career advancement Being sexually exploited or "played for a fool"
AWs: 54*	*FIWs: 72**	*AWs: 47**	*FIWs: 34**
Sensitivity (gentleness, warmth, empathy, compassion, supportiveness) Ability to express emotions	Interests/ concerns around being a housewife, creative homemaker, mother Maintaining an attractive appearance Being a good listener, compromiser, peacemaker, ego-builder	Helpless, passive, dependent behaviors and domestic housewifery activities	
		Generalized dislike of domesticity Flirting, appearing stupid or empty-headed	Specific activities like baking bread sewing, gardening Gossiping

*Total number of responses made in this category.

I remember one thing . . . this is just a little thing—but my dad, when my mom couldn't open a jar, she asked my dad to open it . . . and ever since then I've always, you know, it had been my idol for a while to be able to open a jar that my mother couldn't open, and I really think I've gotten pretty good at opening jars, I really have [laughs], even [at work] . . . there have been times when other guys . . . couldn't get the top off a bottle it was stuck so tightly, and I could go over there and I could get it off . . . I've really enjoyed that [laughs].

The emotionally-charged quality of even minor "masculine" behaviors is suggestive of the impact of the larger, more significant ones.

Although androgynous women are generally very positive about most of the "masculine" qualities they mentioned, it is noteworthy that some of these women added the parenthetical comment that many traditional masculine traits had potential drawbacks if used in the extreme. In fact, some of the traits might even be detrimental, although these women felt they needed to demonstrate these traits to fit into and succeed in certain work settings. For example, one androgynous woman spoke of the following traits:

Never revealing that anything is getting to you for one thing . . . I don't ever let anybody get the impression that the work is too much . . . You don't ever show your weakness, because I really think you get attacked if you do . . . just not really revealing yourself as an emotional person . . . I think it's a horrible way to live, but it's what's demanded by the situation . . . You stick to doing a lot of things that maybe you don't want to do because you know on principle you should do it or because it's going to help other [women] . . . [Being] independent or autonomous, not asking anybody for anything which again . . . I've always tried to develop, even though it may not be useful in the long run to do that.

In general, androgynous persons appeared the most vocal about unwanted or undeveloped "masculine" characteristics, with androgynous men making the greatest number of comments in this area (see Table 1). It is possible that androgynous persons have a more differentiated view of the traditional values of masculinity, being able to articulate both positives and negatives. It is probably not surprising, though it is striking, that masculine-identified men mentioned more "wanted masculine qualities" than any other group.

A careful study of the matrix for feminine characteristics given in Table 2 also draws attention to the variations in associations or cognitive maps differentiating androgynous and same-sex-identified persons. The abstract summaries of key comments by the various groups could again be elaborated by subtle comments made by the groups, teasing out the tone and details of the way "feminine" dimensions enter into daily life. For example, the quality of being a peacemaker and ego builder was stressed by one feminine-identified woman in the following lively way: "I try to be an ego builder for [my husband and sons] 'cause I don't know, the world is really kind of a shitty place, you know everybody's out to rip you off and I just feel like when they come home, if they can't come home to just a little bit of peace, . . . I guess maybe that's my most typical trait that I think that's a woman's job." Although feminine-identified women mentioned some specific aspects of typical homemaking as undeveloped feminine skills (for example, baking bread, sewing, or gardening), androgynous women appeared stronger in their general dislike of "feminine" domesticity and dependence:

> I have avoided everything that's been just overtly domestic . . . because I thought, all right, I'm not going to be a little wifey, homey type. [I've not wanted to be] dependent on X [man she married] in any way, and maybe in some ways I overreact to that one, being really hard nosed about paying for half and keeping a separate savings account . . ."

Several feminine-identified women mentioned gossiping as an unwanted traditional feminine trait, while androgynous women included flirting and appearing stupid or empty-headed as unwanted feminine characteristics, mentioning, for example:

> Going out of your way to avoid . . . any implication at all that you were taking advantage of being a woman [in succeeding at work] . . . So that has been really an important kind of thing to me too, to try to develop a quality that says you are absolutely straight. There's no way anybody could imply that you are trying to worm things out of somebody with personal charm.
> I didn't want to be thought of as a stupid person . . . [the] kind of senseless, giddy type thing.
> I never stoop to losing any game with a boy or a man just because I thought I would make him feel bad. I know girls used to talk about that

in high school and I just thought that was the most ridiculous thing I had ever heard of, and I absolutely refused to be any part of it.

It is interesting to note in Table 2 that the two groups most articulate about unwanted "feminine" characteristics were the androgynous women and the masculine-identified men, with the androgynous women only slightly more vocal. Could it be that these two groups, in avoiding or wanting to downplay the feminine aspects of behavior in their lives, are more differentiated and aware of behaviors or characteristics that hint at the unwanted feminine? Note, too, in contrast, that the feminine-identified women report the most wanted feminine characteristics of all the groups and are most verbal about the positive feminine dimension.

Further inspection of Tables 1 and 2 also reveals that masculine-identified men and feminine-identified women mentioned far more wanted than unwanted same-sex behaviors than did androgynous persons. In contrast, androgynous persons gave more examples of wanted than unwanted cross-sex behaviors, compared to same-sex-identified persons. Although this data only lends further support to the differences in cognitive maps and potential behavioral flexibility between androgynous and same-sex-identified persons, it is interesting that these differences show up in so many different ways.

The types of questions exploring this aspect of cognitive maps and images were perhaps the most difficult of all the areas examined in this chapter. Not only did androgynous persons have to stretch themselves to think in traditional categories of masculinity and femininity and compare their own views with conventional ones, but masculine-identified men and feminine-identified women had to wrestle with the concept of "wanted or developed" cross-sex behavior. It was at this point that many of the dichotomous assumptions held by same-sex-identified persons were expressed overtly. One feminine-identified woman commented, for instance, that "I guess maybe I accepted most of the feminine things . . . I can't think of anything that's traditionally masculine I felt I did want . . ." The masculine-identified men were even more likely to comment to this effect:

I can't think of any more [masculine behaviors not wanted]. All the ones that I know about, I've gone after.

That's hard because I think I was shooting pretty much for the masculine image . . . I was trying to develop most of the masculine characteristics that I could think of.

I would say most things I value as feminine I try not to do and I wouldn't want to do . . . they're . . . taboo.

I'm a red-blooded all-American boy. There's nothing at all feminine about me!

In summary, we can point to a wide range of subtle differences between androgynous and same-sex-identified persons in terms of their sex role attitudes and cognitive maps for masculinity and femininity. One senses that androgynous persons have struggled or arrived at cognitive schemas freed of traditional sex-bound imagery and associations, allowing them, perhaps, to push into more flexible sex role behavior and wider experimentation with cross-sex alternatives. They appear to be more negative and dissatisfied with the traditional sex role norms and concepts, despite liking being male or female, are more affirming of changes in the roles for both sexes, appear to place fewer taboos on cross-sex alternatives, and are less likely to be unaccepting in subtle ways of the women's movement, working mothers, female initiating of sexuality, and homosexuality in general. Androgynous persons seem to anticipate an evolution of their views over time and do not expect any clear endpoint to this growing. These many differences form the backdrop for an exploration in the next two chapters of the concrete ways androgynous men (Chapter 3) and androgynous women (Chapter 4) differ from same-sex-identified men and women in terms of their life development. We will be moving away from an explicit exploration of cognitive maps, feelings, and images to an examination of external life events from childhood, adolescence, and adulthood, searching for clues that appear to distinguish androgynous development for men and women.

3

BECOMING AN ANDROGYNOUS MAN
*Patterns of Development
and Keys to Change*

The process of becoming a fully androgynous person is the goal of a lifetime, an evolution towards wholeness and full expression of potentiality. The process can begin at any point and continues indefinitely. There appear, however, to be precedents and predispositions towards androgyny in the life experiences and developmental patterns of people who emerge in adulthood as androgynous persons. These life experiences and incidents are not necessarily the only experiences which lead in androgynous directions, nor do they exclude influential factors which might affect movement in androgynous directions at later points in life; however, it is interesting and noteworthy that androgynous patterns appear even as far back as childhood and that androgyny does indeed appear to be a developmental, gradual process that is grounded in life history, critical incidents, and significant personality patterns and preferences.

      The present chapter investigates the development of androgyny in the lives of men, contrasting androgynous men and masculine-identified men in terms of critical shaping experiences and tendencies in childhood, adolescence, and adulthood. Numerous differences emerge which can serve as stimuli to the kind of self-exploration begun in the last chapter on cognitive maps. In this chapter, the focus is on external behavior and personality styles, day-to-day actions in the outside world. We will be exploring the construct of external androgyny as it appears in overt behavior directed toward coping with the challenges of everyday life. The patterns described may evoke feelings of recognition or remembrance; they may serve as clues toward the kinds of socialization hurdles we all face in sex role development, whether or not one sees these patterns through the eyes of self-recognition. Perhaps the patterns will remind you of someone you know, or encourage another look at children, friends, and other loved ones. Again, the idea is not to use these comparisons in a categorical way to dichotomize the world anew into androgynous versus same-sex-identified patterns, but to stimulate new thinking in this area. Hopefully, too, those persons who see themselves more directly in these descriptions may feel a sense of affirmation that their struggles have been shared by others and that the taboos that keep us silent about the search for new alternatives for male and female development are beginning to ease in today's society.

Whether or not one has shared the past developmental patterns discussed in this chapter, androgynous development appears to be facilitated also by certain kinds of current life experiences and factors. Androgynous men and masculine-identified men differ in the kinds of factors they report as influential in moving toward more flexible sex role attitudes and opinions of greater sex role equality, and these differences will be discussed in the second half of this chapter. The latter section of the chapter gives further clues to ways of structuring one's environment or finding strategies of change to facilitate or support change in the direction of androgyny as men, clues that will be contrasted in the next chapter with ideas and factors drawn from a parallel study of androgynous and feminine-identified women.

PATTERNS OF DEVELOPMENT

As one might expect in a period in which sex role equality was more the exception than the standard pattern, androgynous men and masculine-identified men do not seem to differ, at least within the confines of the dimensions explored in this research, in such factors as parental sex role attitudes, parental warmth or degree of control in relationship to sons, or parental educational level or occupation. We look in vain for simple parental factors to differentiate these two groups of people, at least in present times. It is still the norm that parents of both androgynous and masculine-identified men are essentially traditional in their sex role views and behavior, with the father being the provider and dominant person in household decision-making and finances, and the mother in charge of household chores like cooking and cleaning. Some deviation from these strict role divisions, such as the mother being in charge of finances or sharing in decision-making or the father helping share some of the household chores, was only a tendency among androgynous men, not a significant difference. The majority of mothers in both groups had worked and/or were working, primarily since their children were at least beyond junior high age. They did not tend to be career-oriented, and there were no major differences in types of jobs held. Androgynous men tended, however, to describe their mothers as strong, bright, and independent. Aside from this one tendency, the androgynous and masculine-identified men in this study did not differ in any of the commonly expected socioeconomic indicators or issues of geographical mobility, rural or urban backgrounds, and presence or absence of both parents during the growing up years. Thus we must look further for those differences which did emerge.

Childhood

Despite the absence of other differences in parental characteristics between androgynous and masculine-identified men, one difference does emerge as very significant. Androgynous men report they were clearly and unambivalently closer to their mothers than their fathers in childhood, whereas masculine-identified men report being closer to their fathers. In fact, nearly all the masculine-identified men who felt they were closer to their mother qualified this choice in numerous ways, suggesting either that they felt closer to mother by default, were not really close to her, or had a strong bond with their father too: "My dad . . . worked all day and was gone at night . . . so that's why I said out of necessity my mother was probably closer . . . I would rather have been closer to my father." This difference in closeness to mothers is only the first of many instances in which androgynous men appear to be closer to women in their lives.

Although there were no significant differences in birth order, it seemed suggestive that androgynous men tended to come from families with three or more brothers. Although one would not want to overinterpret this tendency, it is conceivable that in families with several boys, it might be more probable for at least one boy to deviate from the typical male role in some clear way. This comparative difference in behavior or personality might serve as the trigger to more conscious thinking about sex roles and more androgynous development.

Although the majority of contact in childhood for both groups of men was with people who lived very traditional male and female role patterns, with the women chiefly home-oriented and the men chiefly work-oriented, androgynous men tended to differ from masculine-identified men in feeling more positively toward those nontraditional past acquaintances they remembered. Thus they described, in positive terms, a father for whom music was an avocation, a bold, decisive mother who "knew what she wanted and went after it," a professional aunt, an older brother who "never went out for athletics even though he was very physically strong and healthy," the parents of a friend who were teachers and "expanded my [cultural] horizons a whole lot," a bright, intelligent woman who "turned me on to ideas," a male jazz musician in the town, and others.

In contrast, masculine-identified men tended to remember nontraditional sex role patterns in childhood acquaintances in a more negative tone:

> My mother didn't like to work. She would always ridicule my Dad, I shouldn't have to work like this . . . I can remember more of my grandmother being home than I can my mother and it disturbed me . . . there's some negatives that stay with me because of that.

> There was one couple that [my parents] were very close friends with. She was a really fantastic musician and he was an insurance salesman, and I was always appalled because they had separate bank accounts. She earned her money and he earned his and they kept it separately.

> We had . . . one neighbor . . . being in the category that she worked because he was too lazy to work . . . I considered the guy a slob, worthless . . . completely negative.

> I don't have any negative feelings about women getting away from the traditional pattern. I do have some negative feelings about the men that don't follow the traditional pattern . . .

> My aunt took me uptown one time and we went into a card store, and

a man was waiting in the card store, . . . gift wrapping packages or something, and I wondered . . . like why in the hell would he want to work in a card store. Only ladies do that . . . There was a kid in school who played a flute, a boy, . . . and I remember that I thought that was kind of strange . . . why didn't he play a trumpet or a trombone like the rest of us guys.

It is striking that the clearest differences between androgynous and masculine-identified men begin to emerge in childhood, a pattern which contrasts with the tendency we will find among women. These differences involve, most dramatically, personality tendencies that androgynous men carried with them in childhood as burdens in a sense, ways in which they felt atypical from what was expected of boys and men. The pressure and stress of conformity to the sex role patterns of our culture appear to occur very early for boys, and for those boys who do not perceive themselves as fitting the norm, the internal struggle and pain to make sense of one's experience and carry or suppress one's tendencies is a lonely, difficult task. It appears that masculine-identified men either conform more easily to the aggressive, tough image of the male norm, or they act more quickly or successfully to suppress any inclinations toward quietness or unassertiveness, keeping any potential nonaggressiveness fairly private and eventually forgotten. Perhaps masculine-identified men respond more completely to the male peer group in childhood which has been suggested as a primary sex role socialization agent for boys (Hartley, 1959). The male peer group, through teasing and exclusion, is a powerful tool toward the suppression of anything feminine in little boys; in fact, masculinity at this age is often defined as anything "not feminine."

The chief source of stress for androgynous men in these early struggles with sex role conformity centered on their perceiving themselves as quiet, unassertive, and introspective in childhood compared to masculine-identified men. Typical comments included:

I was very quiet, withdrawn. I think, I had a lack of confidence in myself.

I was quiet, shy, mischievous . . . introverted.

I've tried to play down . . . dominance, like not obviously taking the initiative in certain things or coming across as, you know, I'm-the-boss type of thing.

Well, I was a coward . . . sometimes the kids would gang up on me and rough me up and I would do very little to fight back . . . I will try to talk my way out of a fight and if that doesn't work I'll run . . . I've always been a nonviolent person. So far as being a boy, I was atypical of what was supposed to be.

I knew at a young age, I was pretty sensitive . . . I knew I had strong feelings, I could feel sadness and I could feel pity very strongly, and sometimes emotionally I would cry, rather than just from hurt, and I felt that I was different from other boys in that respect, and I consciously tried to sort of shut that down when I was a kid.

Many androgynous men described with particular poignancy this type of shutting down on their sensitivities. It seemed almost as if, for many, this process could be traced down to particular incidents in time, conceptual turning points: "There was a time, when I was a kid and I went over and watched a TV show with this friend of mine . . . and my heart just broke for this poor boy [in the story] because his dog had been shot, you know, I was just so sad, and my friend, you know, he started, he made something funny about it, and I just felt like I couldn't say a thing about the way I felt, because it just wasn't acceptable, especially for me being a boy."

In addition, androgynous men tended qualitatively to feel more ambivalent about their early memories of being a boy, stressing conflicts with the traditional male role in different forms:

Oh, I can remember I was a bench warmer on the Little League, like I was generally below par at most athletic games; in terms of baseball I'm really C−. I'm just really terrible at baseball. . . And you know that was an unpleasant experience in my life, cause . . . I didn't have the courage to say that this is for shit, if I'm going to sit on the bench, I don't even want to play, and I didn't have the togetherness to do that.

One of the first instances I can remember where I thought I was expected to do something that I didn't feel, and it was a masculine role, we were playing war games . . . and some of the kids would be leaders, you know, generals and things, and after awhile we were going through one of our tactics and attacking something, and one of the guys who was always the leader turned to me and insisted that I be the leader and I can remember feeling very uncomfortable at that. Leadership is a very foreign thing to me, but I did recognize that it is something that I ought to be able to do.

I see myself as being atypical, more, not really a sissy type thing, . . . but I didn't like having to be big and rugged and beat up other boys and be hot dog on the playground. I couldn't see that . . . I always looked down on myself because I wasn't that way.

I was always a cry baby, very emotional and sensitive kid, too serious at too young an age, you know like when I was in second grade, we did our first communion and I was very moved by it, and I remember asking the other kids if they were close to tears when they went into the school, and I took all kinds of shit for that . . . boys just don't do that.

Compared to masculine-identified men, androgynous men showed a slight tendency also to remember or report times when they had wanted to be a girl or wondered what it would have been like. They mentioned such episodes as having two very close childhood friends who were girls and wanting to be like them; dressing up in lace curtains and pretending to be a bride; mystically feeling like a woman on one occasion. One androgynous man mentioned thoughts of wanting to be a girl because of the different way girls were treated: "I was always being dared to do something and they would always get out of it. I remember sitting on a huge concrete stairway and everybody's riding your tricycle down this stairway and you just kill yourself and the girls didn't have to do it. They just watched. Here I am in a cowboy outfit. I have these god damn guns and everybody's yelling at me that it's my turn and I'm thinking my sister doesn't have to do it, his sister doesn't have to do it, just fuckin' ridiculous." Several androgynous men mentioned wondering what it would be like to be a woman during sex, and two described wondering what it would be like to be a beautiful, manipulative woman, envying the indirect use of control: "It had . . . to do with the fact that I had felt for so long very submissive or passive and I wanted that kind of control, but it was a devious kind of control, it was a manipulative, I've got a string on you control. It wasn't direct power; it was indirect, and that's what I wanted . . . I didn't want to be the king of the country. I would rather have been like the prime minister, the guy who pulls the strings."

In contrast, masculine-identified men tended to have more positive feelings about their earliest memories of being a boy, mentioning pleasant episodes around rough-and-tumble play and relatives' comments such as those reported by one masculine-identified man: " 'Oh, isn't he a fine boy,' or, 'He's going to grow up to be a really big man.' or, 'You better be careful or you'll have to eat more bacon and beans,' or, 'He's going to take you.' " Other pleasant memories of masculine-identified men included stress on playing ball in the neighborhood: "Girls couldn't play . . . I can remember being real little, and them making me stand way the hell out of the way, and nobody would ever hit a ball there, and then as you got older you could get more into the action, but you know, the girls, no matter *how* old they got, they could *never* get into the action." Several masculine-identified men mentioned mixed feelings about memories of frequent fighting and resenting playing the piano because it was a "sissy" thing to do and they would rather be outside playing. One masculine-identified man remembered vividly a situation where "a little girl . . . scratched me and I hauled off and belted her one, and the teacher grabbed me and said 'You never hit girls' . . . Oh, I hated that woman, I still do today."

Compared to androgynous men, masculine-identified men tended to be pushed more toward early independent behavior and tended to fight a lot with other children. The push toward independence was remembered in some of the following ways: being forced to take almost full care of oneself at an early age, since parents were gone a great deal; being expected to have a job in high school; and supporting oneself through high school outside the family home. One masculine-identified man described a childhood situation with his mother: "I can remember when I was five years old, the very first thing my mother even did with me, one of the first things . . . we went into [a big city] in front of a department store and she said OK, meet me in such-and-such a department in an hour and a half. If you can't find it, ask a policeman, ask a floorwalker. So right away there was the sense of being turned loose but, yet I knew, if anything went wrong, she would be there or somebody would be around . . . a lot of things that were going to later maybe help us to become more independent." Reports of spending a large amount of time in childhood fighting with others boys are characterized by one masculine-identified man's comment that "I had to fight my way through my young childhood, literally, because boys were that way . . . I suppose it was unpleasant in the beginning, but . . . after awhile I think actually it turned out to be positive because it taught me early in life I was going to have to scrap for anything I got and it carried me through. I think that's why I'm very successful . . . today because I wasn't afraid of a good fight . . . [and] it teaches you that even though you lose, you can bounce right back."

To these contrasting pictures of childhood experience for androgynous and masculine-identifed men, we can add one final and noteworthy difference. Although androgynous and masculine-identified men did not differ in terms of sheer amount of contact with girls in early growing up years (pre-junior high), they did differ dramatically in how they perceived this contact. For masculine-identified men, feelings toward contact with little girls in childhood were more negative or ambivalent, summarized by such comments as:

> They would cry if you fought rough with them, and girls wanted to play in the house when you wanted to go outside and play.
>
> The girls didn't run, play and roughhouse, that sort of thing, and I wanted to run, play and roughhouse.

Androgynous men report in sharp contrast far more positive feelings about girls:

> I had a lot of girl friends. My life was real strange . . . I never went through the stage where I didn't like girls . . . I always liked girls. . . One girl I considered my girl friend in kindergarten and first grades; second grade I was sort of unattached, I knew a lot of girls and I remember going over to girls' houses to play with them.
>
> I was always intrigued by girls . . . I seemed to get along better with the girls in my class than I did with the boys.
>
> I always liked girls better than boys, always, because I don't know, they just seemed to be more real. They could talk about how they felt and stuff like that.

This difference seemed even more striking in that androgynous men who voiced positive feelings about girls sometimes also spoke of choosing to keep quiet for awhile about these positive feelings because of peer pressure. For example, one androgynous man sketched the following scene: "I enjoyed girls. I had girl friends like when I was in first grade and second grade, I remember it was kind of a strange sort of thing . . . I found them as pleasant playmates. I remember one time, maybe about . . . fifth grade, having gone up the street and met a girl named [A] and we spent the afternoon playing in her back yard . . . and I remember coming home that evening and my mother says 'What did you do today?' and I said, 'Well, I spent the afternoon playing with [A.],' and I said 'Please don't tell my brothers because I don't want them to know I spent the afternoon playing with a girl' . . . and that was the only time I did play with her." Another androgynous man described that "up to second—third grade, I liked girls, had friends that were girls, and then from third to sixth grade, if I liked a girl, I wasn't allowed to say anything because I'd really get ridden by the guys and finally in sixth grade when I really liked this girl and they started razzing me, I said to hell with you guys, I *like* this girl, and so from there on in, I dated frequently."

In summary, a picture begins to emerge of androgynous men struggling in childhood with somehow being different from the typical aggressive male norm. They report much early pain about being more introspective, less aggressive, and more sensitive to feelings than their male peers. In addition, they seem more comfortable than masculine-identified men with females, having more positive contacts with mothers and having little girls among their friends. These differences and tendencies foreshadow differences which emerge in the school years of preadolescence and the events of adolescence and adulthood, and we will return to their significance in the next section.

Adolescence and Adulthood

During the school years, masculine-identified men were highly active in athletics, especially in rugged contact sports, and tended to be highly active in extracurricular activities and less academically oriented. These areas of activity form a sharp contrast with the experiences of androgynous men during this time. Androgynous men report far more negative experiences around athletics compared to masculine-identified men. Some were pushed to participate and resented this; others felt they were not as good in athletics as other boys or disliked the violence of sports. Many of the androgynous men who reported critical negative experiences around athletics did participate anyway, but their feelings remained unchanged. The following quotations comprise a sample of androgynous men's attitudes:

> I early gave up any interest in competing in sports and athletics and this sort of thing, though I enjoy sports, but I was not interested in the aggressiveness and competitiveness.
>
> I was about average in sports and I can remember a time in junior high when I went to gym class the day after they had tryouts for basketball team, and the coach says to me, 'How come you weren't here last night trying out for basketball?' 'Well, I didn't think I was good enough to make it.' He says, 'Well, that is *our* decision.' So the next year I did go out, and in fact I didn't make it [laugh] . . . there is a certain amount of pressure there, that just because you are a man you are supposed to be good at sports.
>
> I had a cousin who was a football coach, and he was really disappointed when I didn't go out for football. 'I don't want to go out there; I

mean you guys are out to kill. You're out for blood . . . I don't see the value of that. I don't want to go out there and get hurt just so the stupid team can win a game.' 'Oh yeah? The kid's weird,' you know. I always thought of myself as being somehow not as good as other people.

There's a tradition in my family of athletes and I was the first one who said 'fuck it.' I wasn't as good as the others, I was small. I couldn't believe some of the people you'd have to tackle . . . I'd walk off the field saying 'This is stupid.' I hated it and I would attack him [my father] for [pushing me].

It is difficult to tell whether the negative feelings about athletics among androgynous men reflect negative feelings about athletic, physical activities *per se* or whether the negativity is directed more toward the aggressiveness, competitiveness, and other values that were extolled for men as part of the male image. One suspects that the latter is more likely to be true, and that athletic activities, if stripped of their role-carrying messages, might be less negative to androgynous persons. This appears to be true for androgynous women, who sometimes wish they had had more encouragement to be physically active, although they too are critical of identifying the male role with super-aggressive athletics and strong-man body building.

Another important difference between androgynous men and masculine-identified men during the school years is the tendency for androgynous men to be more academically-oriented. Several examples are suggestive of this trend:

I was very obedient, cooperative, and industrious. I studied hard.

I think I came out of the womb serious and introspective . . . a model student . . . the smell of new books and everything always used to turn me on.

I was never as good as the other guys . . . in athletics. . . It was always intellectually where I was better. . . [School] was where I got all my rewards, most of my good feelings came from school . . . I had to work through, in junior high, being a good student and everybody going 'boo, boo, boo,' you know, not being cool, and I'm going, 'Heck with you, you want to be stupid, be stupid. The idea of this game is to get A's and B's and I can do that, and if you can't, tough.'

I wore glasses which meant that I looked a little bit more like an egghead and I was not quite as tough as the other guys . . . basically I was a smart boy in school and that was rewarded.

Although androgynous men had more positive contact with girls during childhood, they tended during later years to date less than average compared to masculine-identified men and to be more critical of traditional male-female interaction patterns. Some tended to stress the anxiety-arousing qualities of the traditional male role requirements in dating: "I didn't know how to act, I was still trying to figure out what was permissible and not what I could do, but what was right and what was expected of me. I was very much aware of what should I do right now if I were going to be the typical male in the courtship, what was my expected behavior, what did I have to do here, and I'd spend a lot of time hassling with that." Androgynous men tended to dislike a woman being dependent on them, to dislike bearing the burden of initiating social relationships, and to avoid the "wham-bam, thank you ma'am kind of sexuality, where you don't really take a woman into consideration." Other examples of their dissatis-factions included:

> The way I was supposed to act toward women, I thought, was un-bearable. I just was not comfortable being that way: being dominant in a relationship, hey, let's go here, hey let's go there, and being that assertive and overpowering . . . *Equal* was a struggle with me . . . not being submissive and leaving it totally up to the woman as to what goes on, which was impossible to do in those days . . . that was a struggle.
>
> Having to cope with the traditional yet still very strong underlying, unspoken expectation that I am to be the social instigator . . . that I am to be the one who is the pursuer, that I am the one who is to strike up the relationships, and this has been very disgruntling to me and I do not like it.
>
> [I didn't like] the way the typical masculine stereotypic male would treat women. 'If you play your cards right, you know, I'll reward you by taking you out . . . you know, come to me for your rewards. I've got all the goodies, you have to play up to me.
>
> Men have to put far more energy into the relationship, especially in the beginning, to get even the most minimal response, like the onus is on you to take almost the total initiative . . . so when thing's don't work out, it seems to me that I've been much more vulnerable than the woman . . .

Androgynous men also stressed the destructiveness, aggressiveness, and duplicity of sexual games played by men.

It does not appear that masculine-identified men felt less anxiety, tension, and discomfort around dating girls than androgynous men; rather, they dated actively despite these feelings and explained their anxiety in different ways. Thus they spoke of girls being somehow "different," of discomfort with sharing sensitive areas of their thought and life with girls, and of greater comfort with confiding in boys or men. Masculine-identified men perceived themselves as highly aggressive throughout their lives, not only in terms of career (for example, "You try to not kill everybody or crawl over everybody, but you certainly try to win, you try to get more points or do more than somebody else.") but in relationships with women (for example, "If I couldn't, in a conversation, convince somebody of my point and if that somebody was a female, you could always curse or scream or yell and scare them to death.").

It is not surprising, then, that masculine-identified men tended to be more positive and androgynous men more ambivalent toward all-male groups in which aggressiveness, so often, is a valued norm. Androgynous men seemed to be more articulate about what they disliked in all-male groups and mentioned such issues as the following:

> Like being on sports teams, you get in a locker room with a bunch of guys and you can go 'Ho, ho, ho, isn't that funny, yah, yah, yah,' you know, and in sort of a rough way it's friendly . . . but I'm not going to find any intellectual, interesting situation in an all-male group, unless the group has been gathered for a specific purpose such as that. . . It's never going to get down to social issues, it's never going to get down to philosophy of religion . . . to anything intellectual, sort of theorizing, which is easier to do with a woman, . . . you can be, maybe it's romantic or something, but you can start talking about poetry . . . about metaphysics as love, things like this.

> I was very ill-at-ease at the aura that prevailed that the fraternity was a bunch of brothers that would give their lives for one another and sign oaths in blood and all this; and that really turned me off, I was really revolted by that and the day of initiation I remember, I left the house and never went back, after I was initiated, . . . I was just overwhelmed by the negative messages that came through in this kind of all-male group. . . I've never felt at ease with . . . the aura of superiority or eliteness . . . and secretiveness which sometimes attaches itself to a homogeneous group, or the effort to get special . . . powers and privileges . . . I think those things are detrimental.

> I don't trust them. I've been with groups of men and . . . like there's

another kind of consciousness ... it's potentially dangerous ... there's something missing, there's a degree of sensitivity that's missing, of quietness.

This tendency to hold more ambivalent or negative feelings about all-male groups by androgynous men did not extend, however, to feelings about consciousness-raising groups for men, that is, groups which focused on exploring the male role, analogous to female consciousness-raising groups where the focus was on the female role. Androgynous men were more likely than masculine-identified men to have participated in consciousness-raising groups or courses on sex roles, and feelings were generally positive about these experiences, the few exceptions being that some particular group had become boring over time.

Interestingly, androgynous men also expressed a dissatisfaction with the traditional lack of closeness among men:

> The male-to-male aloofness, business attitude, that you deal with fellow males as adversaries rather than as ... close friends.

> I resent not having a brother, not a blood brother, I mean men don't meet in groups like women do and talk about their lives or talk about their spirituality very often with other men.

Androgynous men tended to be changing towards a preference for sensitive, self-revealing men as friends than for men with more traditional interpersonal styles:

> [Earlier] I would have wanted ... with men, a good, hearty, laughing, robust energetic person, whereas now if a person's quiet and thoughtful and speculative, they're just as interesting to me, whereas before I would avoid them as being too effeminate, too weird.

> I've come to have higher regard for the men who are open and sensitive and flexible and aren't always 100 percent sure of themselves.

Androgynous and masculine-identified men both tended to have boys as their closest friends in high school. This pattern continued for masculine-identifed men, whereas more of the androgynous men said that their closest or most significant relationships currently were with women. The following quotes from androgynous men stood out as examples of this trend:

> Most of the growth experiences that I value [have been] with women. I would say right now, starting with a new person and going into a deep relationship, it would go much more quickly with a woman than with a man.
>
> I think I'm closer to women . . . it's a lot easier for me to reveal very personal, deep personal fears even, or worries or concerns to women than it is to men.

Many of these same men wished they could have this same closeness with men, but the experience was rare in everyday society.

These patterns contrasted strongly with that of masculine-identified men who tended to describe men, rather than women, as closest current friends, with wives sometimes mentioned as exceptions. Masculine-identified men were more likely to say, for example, "Probably when it comes to the real sensitive areas in terms of my planning . . . goals . . . direction, . . . I would have to say I would seek out another male much more quickly than I would a female, especially a single female."

Not surprisingly, the friends and significant others (wives, girl friends, and so on) of masculine-identified men held more traditional sex role attitudes than those of androgynous men and were less likely to be working or enrolled in degree programs, and masculine-identified men expressed far more ambivalence about their significant others working than did androgynous men. Masculine-identified men tended to discount their wives' work intentions as serious:

> Very often I've discouraged her from working, and once I get to a point where . . . she can no longer live with this attitude, then I back off a little bit and she goes to work for a few months, and then she gets tired of it [laughs] but no, if she had a career, I would definitely say pursue it, but she doesn't really have a career so I can't really see her going out and working for nickels and dimes.
>
> Several times she's wanted to go back to school. By wanted I mean she's filled out her application form but when it's come time to go to school she's chickened out.
>
> Well, she's talked about [working] occasionally, but I've never listened.
>
> Well she's talked about going back to school . . . and updating her teaching certificate, but I don't know whether she will or not [laughs].

Such types of comments, which could be seen both as reflecting and helping to perpetuate their wives' ambivalence about working, were absent among androgynous men.

In terms of issues of adulthood, androgynous men tended to report more critical incidents around whether or not to be in the military service although only half as many androgynous men as masculine-identified men actually participated in the service. The masculine-identified men also tended to see their experiences in the military (several were in the Marines) as positive or neutral, whereas androgynous men tended to see those years more negatively. One androgynous man felt that the service was a very strong factor in changing his views about male and female roles in a more nontraditional direction and reported: "I was horrified at the expressions of the macho image that I saw there, and that, I think, aroused a great deal of resentment in me in terms of the way men live . . . how vicious they were toward one another, destructive and hostile." Several androgynous men (but no masculine-identified men) stated that they were pacifists, and although this was not a significant difference, it seemed noteworthy in that some androgynous men described the process of deciding to become a conscientious objector as a very significant part of their lives. For one androgynous man this meant "I had to decide whether that was not being a man, and I had to define . . . what was manhood to me, and to find that, and it didn't necessarily include toting a gun. . ." Two androgynous men had wanted to join the Green Berets or the Marines and had flunked the physical; looking back, they tended to feel this was possibly a major choice point in their lives, forcing a kind of reexamination of themselves and freeing them from a strong traditional male socializing process. Flunking the draft physical obviously did not seem to have the same refocusing effect unless the person had wanted to join.

In addition to differences in military service, androgynous men tended to show more career indecision than masculine-identified men, involving such trends as major career shifts from one field to another, dropping out of college or professional programs, interrupting their education in some way, and changing majors or transferring schools frequently.

Finally, the two groups of men tended to differ also in their views of marriage and children, although one must be cautious in interpreting these differences in light of the fact that masculine-identified men in this research sample were more likely than androgynous men to be married and have families. Although these differences may color their responses, masculine-identified men tended to be more positive about marriage in terms of its potential impact in decreasing role stereotypes. They tended to mention marriage as a humanizing institution, making them more aware of the dilemmas and traps of the female role, more sensitive to another person's needs, more aware of their wives' and hence women's capabilities, and more capable of sharing in a relationship. This is a very striking and interesting observation that we will return to in the second half of this chapter.

The possibility that marriage might decrease, rather than increase, sex role stereotypes seems to escape the attention of androgynous men who tend to be more ambivalent about marriage. Despite their general wishes for a nontraditional relationship of shared responsibilities and bordering on concepts of "open marriage," androgynous men felt more cautious or negative about marriage, anticipating or feeling that marriage had heightened or would heighten issues of responsibility or financial independence. One androgynous man was totally opposed to marriage as a legal contract that reinforced traditional sex role patterns. Androgynous men did, however, tend to find the idea of a close relationship over time appealing, and their views on marriage would be better described as cautious or .
focused on responsibility themes rather than purely negative.

Not surprisingly, then, androgynous men more often than masculine-identified men stressed the responsibilities and burdens of raising children although they also were more likely to mention the joys, rewards, and pleasures of being around young children. These responses appear to reflect a real ambivalent bind for androgynous men who tended to be both more positively attracted to children and more wary of subsequent issues of responsibility.

Again, it is interesting that it is the masculine-identified men who call attention to the potential role of children in liberalizing the views of their parents toward less traditional sex role attitudes. It is true that masculine-identified men were about equally divided in terms of whether they saw or would see children as heightening or lessening traditional male and female roles in the home. On the one hand, many masculine-identified men suggested that they would tend or had tended to leave more of the child care responsibilities to their wives, hence increasing sex role distinctions. Sometimes this occurred in subtle ways, such as by doing only what they felt comfortable with in terms of children and letting the child then "go to whichever [parent] he feels like, . . . usually that's the woman." What seems more noteworthy, however, is the equal number of masculine-identified men who mentioned children as having the impact of decreasing sex role distinctions among the parents by necessitating more sharing of chores, by heightening their consciousness of typical male and female socialization processes, and by the children bringing home the less traditional currents of a changing society. Concerns for their daughters' futures, in particular, were mentioned as influences in moving toward more nontraditional views of female career roles. The possibility that children might move parents in a less traditional direction in their attitudes towards male and female roles will receive additional attention in the second half of this chapter, in a discussion of marriage and family as a potential—and perhaps not immediately obvious—locus of sex role change.

Developmental Patterns

The most striking observation that emerges from a comparative and longitudinal look at the development of individual people over time is the considerable uniformity of development that appears to characterize masculine-identified men in contrast to androgynous men. Masculine-identified men, almost without exception, outwardly pursued active, aggressive, and often athletic or achieving lifestyles from childhood onward. Although there were several subpatterns that could be identified in a tentative fashion, these patterns refer more to differences in internal self-concepts and descriptions than to external behavior patterns.[1] Even when masculine-identified men expressed some degree of early disparity between their personal tendencies and the demands of the aggressive male role, they pushed themselves to assume more of the traditional role expectations. Typically, they were successful in this without much pain or concern about any price they might be paying. Thus, a masculine-identified man who retained his quiet manner embedded this trait in an otherwise highly traditional male role. It appears that few of these men allow personal tendencies that deviate from the male role to persist long or publicly without pushing themselves to adhere more tightly to the male role. Androgynous men, in contrast, appear to show far more significant variations in longitudinal development and more diversity of developmental pathways toward the expression of androgyny in their lives.[2]

KEYS TO ATTITUDE CHANGE

Androgynous development does, indeed, appear to represent a gradual process over time, with significant underpinnings in the events of childhood, adolescence, and adulthood. For men, childhood emerges as the period of most acute conflicts over conformity versus deviance from traditional sex roles. Masculine-identified men push quickly for resolution or find themselves more in harmony with expected behaviors; those who will perhaps move in androgynous directions struggle with the dissonance of knowing their own personality tendencies set them apart from the typical male image. The price of secretly or publicly carrying this "differentness" is heavy, and many androgynous men pass through a period of feeling insecure or uncertain about themselves. Without cultural supports for affirming all one's potential personality traits, those who deviate from the imagined average label themselves as the ones with problems, rather than questioning the norms themselves. For some, however, this period of dissonance does begin to open up thinking about sex roles in general and brings immediate awareness of the limitations of the traditional roles.

Whatever the details of the journey, the paths toward androgyny appear to be more variable and diverse than the traditional option, despite the many similarities that seem to characterize most androgynous men compared to masculine-identified men. There are many ways to become androgynous; there are many starting points. Thus, although there are many precedents to androgyny that can be seen in the first half of this chapter, the fact that there are patterns of androgyny which begin only recently in near-adulthood or adulthood alerts us to the fact that the evolution toward more flexible integrations of sex roles can begin anytime.

What, then, are the factors that seem to move persons towards more flexible and equal sex role attitudes and more androgynous practices, whatever the starting point? Again the focus of this section will be on men, and we will be exploring how androgynous and masculine-identified men differ in the kinds of factors which they report as significant influences in any movement of their sex role attitudes in non-traditional directions. In a sense, then, we are examining some of the factors involved in natural change processes with an eye to identifying not only crucial factors that may serve as part of deliberate broad-scale change efforts in the sex role area, but more importantly, those factors that individuals can draw on to strengthen and design their own strategies for self-change.

One factor stood out overwhelmingly as the primary influence or mediator of sex role attitude change away from traditional patterns for both androgynous and masculine-identified men: the impact of key women in their lives. Although androgynous men and masculine-identified men differed in the nature of this impact, the importance of the role of individual women as change agents seems especially noteworthy in light of the general tendency among advocates of sex role change to devalue personal impact as a viable vehicle for such widespread change. Perhaps, instead, it is a crucial starting point or concurrent buttress to whatever large-scale efforts are undertaken to confront institutional sexism.

The impact of women for the androgynous men came chiefly through the influence of positive, personal relationships with strong, career women or feminists. For example, typical responses of androgynous men included:

> My introduction into the women's movement was smooth . . . I got a very nice confrontation from this woman that I knew who did it in a nice way, didn't hit me over the head with it . . . if it had been more angry, I wouldn't have listened to it . . . I could see that it [women's movement] was affecting her, and it meant a lot to her, so I paid attention to it. It was like saying, something that is really moving me in a deep way, really affecting me, it is important to me, so I say, well, maybe it has some importance for me too, and sure enough . . . it just sort of built from there . . . I started to get involved with the women's movement myself . . .

> An old girl friend of mine probably did as much to awaken me to sex roles as anybody . . . I found it very stimulating to find someone who wasn't locked into all the [traditional feminine] things, because it made me behave differently. It made me feel less like I had to be 'big, strong, he-man protective,' making all the sexual advances, making all the decisions . . . and I liked it. I liked associating with a person instead of a role. Intellectually, she was very sophisticated and so she favorably impressed me as a person and . . . it was very easy to accept her attitudes. If I didn't like her, . . . maybe I would have started on a different foot toward women's and men's roles.

> I think probably the greatest single factor was that I married a woman who was very independent, very assertive, had a lot of abilities, and was very intellectually alive and interested in having a full functioning role in society.

The nature of the impact of women on the lives of masculine-identified men occurred in a different context. Masculine-identified men were more likely to mention the influence of competent, professional women peers and supervisors in their work settings and of their wives' demands for more rights at home. The influence of wives seems particularly instructive:

I think that I needed to learn that a wife was someone to be reckoned with. It never entered my mind [laugh] that when a man took on the responsibility of a wife that, you know, she had any say. I made the decisions and said this is the way it's going to be and that's the way it was, so it came as a shock to me that that was necessary [to let her have a say], and she had to remind me.

What contributed to that was I had to decide whether to continue my career . . . and I felt at that time that was strictly *my* decision, and my wife got, my wife and I had long discussions about that and I soon realized that it wasn't really my decision only, that I wasn't the only one to contribute to that decision, it had to be her too . . . I felt that my wife was demanding more equality . . . she achieved it from me. I was willing to give up some of my earlier conservative viewpoints . . . for example, financially I used to make *all* the decisions, but now, I actually ask her [laughs] what do you think in most cases now. I'm actually weighing what she says very heavily . . . I don't think I'm decreasing my role as a man . . . just getting more of the facts before I make a decision.

Trying to develop a relationship with my wife that is conducive to meeting not only my needs but her needs, I've had to change my expectations of what her role was to allow her to emerge, to have her needs filled.

Masculine-identified men were also more likely than androgynous men to mention demands in their professional settings as one of the prime influences on their beginning attitude change. For example, they made such comments as: "Well, first of all, one reason I'm changed is because the government said we were going to change, and recognizing I'm not going to fight the government, I figured if that's what they want, that's what they're going to get [laugh]. If I'm going to fight something, I'm going to fight something where I can win." Other masculine-identified men mentioned increases in sensitivity toward more sex role equality resulting from the heightened interpersonal focus of the manager's role, from job-related travel and broadening of perspectives, and from working in a professional area which trains more women than men:

In the type of work that I'm doing in management I've gradually become a lot more in tune with the people I'm working with and just getting more sensitive to them has helped me be more sensitive to a lot of other things.

Since I've been out in the world a lot more and doing a lot of traveling [for work], I've just changed my opinions about a lot of things like that. I think another thing that contributes to my changing view of roles is that there are more gals working [and studying] in my professional area than there are males . . . in that group of people you have some very fine people and you want to accept them whether they are masculine or feminine.

One masculine-identified man mentioned, in a related way, that holding a position of responsibility on a community committee had influenced his views toward greater sex role equality: "You could take a different view if you stay along the sidelines. You can take a negative view and tell everybody, 'Well you're all wet' . . . But once you find yourself in a position of responsibility, you really change your outlook. You may not change your personal feelings but you tend to recognize what has to be done and you do it."

Beyond the influence of individual women in their lives who mediated the effects of the women's movement for them, androgynous men were more likely than masculine-identified men to mention that changes in their sex role attitudes had occurred as a part of a general evolution of their religious and political convictions in nontraditional, anti-materialistic, egalitarian directions. They also tended to mention the impact of courses, groups, and workshops in the sex role area as well as the impact of living in other cultures.

In light of the fact that androgynous men have been exposed to more nontraditional models for sex roles in terms of current friends, significant others, and consciousness-raising courses or groups, and have felt more positive about past acquaintances who showed nontraditional sex role patterns, one might argue that androgynous persons evolve new reference groups during their lives to support their experimentation with sex role alternatives. Friends become not only models for new behaviors but mutual support systems which help compensate for the relative scarcity of androgynous models in society. Thus friends and significant others model and reinforce each others' discoveries and creations of sex role alternatives.

The relative absence in our society of androgynous models, especially for men, may explain the relative lack of emphasis on male models of role change in the comments of both androgynous and masculine-identified men. It is conceivable, in fact, that highly masculine-identified men would perceive such models in a negative light and reject them out of a fear or conviction that integrating "feminine" characteristics into "masculine" behavior is unacceptable. It is suggestive that the only men who mentioned the impact of male models for nontraditional sex roles were those who were struggling to make transitions to careers or lifestyles characterized by more interpersonal sensitivity and sharing of emotions. Thus, they had already made some commitment to allow more of the traditional "feminine" characteristics into themselves in the context of their work, and were seeking models and reassurance from men to see how it could be done, finding such men in nontraditional male counselors, friends, or professionals.

Overview

The importance of individual women as change agents remains the most intriguing factor to emerge from this study of the influences on sex role attitude change in androgynous and masculine-identified men. In fact, in terms of male androgynous development, the presence of positive contact with women throughout their lives appears to be one of the key characteristics of androgynous men. When examined in overview, there seems to be considerable support for hypothesizing that positive contact and closeness to women facilitates the development of androgyny. Not only were androgynous men closer to their mothers as children, but they also reported more positive contact with girls while growing up and tended to feel closer to women currently as well as more ambivalent about all-male groups. Androgynous men regretted the general lack of closeness to men and valued gentle, sensitive men, but the dominant trend in their lives was towards greater closeness of contact with women. This contact appears to have been rewarding to androgynous men and may have served as a potential model for important cross-sex traits like emotional and interpersonal sensitivity. Such positive learning experiences with women as models of these alternative characteristics may be especially important in a society which offers so little reinforcement for traditionally feminine characteristics in men. The rewards from contact with girls may have been part of the factors allowing androgynous men to be less dependent as boys on the male peer group which advocated a rigid male role, and therefore to less severely repress any of their behaviors that deviated from that male role.

In contrast, masculine-identified men appear to receive much less significant cross-sex contact. Their predominant contact seems to be with other men (fathers, male peers in childhood and currently) and this same-sex contact may make it less likely that they would learn much in detail about the diversity of real women and the degree to which actual men and women show overlapping characteristics. Masculine-identified men would also appear to be less likely to turn to women as models or reinforcers for any personality characteristics which might broaden their traditional masculine repertoire. For many masculine-identified men, marriage may be one of the first significant relationships with a woman, and it is indeed congruent with this line of reasoning that some of these men tended to report marriage as a key "humanizing" influence leading to more flexibility in their sex role behavior.

It is intriguing to ask whether contact with women must occur in nontraditional contexts in order to facilitate androgyny. The data that androgynous men tended to date less and be more dissatisfied with traditional male-female interaction patterns can be seen as partial support for this hypothesis. Certainly the contacts with significant others and friends of androgynous men were more likely to be characterized by nontraditional values, although it must be noted that women who were most influential as change agents approached the issue within the latitudes of acceptance of the men in their lives, rather than aiming for a full-blown confrontation of ideologies. It is intriguing, however, that even relatively traditional wives had an influence in moving masculine-identified men toward less traditional sex role attitudes, and it is tempting to speculate that close contact with women in itself may facilitate more flexible sex role attitudes in men. In any case, the tremendous importance of close relationship and/or marriage and the family as contexts for significant sex role change cannot be underestimated or devalued in discussing issues of wider social change. Exposure to the "feminine" values in some form seems to be at least an initial starting point for moving toward androgyny.

In addition to the importance of relatedness to women and exposure to women who are seeking more equality in relationships, the importance of opportunities to actually discuss and explore new attitudes and behaviors in the sex role area seems especially important to the development of androgyny in men. Thus androgynous men reported positive experiences with consciousness-raising activities and one suspects that the emphasis on feelings, intuition, sensuality, relaxation, play, massage, and meditation of the human potential movement and the consciousness-exploration movement may have been, at least in part, an attempt to allow our culture to explore alternatives to our "masculine" preoccupations with task-oriented achievement, competition, and logical rationality. As such, these movements may in fact have had far more to offer men than women. Women often risked overdosing on the feelings and intuition which were often already well developed in them and they might have done better to enter assertiveness training, problem-solving, and conflict management workshops to complement those dimensions they already had developed.

Therapists have often commented that it is harder for a man than a woman in our culture to grow whole, for a woman need only add on the traditional and highly esteemed "masculine" qualities to her grounding in a rich emotional life; a man, in contrast, has been trained by culture to devalue those very aspects he needs to complement his strengths, and for him, the attempt to develop his feelings or his intuition may feel like a regression. If a woman has to "grow up" from her childlike state in order to be a full adult in our society, a man first may have to "grow down," recovering some of the spontaneity of his childhood, before he can return to full adulthood as a complete being. This search for wholeness and the exploration of one's undeveloped potential will be the subject of the later chapters on "internal androgyny" where we will focus on explorations of the cross-sex side of each of us, the metaphorical realms of "masculine" and "feminine."

Finally, the development toward androgyny appears to be facilitated by work environments which provide opportunities for collaboration and exposure to competent women peers and models of equal status, a powerful source of breaking down traditional stereotypes for masculine-identified men. Since there is a little bit of "masculine-identified values" within us all as members of a society of dichotomous sex roles, this dimension of attitude change cannot be underestimated. Social psychological theory and research support this factor in particular, arguing that forced behavior changes, sanctioned by legal requirements of affirmative action, are key dimensions in reversing prejudice and discrimination. It is reassuring, however, that much of the influence in work settings reported by masculine-identified men does not reflect merely this external factor, but speaks on behalf of the power of equal status contact as an opportunity to confront one's own stereotypes and begin to move in less traditional directions. The work environment may, in fact, offer the first avenue in which many masculine-identified men will feel challenged to take a second look at dichotomous sex role assumptions, and although it does not seem to be as important a factor once one has begun to move in the direction of androgyny for men, it may represent a crucial starting point in attitude change.

Opportunities for exploration of sex role attitudes and behaviors do not need to be elaborate or extensive to be helpful. Even a brief opportunity to share openly with others some of the struggles of androgynous paths may play an important role in clarifying one's cognitive maps or thoughts in this area. Even the interviews which formed the basis of the research from which these chapters draw appear to have been helpful growth experiences for many of the participants. This seemed particularly true for the men. As one androgynous man expressed: "I like doing this . . . like I have all these things inside me that I want to get out, and you don't often have that opportunity to get it all out, and so it's felt really good for me to express all these things . . . because they come out piecemeal, but rarely do you set down for two hours and you do most of the talking and say what I think about things." Masculine-identified men, too, made comments such as "I think it's interesting to sit down once in awhile and talk about . . . my feelings, because I think about it occasionally but I don't really put it into words, 'cause nobody really asks me."

The exploration of sex role issues, so centrally linked with questions of self-esteem, deserve far more attention in education and therapy. Deviation from traditional sex role behaviors often involves great psychological pain and ambivalence for many androgynous persons who judge themselves inadequate or alone in their struggle with sex roles. Although the androgynous men and women described in these chapters appeared to have worked through their inner struggles and attained a strong, confident view of themselves, this process might surely have been facilitated by some external support and legitimization for a wide variety of ways of being a man or a woman. Surely the ongoing efforts of persons trying to move towards androgynous goals might be aided by knowledge of what has helped others in this search. If androgynous persons derive support and courage from each other's struggles, one can speculate, too, that sex-typed persons might benefit from more opportunity to explore any private doubts they feel about the degree to which they fit traditional sex roles.

Growth in androgyny requires active exploration and experimentation, and cognitive flexibility may well be a crucial forerunner to behavior change. Thinking, reading, sharing, and talking about one's own experiences seems essential especially for men if the taboos of society against the integration of the "feminine" into the "masculine" are to be eased and removed. The difficulty, as Warren Farrell (1974) points out, is that men have been trained to be question-answerers rather than question-askers, to not share ignorance or uncertainty, to remain experts in topics of their own choosing. Movement toward androgyny requires men to tolerate uncertainty, to ask larger questions, and to lean with more patience into a range of alternatives which are just now beginning to emerge as our culture dares to live with new dreams.

ENDNOTES

[1]A first or "consistent" pattern among masculine-identified men represented a consistently active, highly masculine-identified role pattern. A second or "delayed" pattern also represented a continuous external adherence to aggressive, active, and traditional male behavior. However, the masculine-identified men who fit this pattern qualified their external behavior by some reference to feeling quieter or less aggressive inside and needing to push themselves somewhat when younger to be aggressive externally. Those who reported fighting a lot or being pushed toward early independence tended to come from this second group. A third or "quiet" pattern was the exception, differing from the former two aggressive patterns, and consisted of a lifelong tendency toward quiet, relatively withdrawn characteristics. Although deviant in personality traits from the traditional male role, this pattern was associated with the practice of the most traditional behaviors and attitudes towards sex roles. The other most traditional masculine-identified men were found among the first pattern.

[2]Four developmental subpatterns can be tentatively identified for androgynous men, although caution must be exercised in generalizing on the basis of such small sized subgroups. In the first or "compromised androgynous pattern," very early the boy felt himself as deviant from other boys (more sensitive, less assertive, and so on) but tried to conform somewhat, played sports and performed with average ability, but received most rewards from intellectual pursuits. A second or "continuous androgynous pattern" consisted of an early and consistent development of both active leadership characteristics and gentle, nonviolent, and expressive qualities. Both sets of qualities were consistently rewarded and never suppressed. This early androgynous pattern also tended to include liking girls as friends from an early age.

In the third or "deviant pattern," the salient feature of the androgynous man's development was his deviance from his general environment (for example, a radical youth in a small conservative town, a verbal philosopher in an agricultural community) and androgynous tendencies emerged as a part of this general nonconformity. These men tended to be loners, to describe themselves as fairly unassertive, and to feel less close to women than in the other patterns. This pattern was the most likely to be characterized by an actual dislike and avoidance of many traditional masculine traits, and the androgynous challenge for these men was to reown and recover some of the same-sex traits they had previously repudiated.

A fourth or "recent androgynous pattern" consisted of those androgynous men who had been highly involved in the typical male adolescent patterns of dating, sports, and fairly aggressive personal styles. One androgynous man described this pattern in the following way: "The rock of granite image, never crying, never expressing any feeling whatsoever, I worked on that real hard and that was tough, I got pretty good at it too. Then I got into a real heavy physical thing, you know, strength and endurance and be the perpetual warrior, I did that for awhile . . . till I got that down pat." For these men, the shift to androgynous patterns was relatively recent in their lives and involved the effort to broaden their personalities to include more cross-sex traits and to find more comfort in a wider range of behavior.

4

BECOMING AN ANDROGYNOUS WOMAN
Patterns of Development and Keys to Change

The process of becoming an androgynous woman differs from the pattern more typical of feminine-identified women in many ways. This chapter traces these differences in developmental paths and critical incidents in childhood, adolescence, and adulthood and explores the factors androgynous and feminine-identified women cite as most influential in any changes they have experienced in the direction of less traditional sex role attitudes. Although there are many subtle and qualitatively rich differences or tendencies that separate androgynous and feminine-identified women in childhood, the most striking and important events and experiences that affect the development of androgyny appear only in adolescence, a pattern forming a dramatic contrast with the socialization conflicts faced by androgynous men. This and many other contrasts between the paths of androgynous men and women will also receive attention throughout this chapter.

PATTERNS OF DEVELOPMENT

Childhood

As was true for androgynous and masculine-identified men, the androgynous and feminine-identified women who were interviewed in this research were not differentiated in terms of geographical mobility, rural or urban backgrounds, or parental characteristics. Mothers of both androgynous and feminine-identified women had worked since marriage in about the same proportion, and there was only a tendency for mothers of androgynous women to have more than a high school education compared to mothers of feminine-identified women, and for fathers of androgynous women to be described as somewhat nontraditional either in being emotional, sensitive, or helping with child care. Androgynous women did tend more often to view their mothers positively as strong, independent, active, or dominant women, whereas feminine-identified women were more likely to express negative feelings about self-sufficient traits in their own mothers. Nonetheless, these tendencies can only be suggestive of subtle differences in tone between the childhood homes of androgynous and feminine-identified women; for the most part, both groups came from homes where relatively traditional sex role behaviors characterized parents, although there seemed to be slightly more contrast between the two groups in parental characteristics than was true for the men.

Most of the exposure of androgynous and feminine-identified women to sex roles outside the home involved largely traditional male and female patterns, as could be expected from the dominant social norm of the time, however, feminine-identified women were more mixed or negative, and androgynous women more positive, in their reactions to nontraditional past acquaintances they remembered. Thus, feminine-identified women gave more negative examples about career women who never had families or whose children had problems, and a few mentioned they could not imagine men who would reverse roles and stay home:

> A friend's mother, she was very career oriented. She was very much the type to, when her children would bring friends home, 'Don't sit in the living room, don't mess up this,' very much an adult type world even though she had children. It was very hard on them.
>
> I suppose if we'd known someone where the man didn't work and

stayed home and she worked, I would have thought, that's weird and that's wrong, he must be a slouch. He must not be able to hold down a job.

In contrast, androgynous women remembered positively examples of career women (aunts, professors/counselors, friends of the family) who they thought were exciting and interesting, even though sometimes other relatives tried to present these nontraditional alternatives in a negative light or as exceptions rather than real possibilities. Androgynous women were also more likely to mention deviant male roles in a positive light and knew more couples who had somewhat reversed roles, with the woman working full time in her career and the man's career secondary, or where the two people traded off who was working full time:

> Some friends of my parents. . . . the wife did travelogues and traveled all around the world . . . and the husband was just sort of her photographer and kind of a sidekick type person . . . I had very positive reactions. I thought that would be great fun to do that, but . . . that was just seen as an exception . . . that is, somehow luck happened, and she could do that.

> She is . . . a person that I have admired for a long time . . . and that I've identified with a lot . . . because she is a person who's been able to be a professional person but still keep the strength and the warmth about her . . . she hasn't become a hard, harsh person to be a professional, and she hasn't become a soft, helpless, weak person to be a woman.

This latter description comes close to being an intuitive statement about androgyny as it might be lived out in the life of a woman, and may well have served as one of the rare and key models for something like androgyny in this woman's development.

Although feminine-identified women and androgynous women were more often likely to describe being closer to their mothers than their fathers, there were dramatic differences reported in their relationships with their fathers. These differences appear to be among the most intriguing trends which differentiated androgynous women and feminine-identified women in childhood. Feminine-identified women seemed more likely to mention being a "Daddy's girl" or a "father's little girl . . . being loved by your father or being able to sit on his lap or take naps on his shoulder," without any of the strained emotional relationships androgynous women often described with their fathers. One gains a picture of a father who cuddles and rewards his little girl for her soft, delicate, pretty, "feminine" qualities, who protects her and wants her to grow up ladylike and sheltered from the harshness of the world.

In striking contrast to the harmonious role as "Daddy's girl" described by feminine-identified women, androgynous women tended to describe intense relationships with their fathers, extended strivings to please their fathers, and sometimes thwarted attempts to be close and live up to their father's expectations. The tone of the relationship between androgynous women and their fathers is suggested in the following quotes:

> I felt more of a kinship to my father and consequently it was just horribly frustrating because I never could get close to him . . . I was expected to behave and live up to his expectations, whatever they may happen to be, and I never really knew what they were . . . I never felt like I had anything in common with my mother.

> During this period too, I was very caring about my father's feelings toward me. People used to say 'You're the apple of your father's eye,' and I didn't really know what that meant, but I thought it meant I guess I look like him and I'll try to be like him in a lot of ways, and to get his affection, I will do things so that he will be endeared to me . . . I was always dealing with the sissiness bit. I didn't want to be a sissy. My father had kind of said, a couple of times, he had termed certain behaviors that I had emitted as 'That's for sissies,' . . . and I can remember that term being applied and . . . wanting to avoid it very strongly . . . I was very bent on pleasing my father . . . I would gang up with him against my mother when there was the opportunity . . . I never considered it to be a really close relationship, but it was very intense . . . and one scolding from him would be like twenty-five from my mother.

> I was trying to live up to what [my father] expected me to be, and what he expected me to be was to be this really self-sufficient aggressive person, and yet he wanted to control that a little bit, he wanted to control how aggressive, he didn't want me to get too aggressive. . . There was a time that when I was ever afraid of anything, I can remember specifically being afraid to go talk to a teacher . . . and I went in there and I was pretending . . . like I was my father, and I could pull it off.

The importance of contact with the cross-sex parent showed up as an important aspect of the development of androgyny in men, and again, in the female context, a similar trend emerges. However, the nature of the relationship between androgynous women and their fathers seems more convoluted and turbulent emotionally than that described by androgynous men about their mothers. As we will see in later sections of this chapter, it would probably be an error to interpret that androgynous women were any less dependent on the approval of males and especially fathers than the feminine-identified women who were so conscious of being "Daddy's girls." Instead, it is the nature of the model provided by the father and the type of behavior and personality characteristics that are rewarded by the father that seem to constitute the important difference for androgynous women. Thus, not only did androgynous women report the desire to please their fathers, the behaviors that would please their fathers were precisely those which would extend their repertoire beyond the traditional "feminine" realm. Thus, they were provided with a role model from their fathers for cross-sex traits, and with a powerful motivation to become more assertive, achieving, strong, and intelligent. This process reached varying degrees of consciousness during childhood and did not always represent a smooth and peaceful resolution of father-daughter conflicts. In addition to this trend in relationship with fathers, androgynous women also tended to be oldest girls, a phenomenon which might have complemented and facilitated the emphasis on achieving traits that is found in research more often in first children (Kagan, 1971).

Apart from this suggestive tendency in relationships with fathers, it is interesting that androgynous and feminine-identified women are not more different in the types of experiences in childhood they remember or the feelings they had. Earliest memories of being a girl seem to be characterized by ambivalence for almost half of each group of women, suggesting that growing up female in our society holds at least some disappointments for even little girls who will choose traditional life patterns. However, it would also be a mistake to overemphasize the similarities, for there are many subtle differences in the kinds of examples and memories shared by androgynous and feminine-identified women about their childhood, and for the most part, androgynous women tended to be more ambivalent, more vivid and articulate about this ambivalence, and more concerned with general rather than specific disappointments about being a girl.

Typically, the earliest memories of being a girl reported by feminine-identified women were more anchored in female role behavior or imagery. They mentioned such incidents as being a father's girl, learning it was all right to cry if you were a girl, watching a boy go to the bathroom in the road, and an early, embarrassing onset of puberty (for example, "It didn't really dawn on me that I was going to be a woman someday until sixth grade, maybe fifth grade and I was jumping rope . . . and one of my girlfriends said, boy [X], you need a bra and that just, you know I realized, my gosh, and that was it. That did it. I knew right then. I guess that's the first really traumatic thing that happened that I really realized that I was going to be a woman someday. I'll never forget that . . . [It was] unpleasant at the time, because she said it in front of everybody and it really embarrassed me . . . because no one else was like me yet.") Feminine-identified women also mentioned memories related to wishing their clothes were more like a girl's:

> My grandmother made me the most beautiful dresses in the world and in school . . . [I] had to wear high-topped brown shoes and I just hated it and as far as I was concerned, girls didn't wear them and you were subjected to humiliation.
>
> What comes to mind, . . . maybe my eighth-ninth birthday when my birthday cake was a doll . . . with the cake frosted like a dress, because I can see myself standing beside the dress in jeans and an old ratty blouse and maybe I was thinking, gee, I wish I could have been dressed like that in a pretty little dress.

Several feminine-identified women remembered incidents in which they had been excluded because they were girls from highly desirable activities like a fishing trip with father, school and gym events, and playing with a brother: "He [my brother] started to exclude me too from a lot of his activities like when a boyfriend would come over and he closed his door on me . . . As we grew older, I was excluded more and more, and he hated the fact that I wanted to be part of his life . . . I had to learn to become a girl . . . I found out that men do certain things and girls do other things. I had to quit playing cards with him and going playing baseball. I had to find girl friends and play dolls and play house . . . Once I found out that there was a complete different role for a girl, that she developed into something different and had different roles, I just took it for granted and accepted it." These reports of being excluded from boys' activities were more typical of androgynous women, however, who also gave an impression of more actively resenting the exclusion than the feminine-identified woman quoted above.

Both feminine-identified women and androgynous women reported times when they had wanted to be a boy, although feminine-identified women tended more often to mention specific occasions rather than generalized wishes. For example, they reported specific incidents around not being allowed to do something that their brothers could do, thinking that if they were male they would be better at baseball, horseback riding, or athletics in general, and observing that a man works eight hours and is done whereas a woman was "on call" twenty-four hours a day. One feminine-identified woman confided that she had felt guilty at wanting to be a boy, and had never told anyone of these thoughts.

Earliest memories of girlhood reported by androgynous women had a slightly different and more consistently ambivalent tone. A few androgynous women remembered memories around dolls, having hair fixed like Shirley Temple, a brother being born, playing doctor, but they tended somewhat more often to remember incidents characterized by behaviors less typical of girls or by exclusion from boys' activities such as games, sports, or wearing jeans to school:

> Well I was pretty much a tomboy . . . and I would play with the boys . . . and I remember some of the older boys objecting to my presence.

> My very earliest memory was one morning when I was alone in the house with my mother . . . and she had given me some very lovely dolls to play with and I never wanted to play with them. I wanted guns and holsters and cowboy hats and cowboy boots and things like that and my mother was kind of disappointed . . . I remember it at the age of four.

> When I was little, I had two other girlfriends and we used to play-act a lot of things and they had long strawberry blonde hair and I had a short brown hair pixie and whenever we played Romeo and Juliet I was always Romeo, . . . and I didn't like it that much and . . . I felt funny about it, but, you know, they sort of wanted me to be Romeo because I looked more the part than they did.

> Oh yeah, . . . about the realization that there's something different about being a girl . . . when I was . . . in second grade we had to draw a picture of what we wanted to be when we grew up. Well, I just couldn't think of anything besides a nurse and a teacher, so I drew a teacher.

> I remember when we were in kindergarten, the teacher had a habit of every morning . . . she would check for if you brushed your teeth and cleaned under your fingernails . . . and if they weren't clean you didn't

get to play the morning game . . . and I used to walk to school with a neighbor boy and on the way we were picking grass and our fingernails got dirty. OK, we were standing in line . . . together, and she said, '[X], your fingernails are awfully dirty,' and I didn't get to play the game, but he did, and so afterwards, I didn't think enough at the time to rebel against that, I just said [to him], 'Well, [T.], your fingernails are dirty too,' and then I think that's when I sort of thought well that's really unfair . . . She sort of made allowances for him because he was a boy and he could have dirty fingernails, and I was a girl and I couldn't . . . [and] they played a game that they never played before, . . . a very active game, and I didn't get to play it. I remember that specifically.

Other androgynous women mentioned feeling fairly "militant" as a child about why girls weren't allowed to do certain things or frustrated at the role requirements for girls: "Even at young ages, I didn't want to have to do all those things. . . I wanted to be able to do other things too . . . I wanted to do what I wanted to do, but I didn't want to do things that people said I had to do." Although they did not relate their behavior to sex role issues, some androgynous women reported being a behavior problem as a child and described themselves as "mischievous," "rebellious even in kindergarten," "continually . . . laughing too loud," or getting in trouble in most of grade school for talking too much.

Although androgynous women remembered more encouragement to play with dolls, they tended to have more vivid, detailed memories of being a tomboy compared to feminine-identified women who only mentioned this in passing or commented that they had been too fearful to be a tomboy. Androgynous women seemed to give more concrete and vivid images of playing baseball with boys, being encouraged by fathers to be strong and active, or being good in athletic activities:

I remember I was the fastest runner in our class and that was really a neat thing to be when I was in grade school. And we played baseball and we played with the boys and I really liked that.

I really delighted in outrunning any boys ever and I would often beat them up . . . I always wanted to be better than them, especially in athletics.

Despite these more vivid memories of tomboy days, androgynous women did not describe themselves as more athletic today. Instead, if there was any tendency it was for feminine-identified women to make more comments about enjoying participating in sports, although they tended to belittle their skill. Androgynous women more often tended to mention being discouraged from some formal athletics and muscular development either actively by parents or because there were no teams for girls. We will return to this paradox in a later section.

In comparison to feminine-identified women who tended to report "always liking boys" during childhood, more androgynous women tended to mention occasional mixed feelings about boys, chiefly related to the seemingly greater confidence and aggressiveness of boys or, again, to being excluded from boys' activities:

> Well, sometimes I had negative feelings because, oh, they wouldn't let me play something . . . I always thought I had to beat them at something . . .
>
> I wanted them to accept me; I'm not sure how I wanted them to accept me—as a friend or a buddy or a girl or what, but I remember being somewhat afraid of them and I think I felt that they had a power that I didn't, and I think I saw that in my head as strength. I think I thought they could probably beat me up if they wanted to.
>
> There was a period that I remember that the boys started to make a women haters club . . . and I remember that being an annoying experience. I didn't know why they were going through a funny phase like that . . . I got really upset for a little while.
>
> I can remember at least one time . . . they decided to set up a baseball team between the boys and girls . . . I just knew we were going to get slaughtered and it was the most humiliating experience of my life, because we couldn't do anything. I was one of the best baseball players and I couldn't even hit their balls; it made me so mad, and I thought that was a very unfair thing to do to us and I really hated all the boys right then . . . I think once in awhile I was a little jealous because, for instance, they had organized baseball games, and the girls did play some softball during gym class and stuff, but we never had any organized baseball games.

Although androgynous women were not alone in reporting times they wished they were boys, as mentioned above, they tended to report more generalized wishes than feminine-identified women who stressed specific situations circumscribed in time. Thus, androgynous women mentioned wanting more of the privileges and freedoms of boys in childhood, disliking sisters "always telling me to comb my hair," and really wanting to be a baseball player. Several androgynous women also mentioned wishing they were boys during their teen and dating years, either disliking the subservient female role, not being able to ask boys out, or imagining they would have had fewer social problems as a male. It is fair, however, to note that a few androgynous women had judged the male role to be less attractive and more demanding in some ways than roles allowed girls, suggesting some early perception of the costs of the ostensibly attractive roles assigned men.

It seems important to note in concluding this section on childhood that the few androgynous and feminine-identified women who experienced their childhoods as relatively unhappy showed some striking differences in the sources of this unhappiness that may bear on sex role attitudes. The feminine-identified women chiefly described discontent about their distant relationship with their mothers, whereas the androgynous women more often mentioned being relatively deviant in their environment, isolated, or dissatisfied with female role expectations:

> I can remember not being able to go along with a lot of the playing house, and the playing dolls and the jumping rope kind of thing, and . . . having difficulty finding friends who felt the same way I did about those kinds of things . . . especially in grade school, it was a small school, so there weren't that many friends to choose from. I had a lot of difficulty, I guess, defining what roles, because I couldn't cope with the traditional roles but, then, there wasn't any other role that was defined either, so I guess I just kind of [went] limping along.

> I was extremely unhappy and withdrawn . . . I didn't have many friends as a young child. My parents were terribly, terribly possessive and restrictive . . . I can remember being terribly dissatisfied most of my life and feeling there had to be something more than what I was experiencing.

Adolescence

Although suggestive of some important differences in the feelings and lifespace of androgynous and feminine-identified women in childhood, most of the experiences mentioned thus far by androgynous women have not resembled the types of poignant and striking pressures experienced by androgynous men in their childhood years that differentiated them from masculine-identified men even at an early age. One gets the sense that, in our society, the socialization crunch for women to conform to the confines of the traditional female role is merely hinted at in childhood, and pushes into the forefront only in adolescence. This, in fact, does appear to be the case when we switch our attention to the differences which emerge between androgynous and feminine-identified women in their adolescent years. Here is where the paths tend to diverge radically, and the prices paid by socialization or nonconformity to the traditional female role patterns become more obvious.

One of the most crucial and significant differences between androgynous and feminine-identified women emerges during the school years and the transition to adolescence in the area of academic performance. Androgynous women are far more likely than feminine-identified women to report having liked school very much, performed very well academically, and received strong encouragement for this academic achievement. The feminine-identified women, in contrast, were more likely to mention that academic achievement either received no stress or only average performance was expected of them in contrast to brothers who were pushed to achieve.

Androgynous women described themselves as ambitious, very studious, a "real achiever," and "one of the best students":

> In high school I was really much more scholastic, and I was in quite a lot of clubs too . . . but mainly my interests were academic . . . I was an outstanding student.
>
> I always tried to do the best, you know, like I pushed myself too hard probably, and always worry that I'm not doing well enough, but when I get my grades, I'm always doing well.
>
> I was always above average all the way along . . . It was important for me to do well . . . but still having the . . . vague feeling that that was disapproved of, that it wasn't so good to be that good . . . I would rather do well in school than have all the boyfriends, on one side, but still on the other side I wanted to be accepted by everybody.

Androgynous women more often described themselves as relatively introspective, independent thinkers from an early age and appeared to place stress on their intellectual capacities as an important part of their self-concepts, a tendency paralleling their high achievement in academic areas. It is worth noting that however much they may have struggled with aspects of the traditional female role and yielded in various ways, androgynous women never relinquished or compromised their intellectual achievement at any point in their development. This loyalty to and emphasis on intellectual life for both androgynous women and men may have been an important source of strength and support for weathering the insecurities of the androgynous path, and certainly provided consistent support to cognitive exploration which may have carried over into the sex role area.

The second most crucial difference between androgynous and feminine-identified women during these adolescent years concerns the whole character and tone of this period of adolescence. On the one hand is the image of the happy, active, socializing American girl, which described nearly every feminine-identified woman by the time she was in late high school. Compared to androgynous women, feminine-identified women reported a happier adolescence and tended to have had more positive contacts with boys in childhood, liked boys all along, and dated more in high school. Several feminine-identified women also tended to have experienced an early puberty and to have been a cheerleader or active in athletics, although they sometimes seemed embarrassed in mentioning their interest in athletics and either qualified it or struggled to describe their interest in a way that would not seem inconsistent with their "feminine" qualities. Cheerleading appeared to be a way for some to participate athletically in the absence of organized girls' sports, and they did not find the supportive or traditional female role of cheerleader objectionable. Thus, feminine-identified women appear paradoxically, perhaps, to have been more active in athletics and related activities than androgynous women, who lacked the same opportunities for female sports but avoided roles like cheerleader. Finally, as mentioned above, feminine-identified women were less likely to have done very well in school or to describe academic achievement as an important part of their self-image. They tended to be divided fairly equally between those who had tried to be conscientious in their studying and those who had never been very school-oriented.

The picture of adolescence found among androgynous women is outstandingly different from the atmosphere of pleasant nostalgia found among so many feminine-identified women. Androgynous women significantly more often reported an unhappy or insecure adolescence typically related to confronting some aspect of the female role which either they disliked or at which they felt unsuccessful. For these women, adolescence was characterized by feelings of inferiority and worry about deviating from typical social life patterns, even when these patterns were also judged, at least in part, as undesirable. Thus, androgynous women mentioned the following types of feelings:

> I remember being very unhappy and very lonely . . . It was a community that I just didn't fit into at all . . . Most of the people . . . were mostly interested in status kinds of things and . . . who could make the best small talk, and who had the neatest clothes . . . and that never never interested me. I always thought that was so superficial.
>
> I wasn't real happy in terms of being a female because I didn't feel that I fit the typical role as I perceived it . . . or I felt at least everyone else was perceiving it. My family didn't have any money to buy, like, fancy clothes . . . I always felt that I was tremendously overweight, which I really wasn't that much, to the point that I perceived myself . . . I had lots of really rough moments . . . within myself . . . I didn't like myself.

Many of these androgynous women had experienced a striking discontinuity between a relatively happy, active, and confident childhood and their very unhappy, insecure adolescence. Although several feminine-identified women had mentioned the awkwardness and embarrassment of an earlier-than-average onset of puberty, this insecurity extended beyond very early adolescence only for one of these women, and this did not seem to be the typical issue at stake in the transition to adolescence for androgynous women. Instead, androgynous women described the transition to an unhappy adolescence in terms of turning from an active, confident, and somewhat tomboyish childhood to a kind of confrontation with more traditional female role requirements:

> I see such a break from before puberty and after puberty . . . [to] more fulfilling expectations rather than really being me, and so worried about what I was supposed to do and what I was expected to do and what I should do and what I shouldn't do. Oh, it was heavy.
>
> I remember at the time that I went into seventh grade, all of a sudden, just all of a sudden, I was self-consciously aware of myself . . . Everything about me was wrong. I thought I was just super ugly, and . . . I would just constantly look at myself and say, 'This is wrong and your nose is ugly and your eyes are ugly, and everything is ugly about you' . . . In junior high was the first that I ever realized that boys like girls who are cute and things like that . . . I felt I never, was never just going to measure up.
>
> In elementary school, I was kind of happy . . . one of the gang . . . In high school, I had a very difficult time of it . . . I was continually dealing with feelings of ugliness because I had braces and all that. I really had some bad feelings about myself . . . I figured . . . if I were a boy

with braces, it wouldn't be as noticeable, and my social life wouldn't be as bad . . . If I had been in a role where I could be the initiator, I certainly would have initiated [social experiences] but being as I was a female and couldn't initiate them, I didn't and I felt very lonely at times in high school.

Comments and worries about their appearance did not seem to correlate with the objective attractiveness of androgynous women. The insecurities seemed more likely related to the tendency for androgynous women to date less than feminine-identified women, even though they were no less active in extracurricular activities. Androgynous women who dated less than average tended to have been concerned and unhappy about this at the time: "I . . . always just felt awful about myself. I felt like I was undesirable because I didn't date . . . I did have friends, but their acceptance of me wasn't, I didn't 'appreciate' it, I suppose, is kind of a corny word but I felt like I needed to be accepted by a male . . ." Some of the androgynous women who did date frequently reported that they had felt so insecure that they dated one boy only:

> I was feeling so insecure . . . I grabbed on to [X] and I hung on tight. I had this boyfriend that I was involved with all through high school and that was like a big security thing. As long as he was my boyfriend then everything was all right.

Many feminine-identified women also dated one boy predominantly, typically their future husband, but usually they did not report this same kind of insecurity and mentioned dating other people too.

It is important to note in this context that despite this typical excursion through an unhappy adolescence during these years of acute socialization pressure from the female role, androgynous women much more often than feminine-identified women described themselves as assertive, independent, and strong in terms of current behavior. Half the androgynous women mentioned some previous shyness or unassertiveness, chiefly during adolescence, but they had either pushed themselves to be more assertive in college, professional activities, and job competition or they had been pushed or encouraged in this direction by father or husband. Several mentioned wanting to be more assertive in some area of personal or professional development, and one expressed the relief she had felt in learning that what she had previously feared was aggressive behavior on her part could now be seen as assertive and positive. Androgynous women were also more active currently than feminine-identified women in full time careers outside the home, a finding that both reflects and perhaps encouraged their more developed assertiveness.

At the very same time that androgynous women are moving from an insecure adolescence to an assertive, secure adulthood, feminine-identified women appear to be making a transition in the opposite direction. Although seemingly happy and well-adjusted as teenagers, feminine-identified women more often than androgynous women described themselves as currently dependent, insecure, or having low confidence in themselves or their decisions. They also were more likely to describe unassertiveness as a past and present trait with an accent on such qualities as yielding, giving in easily, avoiding conflict and not being so "independent that I don't need a man around." One could note these tendencies even within the interviews where feminine-identified women often belittled the value or quality of their responses to questions.

The apparent paradox of a happy, confident adolescence and adult insecurity among feminine-identified women gives rise to several alternative speculations about the meaning of this paradox. One possibility concerns the implication that female popularity in dating, cheerleading, and other school activities may not provide very rich experiences for reinforcement of independence and assertiveness. Even active, energetic girls might be getting rewarded simply for playing supportive roles, rather than for developing confidence in other areas; in fact, success may backfire and convince the girl that her only skills lie in being supportive.

A second possibility focuses on the relative erosion of confidence that appears to accompany situations which are perceived as removed from the world of action and influence. Women in the home may have plenty of opportunities for demonstrating their skills, but these opportunities tend to be discounted both by society and themselves over time, and many women begin to doubt their abilities to do anything independently of that environment. Androgynous women who move from careers into periods of homelife and raising families often report a loss of self-confidence resulting from the real or imagined lack of opportunity to test oneself against challenges in the outside world and the lack of opportunities to be rewarded tangibly and monetarily for their efforts. Money is not so important only for its exchange value but for its affirmation that someone outside oneself feels one's work merits significant compensation. Since by adulthood, feminine-identified women are less likely than androgynous women to be working in full time careers outside the home, even though as many as two-thirds debate working at some indefinite future time, one suspects that the greater insecurity among these women may be, at least in part, related to their lessened opportunities to feel their independent strength in the world.

Adulthood

As might be expected, androgynous women were more likely than feminine-identified women to have current friends and significant others (husbands, boyfriends, and so on) who were nontraditional in their sex role attitudes. Thus, androgynous women reported that their significant others were questioning traditional male behaviors in many areas and were becoming more involved in sharing household responsibilities, although androgynous women also tended to stress leftover aspects of male socialization in their significant others, especially with respect to having a strong career orientation. While not differing significantly in educational or occupational backgrounds from the significant others of androgynous women in this study, in that all were white collar or professional workers, significant others of feminine-identified women appeared less likely to help with housework, and several strongly opposed their wife's working while children were young. Traditional, yet subtle, male expectations held by significant others were described vividly by one feminine-identified woman: "I think he [my husband] tries very hard to be modern . . . Down deep he's very traditional. I think it turns him on more when I bake something for him than when I engage him in a lively conversation. It's almost sometimes a threat. It's like 'watch it, 'cause you're treading on my territory.' Now he would deny it, but I see a different look in his eye when I'm doing something very traditionally female . . . when I'm down there doing the laundry or when I'm scrubbing the floor . . . and when I make him dinner . . . or sew a button on, there's kind of a little feeling there that this is where it's all at."

Androgynous women also appeared more often than feminine-identified women to be going through changes and evolution in the kinds of men and women they were attracted to over time. Some androgynous women mentioned changes away from previous preferences for dominating men, an interesting phenomenon which formerly may have served to stabilize and slow down alternatives to the traditional male role, if even nontraditional women previously favored traditional men. Thus, one androgynous woman reported: "I've always been sort of opinionated and . . . once I get to know somebody, I won't keep my mouth shut, so since I've always been that way I always felt I needed someone stronger than me to shut me up and put me in my place. Well, now, since I no longer believe that is true . . . I am more attracted to people who won't do that . . . I really like men now who are sort of on the nonaggressive side and it used to be that I devalued them, because I thought that they weren't keeping me in line." Such changes, although not representing a majority of the androgynous women, seem an important commentary and reminder of the mutuality of sex role change and how important changes in the female role must be accompanied by changes in the male role if more flexibility for everyone is to be maintained.

Although some androgynous women mentioned always having been attracted to independent, stimulating women, others mentioned deeper relationships with women than previously, and the trend was toward greater attraction over time to nontraditional women or to women in general. One androgynous woman epitomized this trend in her comment that "I guess I never really liked women before." Others mentioned increased diversity in the women they liked, a feeling of sisterhood, and being more able to find women now who liked to have the stimulating kinds of conversations they formerly had tended to have most often with men.

When asked about relationships with women in groups, both androgynous and feminine-identified women appeared somewhat ambivalent about all-female groups. Interestingly, however, feminine-identified women tended to continue their negative feelings over time, a finding highly congruent with the observation that members of an oppressed or minority group often express hostility toward members of their own group (Hacker, 1951). Thus, traditional women often put down other women, buying into the stereotype that women's groups are shallow and superficial. Feminine-identified women, for example, described such negative feelings about women's groups as:

> I think they're just terrible. You know, you go to these meetings and there's always a few women that are the, well, you've got your president and all your little chairmen, and the same women do the same thing all the time and the rest of them are just a bunch of sheep . . . I just despise women's groups with a passion, I really do. I feel like once they find out your name, you've had it, especially if they find out you don't work. Then you've just got to be on this committee and most of it is no good for anything, just running in circles.

Oh, I suppose at that time [in the past] I thought that [a women's group] was a very natural and worthwhile activity . . . Now I find that . . . if I get in a group of women and they talk about how to get someone to brush their teeth or how to wax their floors or something like that, you know, I get bored

Androgynous women, in noteworthy contrast, were most likely to report a move away from feeling totally negative toward all-female groups in the past (for example, sororities and social clubs) to having significant positive experiences with all-female groups, especially in the context of a consciousness-raising or support group format:

What I used to think of all women's groups were, I can't think of any positive feelings I would have had, I would see them as kaffee klatch kinds of things where people would talk about laundry soap, curtains and kids and nothing else, and I still see that happening a lot in groups composed of women, but when you say women's groups I think of more support groups or encounter groups kinds of things and I think that that experience can be extremely helpful, realizing that women can give other women support and fulfill some needs.

Oh, I thought they [all-women groups] were awful. Couldn't stand them . . . I just couldn't stand all the petty kinds of things that they would get involved with and not really accomplish anything . . . and this year I've been in a woman's group in my class and it's just terrific . . . You can really talk about a lot of things and work on a lot of things and I love that kind of group, and I don't ever want to be without one.

Early in my life, I was very excited about the sharp girls . . . Later, women were boring to me generally . . . the groups of women, like if I went to a club meeting, that bored me . . . When I got to socialize in the evening and there were men and they talked about the world of work and the worldly ideas, that to me was very stimulating and I thought, oh gee, that's where it's at. But then that changed when I became a feminist. Now at this point in my life, the men's groups are boring and the women I get to deal with are far superior and they get things done, and they're sharper and they know where it's at, and they don't play games.

I used to devalue traditional women's groups, like my mother's groups of women . . . I would sort of put them down, and I have much more respect for them now . . . because I think I was sort of . . . buying into the idea that, oh, a bunch of women together, you know there's cackling and things, and I don't any more at all . . . I've had really good positive experiences with all-women groups. One thing I found out about myself that I'd really never realized before . . . I noticed that in an all-women's group I was just so much more spontaneous, I would jump in and talk whereas in a mixed group like a classroom I would hold back and try to think out what I was going to say . . .

It is not surprising, then, that androgynous women were more likely to have participated in formal or informal consciousness-raising groups or courses on male and female roles. Typically, they felt very positive about these kinds of groups, although a few mentioned they saw such groups as not crucial for their development, mostly of intellectual interest, or as dealing with issues they felt they had already worked through. One androgynous woman had previously feared that in such a group she was "going to be singled out as the married woman who was maybe not considered fully functioning [laugh] because I was still married," but she stated that subsequent experience with a consciousness-raising group revealed this fear to be unfounded. The only androgynous woman who felt somewhat more negatively about formal all-female groups explained that she disliked official groups of any kind that discriminated on the basis of sex, although she did enjoy spontaneous groups of all women.

Those feminine-identified women who did report becoming more positive in their views toward all-female groups over time did not seem to express the strong enthusiasm that androgynous women felt for the women's groups they were involved in. For example, one feminine-identified woman commented: "I think I still shy away when I'm planning to attend something that's all women . . . I go in with negative feelings, but then I come out surprised with positive feelings lots of times." Of those who mentioned consciousness-raising groups, only one spoke with positive interest of joining such a group. Feminine-identified women reported such concerns as:

I don't feel that I need my consciousness raised, or I don't want it raised as high, you know, 'cause there's some things that I know . . . adamant feminists believe that I don't want to believe . . . there's a male in my life and if you're going to take me, you're going to have to take me at times as part of someone else's life.

I'm not the type of person that they are. It's hard for you to put yourself into another person to see exactly how they feel because we've all had different backgrounds. I really don't think I could do it very honestly being the type of person I am.

Androgynous women compared to feminine-identified women held somewhat more negative views toward traditional sex role behaviors and life styles in people today. Some described discomfort, boredom, pity, or strong negative feelings towards traditional life styles: "Well [my feelings about the traditional role] are negative, as far as my family is concerned, because they think I'm crazy, and you know my mother still tells me I should see a psychiatrist, and yet my sister-in-law . . . can't sleep at night, [has] horrible headaches, and it's just one thing after another and yet she's healthy and happy and doing the right thing staying home with her two children and having children even, and yet, I'm crazy, and I get so angry at that, so that's very negative." More felt only slightly negative about such life styles unless a clear choice had been made by the people in full awareness of alternatives.

The striking tendency among androgynous women, however, was the evolution of their feelings from previous strong rejection of traditional roles to increasing respect and acceptance of other women's choices. Although androgynous women were strongly positive about nontraditional life styles, this increased respect for other women's choices may be indicative of the greater tolerance and acceptance within oneself and others of the full range of human characteristics, a tendency we might expect to find in a truly integrated person. Those more comfortable with their own masculine and feminine sides might be less likely to project those traits and avoid or dislike them intensely in others. The increased sensitivity to traditional women's experiences can be seen in the following quotes from androgynous women:

> My mother's role in the family has sort of been kind of like the court jester . . . you know, my father is seen to be doing the serious work, and my mother is just kind of the happy eunuch that just floats around and is happy and people make jokes with and laugh at her and [she] is not taken nearly as seriously as my father, and that's negative to me because even as I get older I find out that I have underestimated my mother a lot . . . I see a lot of women who are really into the feminist movement looking at traditional women and sort of degrading or devaluing them, and saying 'Oh, she's the kind that wears all this makeup' or something like that, and that really sort of bothers me . . .

> The one thing that I would hope would come of the feminist movement is . . . that women become more differentiated and that they have all these different options and that other women don't look at other women and classify them as traditional. I don't want to do that.
>
> I wasn't attracted to the sorority, alum type person before, and now I've sort of decided that everybody's got their own worth, and I really shouldn't shut them off anymore than anybody should shut me off, and maybe that has something to do with the sisterhood kind of feeling that's grown out of the women's movement.

It is interesting that, just as androgynous and feminine-identified women both held some ambivalent memories of early girlhood, they also both tended to view the actual or imagined impact of marriage and having children on their lives with a mixture of positive and negative feelings. Both groups spoke with candor of the stresses of both marriage and child-rearing. When one pays attention to the general tone and qualitative level of their descriptions, however, feminine-identified women do emerge more enthusiastic and positive about both areas, whereas androgynous women remain more cautious and less positive about both areas for themselves.

In this light, feminine-identified women seemed more likely to report marriage as a very positive experience for them:

> [My parents] were never real close to me . . . I think I maybe needed something and I found this in [X, my husband] when we got married and so I think I was much happier really.
>
> I think definitely getting married has made me realize a woman's role more, a feminine role . . . To me it's positive, because that's always been my dream . . . to be able to please someone like that.
>
> I think marriage and a family makes a person more considerate . . . more affectionate. I think it just makes you feel, I suppose, more like you're a part of something . . . I think it's been an enriching thing.

Feminine-identified women who reported some negative feelings about the impact of marriage stressed mostly incidents in early marriage or some limitations on their careers or opportunities to be in the world:

> It's just kind of a rude awakening . . . It's just completely different than little girls think marriage is . . . The typical playhouse thing was what I expected . . . when people get married, no matter how old they are, I

always feel sorry for them, because they've got that first year to go through . . . all those little things you're going to find out about somebody.

I was a little bit disillusioned with the fact that I thought everything had to be fun and games all the time . . . That was kind of a shock . . . if you get married a couple of months and here you are sitting at home all the time.

If your husband has things he thinks a woman always did, 'Whether you have morning sickness or not, you cook breakfast . . .' I didn't stand and declare that I have rights too, but I almost had to.

In a way, looking back, I wish I hadn't gotten married so soon, so I could find out for myself what I'm capable of doing . . . I've never really experienced the real world. I've been in my own little nest.

Well, when I got married, I think that the career aspirations took a bit of a back seat. I thought, well now they're not most important because something else is important to me too . . . I didn't have to support myself, there wasn't that pressure of eating, paying rent, so it was more of a 'if I want to get anywhere, I have to push myself just because I am interested, because it's not a necessity anymore.'

In comparison, the mixed feelings about marriage expressed by androgynous women appeared more intense and pervasive in character:

My general attitude . . . it's not negative, but it's negative if you're going to try to be a career person or whatever on your own, then I really don't see how it can work out very well with marriage . . . [that] the wife gets equal time and so on for her career.

I see my first marriage now as just simply reinforcing all those adolescent feelings I had about myself as being inferior . . . we were just caught in those roles that we were expected to play, [he] being the superior one, liking himself, feeling himself very intelligent and then I playing the traditional passive, inferior, unintelligent female, and what's so scary about that is I thought I was happy and I really thought it was 'what was wrong with me that I cried so much, and that I was depressed so often and why couldn't I change and be the way I was supposed to be?'

I can remember feeling dissatisfied even during the first year of my [former] marriage but not knowing what was causing that lack of satisfaction . . . I think I felt pretty desexed. I just felt like an object . . . I was just the smaller portion of a marriage . . . fulfilling the particular function. I was a symbol.

> [Marriage has] really brought it home to me that I am going to have to do some real thinking about roles. It was easy when I was working because I . . . had roommates that were also professional women . . . and I really didn't have to do too much thinking about women's roles aside from work because at home . . . we were all equal. But now, I find myself having to deal with it daily . . . I'm really still dealing with this now . . . how much freedom can I have as a married person, what have I to compromise.

One androgynous woman mentioned that her former marriage had had a negative impact in the sense of confirming her traditional concept of femininity, but she felt that being married "did allow me, though, the chance to work through what people had always told me femininity was and what your role as a woman in marriage was. So it was good in that . . . it brought me to the point where I could go on from that."

Androgynous women tended to like the companionship and commitment of a long term relationship, and several mentioned the legal advantages of marriage, but some did not intend to marry or were living with a man, working out nontraditional role arrangements, and not intending marriage in the near future at all. The other single androgynous women saw marriage as a possibility at some point but, like the already married androgynous women, felt that it would have to be a nontraditional arrangement in terms of roles and the importance of their own careers.

Several androgynous women and no feminine-identified women reported previous divorces, and it seemed significant that each of these women felt that the divorce was a very positive experience in the long run and had a constructive impact on her views of herself over time:

> It allowed me to take stock of exactly . . . who I was and how I felt about myself, and to work through the feeling that maybe I wasn't really that bad a person and that . . bad at being female, and also to say, well, maybe the expectations of myself and of society in that feminine role in marriage were not so good either.

> I think what it mostly did was free me up to be me . . . I really felt like I could make my own decisions about relationships, about my job, about where I would live, how I would raise my child . . . I just felt more of a person and somehow or other, my femininity got a lot more comfortable along with that . . . Being more of a person, I can be a lot more comfortable with being a woman.

> I didn't think I could survive without . . . my first husband. I really

thought that if he left me, or he didn't love me, that just my life would end, that it wouldn't be worth living. And when I finally started living alone again, and I had a good job, and I realized that I could survive, I was even happier and I was not only even happier, I just really enjoyed life and got turned on to life and . . . to myself and I just can't believe the kinds of things that started happening to me . . when I started living alone . . . I didn't ever want to be married again. And that's why I have a lot of trouble when I'm asked now if I'm married [she is legally married now] because I don't ever want to be married again.

Finally, although one androgynous woman spoke of "becoming more aware of myself as a woman . . . [and beginning] to feel beautiful for the first time ever" during her pregnancy, it was the feminine-identified women who were more likely to describe the impact of children in such unqualified positive terms. This tendency is underscored also by the fact that giving birth to a child or being a mother were the most often mentioned satisfactions of the female role for feminine-identified women. Those feminine-identified women who qualified their positive feelings with some negative ones, however, mentioned the following areas: an increase in traditional role divisions and "shoulds" around being a mother and "supermom," felt or anticipated guilt at possibly working outside the home, being tied down more ("I thought I was going to be pregnant the rest of my life"), feeling insecure and inadequate at first in the face of the added responsibility of raising a child, and not really enjoying very young children.

As was true of their views of marriage, androgynous women tended to be qualitatively less positive and more cautious about the impact or anticipated impact of children. Some did not intend to have children chiefly because of the "disruptive" or limiting impact that children would have on their own careers and roles given the context of current society. Half of these women were making this choice despite feelings that they would enjoy children and being mothers. Several single androgynous women tended to be more positive, but still somewhat ambivalent about having children, concerned mainly with the added responsibilities, the risk of slipping into traditional roles more easily with children, and the issue of what would happen to their careers. Several married androgynous women felt that having children had been positive or fulfilling but also qualified their comments in the following ways: One regretted that she had stopped working while her children were young because she had lost a great deal of confidence during that period, one had actively made efforts to protect herself from the potential isolation of being around children all the time, and one mentioned that it was "a reasonably hard adjustment" in the beginning to get used to the restrictions involved in having a child, although the positive aspects came to outweigh the "hassles." The issue of attitudes toward children seems particularly ambiguous and susceptible to change in light of today's increasingly greater social acceptance of both childlessness, only children, single parent families, and childbirth in women over age thirty-five (Bird, 1979; Chesler, 1979). The increased options available to androgynous men and women may affect attitudes toward the raising of children in the future; currently, however, androgynous women appear more cautious and alert to the potentially negative impact or challenge of children compared to feminine-identified women.

Developmental Patterns

As was true in a comparison of androgynous men and masculine-identified men, a look at the longitudinal development of individual women reveals considerably more variability of developmental patterns among androgynous women than feminine-identified women. For feminine-identified women, most of the variety in developmental patterns occurred prior to mid-adolescence, such that, by the teenage years only one woman did not show the typical friendly, outgoing, active, socializing pattern of external behavior described earlier as characteristic of feminine-identified women.[1] In contrast, androgynous women showed more diversity in longitudinal subpatterns,[2] differing from androgynous men especially in experiencing pressure to conform to sex role expectations in adolescence rather than in childhood.

Recall that despite compromising in some areas of sex role behavior, however, androgynous men and women resembled each other in tending not to compromise their intellectual achievement at any point in their development, a finding which constitutes a noteworthy exception to their partial yielding in other areas. It is also possible that androgynous women had a solid grounding in childhood self-confidence and independence, judging from their more vivid recollection of tomboy days, and that this base of confidence, combined with their intellectual competence, provided the sources of self-reinforcement and approval which helped them emerge from the insecurities of adolescence as assertive, confident women. Likewise the emotional sensitivity of androgynous men may have given them a kind of resiliency and skill in interpersonal areas which may have allowed them to nourish themselves during the long years of feeling different from the traditional male image.

This analysis of the developmental patterns of androgynous persons and same-sex-identified persons should also alert us to the possibility that insecurities around sex role conformity are no necessary sign that something is wrong developmentally. Many advocates of dichotomous sex roles who argue against social change in this area assert that the pain of deviating from sex role patterns is dangerous to the psychological health of young people, that they will become confused and insecure in their identities as men and women if anything is changed. Instead we find, especially in the case of women, that it is precisely those women who most try to stay close to the traditional feminine image who encounter the most insecurity as adults. Androgynous persons may struggle with insecurity during the period of transition to a new confidence in their own choices and affirmations, but this appears to give them a strength which builds a confident and flexible adulthood. One would hope that it is not only the struggle to be an individual against the traditional restrictive social norms that gives them this confidence as adults, although this is likely to be part of the picture. One would hope that even if society supported androgynous patterns and persons did not have to struggle to invent them, that it is the moving toward wholeness, the integration and balance of the "masculine" and the "feminine" characteristics that is the source of strength, not the struggle alone. Thus it would be the search for wholeness, not merely the search for autonomy, that provides the safest guarantee that the androgynous path can bring fullness and confidence of living.

KEYS TO ATTITUDE CHANGE

In addition to the developmental life patterns and incidents that differentiate androgynous and feminine-identified women, these two groups of women also differ in the kinds of factors they mention as important influences on past or current attitude change in the direction of less traditional sex roles. These are the factors most worth examining as clues to the types of structural supports one might seek to create to buttress or enhance conscious change in androgynous directions. No matter where the starting point, these factors appear worth considering in any design for planned change. It is interesting, too, to note that a third of the androgynous women describe that in their own evolution toward androgynous values, they had passed through a period of first becoming more radical and negative about traditional female roles than they were currently. This possibility of balancing by overshooting, giving conscious emphasis to one's "masculine" side at the temporary cost of one's more accustomed "feminine" side, may indeed be an option along the path toward androgyny and one needs to be alert to the possibility that some factors may encourage change in this direction in the short run. Androgynous development may demand a longer time frame and passing through a period of imbalance in the direction of one's least developed side.

What then are the factors mentioned most often by androgynous women as influences on their sex role attitude change? As was true for the androgynous men, androgynous women mention first of all the influence of other women as nontraditional models, for example, a strong, intelligent, competent female friend, boss, professor, mother, or aunt. Not only is the importance of individual women as change agents a particularly noteworthy finding throughout this study, but it also appears that women have become increasingly important reinforcers for women over time. Androgynous women show tendencies to value women more than previously in their lives, and report increasingly positive feelings about individual women and all-female groups. If women are becoming more important to androgynous women as both models and reinforcers for their nontraditional behaviors, this may allow androgynous women to become less dependent on men as reinforcers, a process which may speed up the development of androgyny and build more confidence in the kinds of independent self-affirming lives women can build for themselves.

This growing importance of other women as positive models and reinforcers appears particularly crucial in light of the tendency among the women to turn to men for their support systems. As mentioned before, androgynous women were equally dependent on their fathers for approval compared to feminine-identified women. They also tended to feel very unhappy in adolescence at not fitting the typical dating patterns, and the degree of their unhappiness suggests the strength of their desire for male approval. Likewise, they report the approval of husbands or male significant others as an important support to their non-traditional aspirations. Thus, if male approval affects even androgynous women so deeply, one suspects that androgyny may only develop as fast as there are nontraditional male supports for it unless the experimentation and support from other women can be seen as positively affirming to women. As women begin to like themselves more, they begin to like other women; as they begin to affirm and enjoy other women, they in turn enhance their own self-image. Androgyny buttressed only by affirmation from external male approval can never ring as deeply as an androgyny emerging from self-affirmation and the celebration of being a whole female. Likewise, androgynous men benefit from the support of androgynous women, but it will be the cultivation of new male-based approval for sex role alternatives that brings androgynous men the kind of self-affirmation found in the parallel women's movement.

In general, androgynous development in women appears to be facilitated by avoidance of reinforcement for traditional sex role behavior (for example, androgynous women tended to remain outside the typical adolescent dating situations and hence were not reinforced for many traditional female behaviors) and by positive reinforcement and support for atypical cross-sex behaviors. This support for atypical behavior most often takes the form of support by family and teachers for achieving, intellectual behavior, the factor mentioned by androgynous women as the second most significant influence on their sex role attitudes, next in importance to the impact of nontraditional female models on their lives.

Half of the androgynous women described coming from high-achieving, striving, or radical intellectual families and cultural heritages, of having fathers who pushed and rewarded achievement or assertiveness, and mothers who encouraged them to be able to support themselves and advance in school:

> In general [my family] was a very open environment, questioning everything about society's values.
>
> All my life my mother has said, 'Oh, I'm so glad that you're getting to do this, . . . to learn these things, because I would have just loved to do this,' and even now I take my books home to my mother and she reads all of them.
>
> I know the day I was born, they [my parents] said you are going to college.

Other androgynous women reported never being discouraged in their goals or behavior along traditional sex role lines:

> I was an only child for four years, so I was given indefinite reign to do anything I wanted to and I suppose that allowed me to just explore . . .

That would probably tend to make me think I could do anything and make it less likely that I would fit into a structured role that society had set down . . . Then when I did get to school, . . . I was reinforced in my achievement . . . all the way along and was confident of that identity. I don't remember anyone ever discouraging me at all . . . I was always the best student in the class consistently . . . so I think that the teachers didn't stereotype me as a passive, non-achieving female . . . and therefore they never asked me to do the little feminine things or kept me from doing the masculine things . . . I was also encouraged, because I was really good in arithmetic . . . to be an accountant, for instance, when I was in seventh grade, which I think is a little unusual . . . I can't remember anything anybody ever said to me that gave me an impression I couldn't do whatever I wanted . . . My mother was working, was obviously good at it, really liked what she did. When we would go and see her at work, all the people obviously thought she was great and . . . then my dad . . . he always thought I could do whatever I felt like doing . . . He never limited me at all.

Another aspect of this stress on achievement was the slight tendency for androgynous women, more often than feminine-identified women, to mention that they had been influenced to think of themselves as intelligent: "I was pretty much raised by my parents to believe that I was intelligent. They always told me I was really smart, and that gave me a lot of self-confidence."

Androgynous women tended more often than feminine-identified women to mention several other factors influencing their sex-role attitude change: (1) the importance of support for nontraditional behaviors given by husbands or male significant others, (2) the influence of the women's movement in general and more specifically through reading, courses, consciousness-raising groups, or professional involvement, and (3) the impact of experiences which required greater independence. Androgynous women described with much detail the importance of such events as leaving home, supporting themselves, pursuing jobs that allowed opportunities to grow, travel, and have new experiences, and divorce, as challenges which strengthened their self-confidence and ability to choose more nontraditional female life styles:

When I decided to go to graduate school my financial support was cut off [by my parents], because they told me . . . if I wanted to go to graduate school which was deemed unnecessary that I would do it on my own funds . . . So that was a very significant influence on me. It was at that time that I realized that I had to be on my own. I had to be able to support myself and do things for myself to survive.

Probably the biggest event was my divorce . . . I was going to have to accept the consequences of what that would mean to me—in other words being on my own with a child, having to support both of us financially and emotionally by myself, forever, for all I knew at that point.

In my senior year . . . I was worried what was I going to do when I graduated and all of a sudden, he [my father] wasn't going to be able to take care of that anymore. I was going to have to take care of that, and after my senior year . . . I moved to a small town, where I [had a job] and lived by myself and that was a great experience for me, because all of a sudden I just packed myself up and moved away and was doing all these things, and I just felt just super independent . . . [it] spurred me on . . . to want to be more independent.

Androgynous women described several other influences on sex role attitude change that feminine-identified women did not mention. These factors included changes in sex role attitudes as part of a generalized change toward more liberal attitudes regarding religion or politics, a transition in college to deciding a career was a primary goal and being able to see oneself positively "as an unmarried female who could make it," and negative or frustrating experiences with traditional men who wanted to define for the androgynous woman her identity and degree of independence. With respect to this latter factor, androgynous women mentioned the following:

I really think that the big change started taking place because of my relationships with men . . one in particular who I had become involved with and he was really the traditional male . . . He wanted me to be the traditional female in the sense of relying on him and being really dependent on him, and I was almost really sort of buying him into that too . . . I knew that he would take care of things and that I didn't have to, and that was easy. And gradually . . . I decided I just wasn't feeling good about myself. I thought I can't do anything. I was just really getting locked into that, and I think that's where it really started changing. And when it started changing I felt pretty much like I was starting to have an identity about myself that I really liked and that was different than what he wanted, and that is when I started talking to other women about it . . . and seeing other people not act the way I was acting, and I liked it a lot better.

It gets disappointing over and over again to run into . . . men [who] really think you're neat the way you are and they're really glad you're independent and stuff and then when they get to know you, they realize they don't really like a woman who is that independent or wants that much equality or something.

It is striking to note that in contrast to this great diversity of factors androgynous women report as impinging on their movement toward nontraditional sex role attitudes, feminine-identified women call attention to a whole different set of influences on their own sex role attitude change. Comments by feminine-identified women suggested that some of their movement in the direction of less traditional sex role attitudes was connected with a concern for the greater choices and welfare of their daughters: "You have to be more open-minded about this . . . because of the way the girls are growing up . . . in a society where most women work. I can't take this child aside and say, 'Now you're going to be a little lady and you're going to grow up and learn to cook and sew and that's the way you're going to be.' I can't do that because that would make her an outcast in society."

Feminine-identified women also mentioned revising their views of male and female roles in a less traditional direction after witnessing crisis-type situations where traditional divisions of roles had proved to be inadequate or unproductive. Examples given by feminine-identified women included watching numerous friends go through divorces after many years of marriage, or being sick and seeing a husband's "helplessness" and inability to take over the typical female roles around the house. One feminine-identified women mentioned her father-in-law's death and described how discovering that her husband "wasn't all as strong as he tried to be" had helped her "to grow up." Also, watching her widowed mother-in-law's inability to cope had led her to decide that she was "never going to let myself get that dependent on somebody else."

Overview

In general, the previous two chapters remind us that the paths toward androgyny for men and women hold many important similarities, but that significant differences exist as well. The timing of struggles and conflict around conformity to sex role norms appears to center on childhood for men and on adolescence for women. In addition, there are important differences in the factors which lead to nontraditional sex role attitudes for men and women, and persons seeking strategies of conscious attitude change can take guidance from these differences. General contact with women, equal status contact with women professionals, and sanctions at work for behavioral conformity to norms of sex role equality seem important intervention points for influencing the sex role attitudes and behavior of men in directions of greater equality and/or androgyny. For women, similar changes might be facilitated more by decreasing participation in traditional male-female interactions, increasing the attractiveness of women (especially nontraditional women) as reinforcers, and providing opportunities or jobs which encourage and require independence and assertiveness.

Consistently the importance of contact with nontraditional women models stands out for androgynous persons. As we have seen, androgynous women were more likely than androgynous men to also mention the importance of men, both as sources of support for nontraditional attitudes and as negative influences propelling these androgynous women away from traditional roles. Reinforcement by men for nontraditional female behavior such as high academic, intellectual achievement may also be seen as an important part of androgynous development in women.

Like androgynous men, androgynous women tended to mention their attitudes toward sex roles changing as part of a more general liaberalization of religious and political attitudes. However, this trend did not appear as important as another influence reported more often by androgynous women: the impact of experiences requiring greater independence (for example, leaving home, living alone, jobs, divorce). Such opportunities appear to provide learning arenas for overcoming the typically greater insecurity accompanying traditional female sex role socialization and for developing skills in assertiveness. Without such opportunities or challenges, women may be less likely to take the risks of experimenting with alternative sex role behaviors and thus may never establish sources for a stronger self-confidence. These types of experiences in independence seem particularly significant as a potential vehicle for the development of androgyny in women, and were even mentioned by a few feminine-identified women as valuable influences toward gaining more confidence. Androgynous women also tended to report struggles against discrimination in their jobs among their chief dissatisfactions with the traditional female role. It is possible that the very process of holding a job, particularly a nontraditional one, may tend to heighten awareness of sex role inequalities as well as teach nontraditional skills to women, thus enhancing the potential for change in both sex role attitudes and behavior. Work settings, then, may be among the chief vehicles for women to develop the kind of personal confidence that appears important for any deviancy from traditional sex roles in an androgynous direction.

For those discouraged with the slow process of social change, it seems encouraging that even traditionally identified men and women report some changes in the direction of less traditional thinking about sex roles. Such changes appear to be facilitated for feminine-identified women by concerns for their daughters' welfare. This factor was similar to the "humanizing" influence of marriage, wives, and children reported by masculine-identified men as increasing their interpersonal sensitivity and awareness of some inequalities in sex roles. Emergency situations which invalidated or revealed the shortcomings of traditional male or female role divisions also tended to be effective influences toward nontraditional attitude change for feminine-identified women. It appears that only in their exaggerated forms are the drawbacks of traditional roles made clear to same-sex-identified persons. Since the family unit has frequently received criticism as an obstacle to equalizing sex roles, it seems particularly important that interpersonal concerns for family members would be mentioned this often by same-sex-identified individuals as factors influencing them towards somewhat more nontraditional sex role attitudes than previously held. Perhaps the most important first steps toward androgyny are those small scale, everyday changes that occur close to home in the friendships, relationships, marriages, or families that form the daily context of most lives. Enduring changes do not always follow from radical collision; the most powerful influences often follow attempts to push the fringes of the acceptable, to stretch the latitudes of acceptance for new behaviors, to affirm rather than deny, and include rather than exclude. Patience and subtlety seem somehow consistent and intrinsic to the process of androgyny; hopefully this can feel like an affirmation rather than one more frustration on the way to a new look at sex roles.

ENDNOTES

[1]Despite general similarities, three developmental patterns could be tentatively identified prior to mid-adolescence for feminine-identified women. A

first or "consistent" pattern consisted of an extroverted, highly active, fun-filled youth, involvement with lots of friends, and enjoyment of sports. A second or "delayed" pattern, represented by an equal number of women, could be described in nearly identical terms and qualified by only one difference. The feminine-identified women in the second pattern differed from those in the first in describing themselves as having a somewhat insecure childhood for a number of reasons, including bad feelings about being fat or entering puberty earlier than average. By mid high school, however, these women apparently were as happy, active, and popular as those in the first pattern. Some deviation in body image from the norm for attractive girls rather than some general discontent with being female seemed one of the chief sources of discontent for those feminine-identified women experiencing an unhappy childhood. It seems possible that when bodily changes became more congruent to the norms, these women could enter the traditional female role in adolescence with enthusiasm and possibly relief.

The third or "introspective" pattern was represented by only a minority of feminine-identified women. These women described themselves as relatively introspective thinkers as children and teenagers who maintained a certain amount of distance and perspective on typical adolescent activities and preferred only one or two close friends rather than a group of friends. They either had not participated in much dating or extracurricular activity or were rather scornful of most of the clubs and activities, despite active involvement in a few key areas. Again, recall that despite their reports of a generally happy adolescence, the adult feminine-identified women in all patterns tended to resemble each other in describing themselves currently as relatively dependent and lacking self-confidence.

[2]In contrast to the relative homogeneity of developmental patterns found among the feminine-identified women, four different patterns of androgynous development could be tentatively identified among the androgynous women, suggesting again the variety of paths that lead to androgyny. As was the case for androgynous men, one pattern represented a "continuous androgynous" pattern in which androgynous women reported having been continuously rewarded throughout their lives for both achievement and nontraditional female ambitions as well as developing qualities of sensitivity. These women might have been tomboys, were continually career-oriented, and had not been heavily involved in the women's movement. These androgynous persons, both the women and men representing this pattern described in the last chapter, did not compromise their basically androgynous tendencies at any point, and with one exception, tended to come from among the younger persons interviewed. Although other patterns were represented among the younger participants in this research, one suspects that a continuous androgynous pattern would become increasingly possible and hence more fre-

quent in a society whose sex role norms are changing toward more egalitarian values.

A second or "internal androgynous pattern" consisted of androgynous women who reported being rather independent and unrestricted in their ambitions as a child and who had continued their ambitiousness and nontraditional style of questioning sex roles quietly and internally, although they behaved outwardly according to many traditional female role patterns. These women reported holding some traditional beliefs about appropriate female behavior simultaneously with inner ambitions that they would achieve something in their lives beyond the traditional stereotypes. They also reported feelings of discomfort with some of the traditional female behaviors, even though they practiced other aspects of the female role. The compromises made by these women were thus more subtle and less tumultuous than the abrupt compromises experienced by the "interrupted androgynous pattern" described below, and their chief tendency was toward outward conformity but internal secret deviation from the female norm:

> I really never questioned the stereotype, but on the other hand I was always sort of ambitious in a way . . . it seemed to me all my life I always thought I was going to do something. I didn't think I was going to be a traditional housewife and never work . . . but that's the only part of the stereotype I didn't buy really.
>
> I did [the traditional things] but I also knew in my heart's heart that a person ought to . . . develop themselves so I knew that was sort of tucked away . . . quietly . . . I chipped away on that in a lady-like style [for example, going to night school].

The androgynous women of the "internal androgynous pattern" did not tend to report extended periods of insecurity in adolescence, although several did mention some dissatisfactions around traditional dating patterns. Typically they also had mothers who worked outside the home either during their grade school and/or junior high years. They all mentioned the importance of the women's movement to their personal and/or professional lives, and jobs and divorce were also included as influences in their growth in a nontraditional direction.

In a third or "interrupted androgynous pattern," the salient feature of development was a dramatic transition from a happy, confident, tomboyish childhood to an unhappy, insecure adolescence related typically to worries around not succeeding at some aspect of the traditional female role and abrupt attempts to compromise or struggle with this stress. These androgynous women either dated very little or reported themselves as clinging to one person, and they had tended to feel badly that they did not have more typical dating patterns. Important transition points toward recovering their earlier confidence and assertiveness included decisions in college to be primarily career-oriented, jobs in which they supported themselves totally, divorce, and the impact of the women's movement. A few of these women reported moving initially to a more radical rejection of some traditional female roles than they currently experienced or expected to experience eventually; this tendency had only been present in one woman in the "internal androgynous pattern."

Finally, a fourth or "recent androgynous pattern" could be identified, although this pattern represented only a small minority of androgynous women and should not be overly generalized. This pattern involved following relatively traditional female roles until very recently, but having been vaguely discontent and insecure throughout childhood and adolescence. There were some of the tendencies of the "interrupted androgynous pattern" but without a base of childhood confidence, and isolation and discontent experienced in adolescence had not been clearly focused on concerns with female role requirements. Divorce and becoming more independent were the prime influences toward gaining more confidence to try more nontraditional female roles, although long-term, general unhappiness might have been a possible childhood predisposition to recent evolution in a more androgynous direction. This pattern seemed to be accompanied by a desire to continue becoming more assertive. Thus, despite many precedents and experiences in earlier life that characterize the majority of androgynous women, it is possible to begin the move toward androgyny at any point and the second part of this chapter yields information relevant to this possibility.

Unlike androgynous men, androgynous women do not show a "deviant developmental pattern" characterized by the slow emergence of androgynous characteristics from a general nonconformist lifestyle which had involved avoiding any of the traditional traits of their own sex and only gradually beginning to recover or reown the positive aspects of these traits. It may simply be that there have been far fewer opportunities or reinforcements for nonconformist lifestyles among middle class females until recently, and this pattern of development is thus not represented among today's androgynous women. Perhaps it would be found instead among those women who have identified more fully with their "masculine" sides and hesitated to move in an androgynous direction for fear this would indicate weakness or passivity. For those who have repudiated the "feminine" side of our cultural heritage, whether male or female, the struggle to reown these qualities can be anxiety-arousing and uneasy due to the general lack of cultural support for these values and the resulting intimation that one is moving in a direction away from social esteem and success. Some androgynous women did, in fact, go this route briefly in a kind of revolt against their previous compromises with or insecurities about traditional female roles. They had shifted to a radical dislike of anything traditionally feminine, and only gradually had begun to recover or value some of the traditional "feminine" qualities, some perhaps for the first time, alongside their developing or developed "masculine" skills.

It is important to emphasize that the most significant contrast between the various "compromised" patterns of androgynous men and women appears to be the timing of the compromise or stress of feeling "different" from the norm for the male or female role. As we have seen, the critical incidents around sex role conformity versus deviancy appear to occur earlier for androgynous men than for the androgynous women. Androgynous men in the "compromised pattern" tended to feel their deviancy and tried to conform during childhood, whereas androgynous women in the "internal or interrupted androgynous patterns" seemed to feel most pressures around conforming to the typical female role during adolescence, having experienced themselves as fairly strong, independent, or confident as children. It was during adolescence particularly that androgynous women differentiated themselves most from feminine-identified women and that feminine-identified women launched more securely into traditional female roles. Concern about body images that deviated from the ideal norm had tended to be more frequent in feminine-identified women before adolescence, whereas androgynous women were more insecure about their attractiveness as females and other role uncertainties during adolescence, when their feminine-identified peers were involved in the happy, active pursuit of typical female social activities.

5

IMAGE, MYTH,
AND METAPHOR

Whenever men and women have spoken of Man with a capital M and Woman with a capital W, myth has been called into play—powerful, sweeping, image-rich language and portrayals of what has been seen as the essence of Male and Female. Biological sexuality has provided a fundamental polarity around which to organize or pattern all characteristics of existence. It is not only human qualities which are divided into male or female, but the qualities of the universe itself.

Thus the sun, light, the day have been typically seen mythologically as associated with the masculine, whereas, the moon, night, and darkness are characteristically feminine. As Susan Griffin traces so compellingly in her book *Women and Nature* (1976), spirit, idea, thought, and energy have been imaged through the history of culture as masculine—active and moving toward consciousness. Nature, matter, emotions, the body have been seen instead as feminine—passive, receptive, interrelated and unconscious, undifferentiated.

How one feels about this imagery and the strength of these mythic themes has a lot to do with which side of the polarity holds the dominant power. Myth is not neutral. It is an immensely powerful shaping force underlying cultural, psychological, and spiritual evolution, and where our myths point—if they are living myths—says a great deal about how we will think, feel, and grow as human beings. Myths are not merely descriptive, but prescribe behavior that will maintain existing belief systems in a culture. As Elizabeth Janeway (1971) argues, myths shape our way of looking at the world and ensure that things will happen in ways that match our desires or avoid our fears. The power of myths lies in their universal application; they do not permit questioning or exceptions and their origins are veiled in timelessness.

A careful look at the myths and images associated with Man and Woman reveals a rather high cultural stake in perceiving men and women as creatures of very different status. Not only is man connected to sun and light while woman is connected to moon and night, but we have portrayed the one as superior to the other. The Western, Judaeo-Christian heritage has seen heaven and spirit as superior to earth and matter, man as closer to heaven, woman to earth. It is not much of a step at all from the initial image of Adam and Eve to a belief in women's inferiority, and her inevitable involvement in evil and earthy sexual dimensions, with man as a superior, purer creature whose only error was to be corrupted by sinful Eve. Over and over again, in the mythology we know, men are the heroes, women the victims who need rescuing. Zeus is a strong, aggressive ruler of Heaven; his wife Hera is a quarrelsome, possessive domestic wife. Prometheus dares to disobey the gods and steals fire for man; Pandora cannot resist the temptation of curiosity and unleashes evil into the world.

The myths and archetypes surrounding Woman are seemingly endless. As Simone de Beauvoir (1953) describes, woman has been seen as flesh, as the guardian of sexual powers, the incarnate of nature. She holds the keys to poetry; she is the mediator between this world and the beyond; she is the nurturing mother, bestowing peace and harmony. If she declines these roles she becomes the ogress, the furies, the praying mantis or black widow spider. And the images continue: she is Venus and Cinderella, virgin and whore, madonna and centerfold, amazon and spinster, princess and witch, Snow White and Miss America, Ariadne and Bathsheba, the Mona Lisa and Queen for a Day, First Lady and Gal Friday, Athena and the "dumb broad."

Perhaps the image of Man in myths does not really fare much

better, but most people have a harder time coming up immediately with as rich an array of imagery for the human male. The mythology of the male appears to carry fewer contradictions, negatives, and inconsistencies, except where the images portray deviations from the preferred myth or image. Thus we find the god Atlas and Charles Atlas, Hercules and Jason, Theseus and Perseus, Zeus and Apollo, the Marlborough man and the Playboy connoisseur, cowboy and corporate head, Ralph Nader and Robert Redford, Evel Knievel and the jock, Indian guru and astronaut and, at least to some extent, Jesus and God. The well known alternatives are few: Casper Milquetoast, Walter Middy, the drag queen, the monk, the hermit, and Santa Claus.

As we have seen in earlier discussions, such images and myths provide territory ripe for projections and distortions. In addition, the particular danger of imagery as the carrier of social stereotypes is its tendency toward remaining hidden from awareness and, hence, resistant to change. The vehicle of the visual, the storied image, is perhaps the richest context for the binding power of words. Myths encircle us with collective images from which the individual woman or man must emerge with effort and stand alone.

Given such significant dangers inherent in the role myths can play in stabilizing a world view, it is not surprising that these myths have been challenged, condemned, and abandoned by many of the advocates of new roles for men and women. Social myths and stereotypic images of Man and Woman have rightly been challenged by the women's movement and, more recently, by the emergent men's consciousness-raising movement. It is indeed time to demythologize our myths of their self-justifying inequalities and simplistic portrayals of superiority and inferiority; it is time for men and women to insist on the right to become unique and individual rather than to remain patterns taken from a two-option mold.

Yet even if we were to cleanse our mythology of its assumptions of inequality between the sexes, the question remains whether the myths surrounding maleness and femaleness capture any glimpses of important modes of being in the world. Do our images of masculinity and femininity carry in their essence any clues to different modes of consciousness and value systems, each of which is crucial to a total world view and a fully-functioning human life? Could our myths of Man and Woman have once been living myths and metaphors for ways of integrating the polarities of existence into one whole? Could the imagery that is played out externally as if referring to men and women in the world be meant instead to say something symbolically about two parts within the self, a metaphorically masculine and metaphorically feminine side within the individual person? Is it possible that the problem we face as persons interested in exploring new alternatives to old sex roles is not simply one of demythologizing and getting rid of old myths but of remythologizing, finding the thread of the symbolism and richness within the myth and letting it live into new imagery for our time?

These are the questions we will be exploring in this chapter, which serves as a transition to an exploration of internal androgyny, that is, androgyny perceived not solely in terms of an integration of external behaviors and personality characteristics in the world of everyday life, as we have looked at it thus far, but androgyny as an integration of modes of consciousness, conceived within the self through the deepening of contact with one's masculine and feminine sides. Thus we will be looking at androgyny as metaphor, at masculinity and femininity as metaphor—metaphors which point toward important modes of being in the world that deserve attention and integration in our pursuit of wholeness. The myths and imagery of the past may have much to teach us in the present, not as buttresses of the status quo but as clues to key aspects of human existence we need to preserve.

To proceed in the direction of an understanding of masculinity and femininity as metaphor, however, requires a recovery of the meaning of myth and imagery in human life. We have largely lost touch with the significance of the mythic dimension today, and have dismissed myth either as a kind of idle fantasy and children's story or as a supposedly "prescientific" and primitive attempt to explain the universe before humans evolved the modern tools of science and the clarity of rationality. Thus myth has dwindled into an inferior status as an unsophisticated, childlike attempt to grope in the dark after answers that eluded us before we came of age. There is no recognition that myth may, in fact, be a highly sophisticated attempt to represent the kind of knowledge that inevitably eludes linear and logical thought. There is no suspicion that in fact, even in the hands of science and modern thought, we are still like children groping in the dark before the great mysteries and that perhaps we have no better way than myth and imagery to speak of these unknowns.

This chapter, then, represents an introduction to the role of myth, image, and metaphor in the search for knowledge and understanding. We will be exploring the work of comparative mythologists, scientists, and psychologists of the Jungian tradition in an attempt to recover some of the sense of what it means to call the human being a myth-making creature, a dreamer, a story-teller, and a searcher; we will seek clues to some of the significance of the mythic dimension for our time. Then, drawing largely from the work of Carl Jung and related writers, we will return to the metaphors provided by the concepts of masculinity and femininity and to the mythical task of their integration, the image of androgyny.

Because this chapter offers a complementary alternative to the dominant paradigm's appeals to logic, linearity, and the scientific method in the search for knowledge, this chapter may pose a real challenge to you as reader. It may help, then, to treat the chapter in itself as a metaphor, to try it on "as if" this might be another way of looking at the world, to see what it might offer by way of insights into ourselves. This approach is similar to Ursula LeGuin's (1976) suggestion that one read her science fiction not as a proof or prediction of possible external reality, but as a reflection or metaphor for capturing truths about the present human condition. The present book has been constructed on the bridge between two paradigms in an attempt to wrestle more deeply with the problem of polarities in sex roles and consciousness. As will be discussed in the final chapter, it is my belief that the challenge of developing an appreciation for the metaphorical and mythical approaches to knowledge is related to the problem of unequal sex roles in our culture, and that the traditional assumptions of male sex role superiority go hand in hand with the dominance of the linear, logical model for discovering truth. If androgynous persons are to break through to new and equal valuations of the masculine and feminine dimensions in themselves, they may also need to recover for themselves a full range of approaches to human inquiry, including the legacies of both the quantitative and the qualitative, the rational and the symbolic.

RECOVERING A LIVING SENSE
OF MYTH

There are many ways to approach an appreciation of myth. One might turn to writers like Laurens van der Post whose accounts of the dreams and lives of people in Africa, as in *The Heart of the Hunter* (1961), brings into vitality and freshness the mythology of a living and fast-vanishing culture. One can return to the myths themselves, myths from all the world's cultures and the greatest religious symbols of the ages. The problem with this approach, however, is that we often lack the keys to decoding the richness of myth; we have forgotten how to let the myth play on our hearts as well as our minds; we have grown accustomed to calling myth false rather than waiting with the possibility that we might instead have something to learn. We act competitively with myths, perceiving one as a challenge or threat to another, rather than seeing them potentially as complementary insights on the path to higher knowledge.

Perhaps before we are ready to approach the realm of actual myth, then, we must speak abstractly for the sake of our modern ears, struggle to grasp what myth is about in general, listen to the scholars of myth, turn to words to go beyond the realm of words. According to Greeley (1972)—who argues for the pervasiveness of the human need to create myth—myths are integrative views of reality, attempts to pull together and confront the complexities of human experience, and thereby to find meaning in human existence and the wider universe. Meaning versus meaninglessness is perhaps, as Carl Jung points out, the basic choice of myth (Jaffé, 1971), and Jaffé goes on to point out that whether the myth is that of religion or science, the basic search is to create an answer for the "unanswerable." Meaning encompasses the "totality" of that which is within time and beyond time, within individual experience and within the greater whole (Jaffé, 1971). Myth represents an attempt to look at the more encompassing picture, to sense the overview in terms of which individual action makes sense.

Myth does not turn, however, to rational language and linear logic when it attempts such descriptions of reality. In fact, myth is not really a description so much as it is an evocation, a "standing for" or witnessing that brings into living feeling and reality a sense of what is being portrayed. It is to symbolic language instead that myth turns for imagery which can capture the essence of an interrelated world. Symbolic language uses metaphor, imagery, and analogy in an attempt to represent the subtleties of complex reality and phenomena that cannot be apprehended directly or do not easily lend themselves to linear measurement and analysis. Whether the reality or territory being represented is the outer world or the inner psychological realm, symbol, myth and metaphor become the critical mediators and vehicles for understanding.

It is important to note that myth is truth told "concretely," not abstractly as in scientific rational language (Greeley, 1972). The use of immediate, subjective imagery condenses experience and heightens impact, much as in a haiku poem. Myth offers a kind of feeling-truth that touches multiple levels of our being, that grasps attention from mind and body, that feels like a recognition, a remembering rather than the result of a newly reasoned argument. Watts (1963) argues, in addition, that the language of myth is ambiguous, allowing for the full contradictory complexity of reality, the dark and the light, the good and the evil, the figure and the ground. The language of fact, in contrast, is an "either/or" language that divides and categorizes into unresolvable dualities (Watts, 1963). Metaphors release and transform polarity, revealing the similarities hidden by ostensible differences (Miller, 1970).

Myth thus clearly represents a different mode of looking at the world, a different language system, one that surrenders to the whole rather than grasping for the main points and letting fall the supposed inessentials. In myth, there are no inessentials. All is interrelated, important to be witnessed and seen within the context of the whole. It was, in fact, scientific Newtonian physics, which tried to identify things in terms of specific coordinates, that turned out to be more removed and abstracted from the web of interrelated fact than primitive myth, an irony identified by Whitehead (1925) as the "fallacy of misplaced concreteness."

Humans have always turned to symbolic modes when they have sought to express reality as "emotionally experienced," rather than as rationally analyzed (Campbell, 1951). Ann Belford Ulanov (1971), drawing attention to the widespread use and power of symbols in human history, argues that the image emerges less of Homo sapiens than of "homo symbolicus." The language of myth is the language of pictures, of images, of dreams, a language with power to condense and augment experience in ways that are only now beginning to be explored with seriousness. Images seem to carry more information per unit than does linear thought, and can often release stored memory in ways inaccessible to linear probing (Masters and Houston, 1966; 1972; 1978).

So widespread is the tendency to create myths and so similar are the basic themes, that many have argued that the human being, in a sense, is coded to turn to certain symbolic dimensions in the search for understanding. Joseph Campbell (1951) calls attention to a myth-producing dimension of the psyche which reflects the great patterns and themes of human existence that guide our individual journeys. In his writing one senses his conviction that the human being is born too soon, without the well-wired instincts of so many animals, and that we need to be "twice-born" (Campbell, 1972), taught and guided by the "image-language" of the human spirit that gives rise to our myths and folk tales (Campbell, 1951). With the guidance of myth we live, we remember how to live, and we witness to that living.

Others who have written of the power of myth to shape our destinies are equally articulate about this power. As Ernst Cassirer (1946) argues, our mythic forms do not just imitate reality, but are actually "organs of reality." In other words, all that we are capable of knowing of ultimate reality is mediated via the structures of our symbols; we cannot grasp reality in itself and we shape it in the very act of attempting to understand. All witness is at least partially self-witness and inevitably obscures what it attempts to portray, remaining a pale reflection of the original richness toward which the symbol points (Cassirer, 1946).

Despite these precautions, myth may still come closer to portraying the nature of reality experienced inwardly by human beings than many other forms which forget that they, too, can only suggest and point beyond the immediate reference point. This is particularly true, as Erich Fromm (1951) points out, if what one is trying to express is the nature of inner experience. Take, for example, the myth of Odysseus, pausing for a moment to transcend the typical external approach to this tale, and trying on the possibility that this story of a man's search to return to his homeland might be a metaphorical way of portraying the conflicts and struggles along the road to maturation and individuation, a coming home to the true self. As Susanne Langer (1942) writes, myth offers fundamental insight into the conflicts and moral dilemmas of life, not an escapist individual fantasy.

If the analysis of myth thus far sounds unduly psychologized, portraying myth as a guide to the unfolding and orientation of human life, it is important to turn to Mircea Eliade's writing for balance. Myth does not just struggle with the meaning of human growth and death, but places the human within the cosmos, creating a way of being at home in the wider context of the universe (Greeley, 1972). But more importantly, myth is not just an integrative explanation or remembrance; it is an "actuality," a "testifying," a "resurrection" (Eliade, 1959). Through myth, humans "reenact" and participate in the power of beginnings, of creation, of sacred time enfused with reality, meaning, significance as opposed to neutral, chaotic, and meaningless profane time. Myths allow access to eternal significance, to a greater reality, to the realm of the gods, and through myth, as Eliade (1959) writes, all of life becomes capable of being transparent to broader meanings and wider presence. Symbols open up a new level of awareness, a new way of "seeing through," seeing at several levels at once, seeing, as Alan McGlashan (1966) so beautifully writes, "translucently."

METAPHOR IN THE PURSUIT OF SCIENCE

It is easy to forget, in the historical separation of science and religion we have inherited and perhaps even struggled to obtain, that all search for knowledge can only be an approximation of what is "really real." Whether we begin with science or religion, the world recedes before the investigation, casting off partial truths as if to entice, beckon, foil, and frustrate us from the pursuit. Whether we turn inwardly or outwardly, we cannot know things as they are in themselves, only as we are capable of experiencing them. Even those who decide to stay close to sensory data are very soon taken beyond the world given us by the senses and introduced to a different dimension, whether it be the dissolving of matter into the energy fields of physics or the abstracting of stimulus-response connections of the behavioral psychologists. Both worlds are arcane, dependent on a new way of seeing, built on new assumptions and ways of looking at the world.

We have been encouraged to think, however, that religion is speculative and appeals only to the authority of personal faith or the experience of some more ultimate dimension, whereas science is grappling with something more tangible, provable, testable, touchable. Science, we trust, will take us to the "facts." Yet to take this faith so naively, so enthusiastically, is to be blind to what philosophers of science have been telling us for some time. There are no neutral findings or data unaffected by theory or assumptions. As Laing (1967) argues so graphically in *The Politics of Experience,* we should cease speaking of "data" and speak instead of "capta," events seized according to some framework or design.

The scientific method, so long contrasted with religion as the only way to sure knowledge, can no longer be seen as immune to subjectivity. Even in the use of the scientific method we make certain assumptions about what questions are worth asking and how we will study something. An operational definition, however much it helps us quantify or replicate a measurement, is still a reflection of a choice of focus: for example, we will define "love" in this way rather than in that way for the purposes of the experiment. We rarely pause to consider that there are perhaps as many findings or outcomes as there are ways of defining or approaching the material. Modern physics discovered, in the Heisenberg principle of indeterminancy, that our experimental methods are inextricably bound up with what we will find externally. Research can never escape the influence of our humanness and our assumptions. Our methods of measurement will always set limits on what we can find, for we affect phenomena in the very process of studying them.

As modern humans we have become enamored with quantification and numbers. They give us confidence and are, indeed, partly responsible for our technology which has given us so many of the successes, though one might also add the blights and dangers, of our modern times. The computer and its interpreters and programmers are increasingly the common backdrop of our daily lives, rapidly receding from our consciousness as we whisper only in science fiction or behind closed doors about the invasive implications. Yet numbers and "facts" suggest an exactness that is misleading. The physicist Niels Bohr has been quoted as pointing in physics to the danger of "excessive clarity" as a sure indication that something is false (Jaffé, 1971), and Jaffé adds, in Jungian analogy, that even from the perspective of science, knowledge that ignores the subtlety of the psyche is in some way distorted. To choose the simple, at least on this side of complexity, is to risk the error described so well by Georg Groddeck (1961, p. 78) in his marvelous analogy between academic research science and a yarnshop where busy workers in the back room struggle for years to tease out strands of yarn from the chaos, with customers periodically coming in to request a piece of some specific color:

> The shop assistant takes out his scissors, cuts off this smooth piece and twists it cleverly into a skein . . . And you buy it with the smug belief that you understand something about mankind.

Wherever humans struggle to say something definite about the world they study, especially when the reality they probe keeps giving back the message of its interrelatedness, they turn eventually to metaphor, to analogy, to models and myth. We are quick to see the role of myth in religion, although we are so out of touch with the vitality of our own traditions that symbols and myths lie draped like funeral trappings across our churches and we pump in electronic sounds and sights to jazz them back to life, never quite making the connection. It is more difficult to see the role of metaphor in science, but it is there. The search for cosmic law, laws of nature, the secrets of the universe might be undertaken by scientist or alchemist; their metaphors will be different, but there will be metaphors for each. The search for a hidden order behind the world of appearances is a search that can tempt scientist or religious seeker.

Physicists will be the first to alert us to the transiency of their models to describe the universe, the sense in which the traditional model of the atom both helped and then hindered an understanding of the basis of energy and matter. The image of electrons neatly cutting planetary orbits around a nucleus has given way to metaphors of electron fields or clouds where electrons have varying probabilities or tendencies to exist. The universe has become a space-time continuum in which matter is process rather than thing-like substance and all is interrelated in a dance of changing energy (Barnett, 1957; Le Shan, 1966; Postle, 1976; Toben, 1975). As Fritjof Capra (1975) writes, the modern scientific view of matter is so far beyond that of ordinary sense experience that our common language is inadequate to express it. Physics has had to turn to paradox, the idea of complementarity, the simultaneous existence of energy as both wave and particle. As Capra (1975) adds, physicists have had to turn to "nonsensory" imagery and experience, a realm formerly acknowledged chiefly by mystics.

Capra is only one of many theorists who are beginning to draw attention to the startling convergence of world views carried by modern physics and the insights into ultimate reality found within the world's religious traditions, particularly the myths and metaphor of Eastern traditions: Hinduism, Buddhism, Zen, and Taoism. Not only do both approaches to knowledge find expression via metaphor, but both turn to metaphors that resound with a similar emphasis on interrelatedness and dynamic process. Both science and religion struggle with the problems of abstraction and linear words in describing their insights, and as Capra (1975) describes, the models of modern physics are the "counterparts" to Eastern myths and symbols which can only approximate paradoxical realities. If science and religion have often in history come up with different models and sounded so different in tone, perhaps it is due to their different goals and premises. As Jacob Needleman (1965) points out, one gets a very different feel for the universe, a very different version of truth if one starts from a utilitarian model that seeks to control knowledge for the security of the ego than if one's model comes out of a spirit of witnessing.

One might expect this heightened awareness of the role of myth and metaphor in the physical sciences to find expression within the social science of psychology in a search for its own myths and metaphors as a field of inquiry. One might also expect psychology to take a lively interest in this human tendency to turn to myth and image as metaphors for truth and to ask how this dimension contributes to psychological functioning. However, except at the outskirts of the field, psychologists have been reluctant to turn their attention in these directions.

Compared to the other sciences, psychology is merely beginning to emerge from its infancy as a science since the founding of Wundt's first experimental psychology laboratory in Leipzig in 1879. Dealing with some of the oldest questions asked by humans, psychology has been only too painfully aware and defensive about its origins in philosophy and religion, in speculation about the soul or spirit or the often equally taboo realm of the mind. Modern cognitive and phenomenological psychologists have had to fight their way back to experience and internal events as legitimate terrain for investigation against the dominant ideologies of behaviorism and logical positivism with their stress on external, sensory-based data and events. In a field in which subjectivity lurks dangerously at the edge of every investigation by the very nature of the subject matter, psychology has done well to turn to empiricism and a commitment to objectivity and repeatability in its observations. However, in its advocacy of the scientific method, psychology has often tried to "outscience" science and has practiced limitations not only in what it has studied but how it has studied, limitations which Bakan (1972) feels it is time to outgrow. It is no longer necessary to exclude the important realms of human behaviors like thinking, feeling, and willing from the legitimate areas of psychological inquiry. To do this, as Rychlak (1968) points out is to exclude from our inquiry some of the essential aspects of humanness, and in a sense to be "subjective," in the sense of arbitrary, about what we are studying. The study of internal events and phenomenological experiences does not necessarily exclude objectivity, the ability to understand and replicate the data of others. As Tart (1973) also points out in the concept of "trait-specific science" and investigations into specific states of consciousness by trained observers, one can be objective about internal events, making repeatable investigations much as the early structuralists tried to do via their method of introspection.

At this stage of knowledge, psychology also seems prematurely insistent on valuing only one possible source of data, the experimental method. In confusing experimentalism with the only valid method of empiricism or gathering information from experience, psychology neglects or minimizes the richness that can come from case material or naturalistic studies. As Rychlak (1968) maintains, we must not confuse the mode of origin of a theory with the method for its testing. The fact that scientific experimental method is the last appeal for theory validation does not mean that we need throw out all theory not directly derived from sensory data. In other words, it is the very nature of human beings to speculate, think, go beyond the givens, actively formulate dialectical arguments, stumble upon the truth; psychology needs to validate both sensory and intuitive approaches to theory formulation. A new insight and idea is a gain, no matter where it comes from. Once you have it, you can test it, but if we rule it out as overly metaphorical or speculative, we may never even be able to examine it more closely.

This book is written under the premise that it is time for psychology to expand its view of what constitutes legitimate inquiry. It is time for psychology to recognize that alternative assumptions and interpretations are built into the very process of our perceptual system (May, 1969) and that it is possible that even our percepts are "mythical" or metaphorical creations which attempt to approximate the reality that may stand beyond the limitations of our sensory coders and screens. Metaphor, image, suggestion, and approximation lie everywhere—in religion, in science, and at the level of the nervous system. One can hope that it will become possible for psychology to take seriously the study of myth and metaphor within human functioning and the psychology of consciousness rather than leave these phenomena on the fringes of inquiry for exploitation as fads. Psychology may be a bridge field which provides a context for renewed communication between the insights of religion and science, but it can serve as mediator only if it too faces the limits of its own one-sided inquiry and dares to push toward metaphor as well as fact in its search for knowledge.

AN INTRODUCTION
TO JUNGIAN THOUGHT

It is in the context of this discussion of the convergence of religion and science in the realm of myth and metaphor that we arrive at the work of Carl G. Jung, perhaps the greatest thinker within the fields of psychology and psychiatry to turn attention in this direction. His theory of personality stands out as one of the most complex and dynamic portrayals of human development and evolution that exists in psychology today, yet the most typical reaction to Jung's work is misunderstanding and dismissal. His concepts are itemized in a static form which betrays their sense of movement, and Jung himself is shelved away in the annals of the history of psychology as a contemporary of Freud's who at one point in his career, before his lapse into mysticism, had the good sense to invent the word association test as his major contribution to empiricism.

Part of the misunderstanding of Jungian theory of personality does, indeed, stem from the largely asystematic nature of his writing. He was a prodigious writer and researcher and moved from one work to another, assuming a background in the reader, and rarely pausing to condense or summarize the main points of his writing in any one spot. His writing, in addition, is rich in allusion and amplification, and Jungians are often parodied as writing one page of text and forty pages of commentary. Much of the misunderstanding, of course, also comes from sheer ignorance and lack of effort before the monumental task of assimilating an enormous amount of supportive material and theoretical argument. Jungian work is best assimilated within the clinical context in which it is derived, and it is ironic that Jung's concepts are more typically separated from his clinical data and thus misunderstood in a way that did not happen to Freudian theory, even at the hands of its worst critics.

Probably, however, the resistance to Jungian work follows most fully from the legitimate suspicion that here is a thinker whose interpretation of science is somewhat broader than the current paradigm and who is willing to admit into existence experiential data that others consider ephemeral or insignificant. It is probably no accident that Freud, disliked though his theory was by operationally-minded behaviorists, was still more acceptable in his linear assumptions of causality and his reductionistic approach to dimensions of human experience like art and religion, areas which seemed to leave the door open to dangerous speculations of hidden potentiality in the human.

Jung considered himself a scientist, but he insisted that all phenomena must fall within the realm of scientific study, including the phenomena of psychological experience: thoughts, feelings, recurring patterns, symbols, dreams, and myths. He was a phenomenologist and carefully guarded himself from making hasty theoretical conclusions. It was only after analyzing recurrent patterns in many thousands of dreams that he felt he could begin to write publicly of his findings and speculations. He searched throughout the world's experiences, myths, and traditions for data, finding similarities across cultures in the ways humans have expressed certain hypotheses and testimonies about the world. The importance of Jung lies not so much in any insistence that these recurring patterns of human experience necessarily corresponded to some dimension of external reality, although he thought that probable. Instead Jung emphasized and argued that these patterns had truth as psychic experiences; they were recurrent, repeatable, and showed regularities from which we could learn about psychological functioning. For example, humans recurrently affirm God-experiences, and though Jung argued one cannot prove anything about the existence of God on the basis of psychological experiences of God, he insisted on studying the God-experience as one clue to the nature of being human. Thus, in his insistence on a scientific approach, he frustrates theologians on the one hand by what sounds sometimes like a psychologizing of religious experience, but he also frustrates scientists who feel he should not even be talking about religious experience at all. By staying in this vital field, however, and not relinquishing respect for either the rational or the intuitive, Jung may have done more than any other theorist to build toward a dialogue of science and religion. As June Singer (1973) writes in one of the most powerful and rich introductions to Jungian thought, *Boundaries of the Soul,* Jung offered a "bridge" between the polarities of rational science and experiential religious feeling for our era.

Perhaps above all else, Jung held a respect for mystery. He was deeply aware that there is a dimension of existence that can only be talked about by approximation. Reality cannot be seen in itself, either the reality of the external universe or the reality of the internal psyche. He took seriously the unknown, and argued that we only get glimpses of the larger picture by symbols, myth, and metaphor. Life's fundamental problems are not so much to be resolved as to be lived with in full appreciation of their ever-changing complexity and vitality (Jung, 1967).

It is this emphasis on mystery and the never-ending process of its exploration that leads us to the deepest understanding of Jung's view of the unconscious. Although with Jaffé (1971) we can describe the unconscious as a transcendent dimension of hidden reality, it is important to beware of conceptualizing the unconscious as a "thing." When Jung speaks of a realm of the vast unknown, he is not implying a spatial concept so much as a dimension of experience or consciousness. The unconscious should perhaps be spoken of as a process, a verb, rather than as a noun, although this is difficult to do given the limitations of our language. The more one explores the unconscious dimension of life, however, the less it appears as the Freudian storehouse of repressed memory or even the supposedly Jungian storehouse of "racial" memory (Hall and Lindzey, 1978). Instead, the unconscious becomes a living force which engages us in dialogue and pushes or draws us toward greater awareness.

Jung agreed with Freud on the existence of a personal unconscious which contained chiefly the repressed, unacceptable side of ourselves, driven there by the early experiences of our lives. He also followed up on Freud's idea of racial inheritance, but developed this concept to a much greater extent. The collective unconscious, as he called this dimension of human existence, is a vast field of psychic energy involving not only sexual and aggressive impulses, as Freud might have argued, but one which gives rise to all potential, unknown, and undeveloped aspects of being human. It is a storehouse only in the sense of actively representing the memories and predispositions of being human. The collective unconscious is a kind of dynamic matrix which crystallizes the experience of what it is to be human—the experience of birth, death, mother, father, child, heroism, the ultimate or God, the wise old man or woman, the trickster-fool, and the sense of wholeness in the Self.

The predispositions towards certain experiences of being human are called archetypes in Jungian theory. Archetype is a concept one must struggle to apprehend for it lies behind the visible world of sensory reality and even behind the realm of myth. An archetype bears some resemblance to Plato's "ideas" and the concept of a "primordial" model that patterns and orders human experience (Jaffé, 1971). Archetypes are predispositions toward the formation of certain images common to all cultures; we never see the archetype, the blueprint itself, but only the myth-motifs and images which appear within each cultural context and bear the striking resemblances suggestive of the archetype itself. Archetypes are like a priori forms which represent basic human needs and experiences; they act like the instincts of our potentiality as human beings or like the latent structure that gives rise to crystal formation (Jaffé, 1971). Joseph Campbell (1972), who also finds this concept tremendously useful, is more likely to draw analogies between the archetypes and a kind of ordering instinct or pattern analogous to those guiding the migration of birds; he speaks of vital pattern-forming elements, "affect-images," and "energy-evoking and directing" signs.

Most psychologists who read only this far in Jungian writing stumble at this point over the concept of the archetype, and dismiss Jung as hopelessly mysterious and unscientific. Although biologists struggle to explain such phenomena as the migration of birds without dismissing the problem as hopelessly mysterious, somehow the equivalent of trying to explain widespread similarities across cultures and persons of myth and dream-motifs does not excite the same kind of interest. Rather than dismissing the concepts of the collective unconscious and of archetypes as impossible to validate at this point and therefore as scientifically irrelevant, I would like to invite you to approach these constructs in the spirit in which Jung himself entertained them: as hypotheses about the unknown principles which may guide human psychological experience. What is at stake is not so much the exact mechanism by which a concept like archetype might be biologically possible; in fact, that rooting of the concept in biology may be a misleading search, given that we know so little about even the gap between "thinking" and the physiological processes of the brain at this point. Instead it seems wiser to ask whether we may learn anything from the metaphor offered us by the concept of archetype, whether we may see new patterns or different insights as a result of this starting point in looking at the human being.

According to Jung, the archetypes themselves are universal, but they are represented to the consciousness by symbols which mediate the unknown reality. Symbols and myths will vary according to the local culture, but central motifs will be similar, offering clues to what it means to be alive, to be whole, to undertake the hero's journey in the world. The archetypes serve as guides to psychological development and thus possess healing and therapeutic power. Since they represent not only the dark and "negative" in human experience, as Freud hypothesized, but also the positive potentiality of being human, archetypes serve as powerful links with the sources of energy and wisdom of the ages, rooting us in what it means to be fully human and whole rather than constricted to only those dimensions of consciousness acknowledged in our individual cultures. The archetypes, through the mediation of living symbols, compensate and restore balance to the human personality, linking consciousness to the depths of potentiality and presence of fuller dimensions and healing perspectives. Access to the archetypes allows, in a sense, access "to the gods," a metaphorical way of saying that the power of living archetypal symbols opens us to witnessing the "numinous" power of the universe, incarnated in the various symbols of the deities or the "God beyond God," to use Paul Tillich's terminology (Jaffé, 1971).

For these connections to be possible, it is crucial that the unconscious have expression in consciousness, that there be symbols which can mediate this potential, bridge this gap. Modern culture, however, with its denigration of the mythic dimension, has misunderstood symbols as mere representative signs rather than clues that point beyond this dimension to other potentiality. When an archetype gets cut off or negatively fixated due to individual life experience which seals the person off from that dimension of experience, it is as if there is a hole in the personality which either blocks off all energy in that area or acts like an emotionally-charged magnet, attracting psychic energy at a largely unconscious level and creating a complex focused on that archetypal area (Singer, 1973). When this blockage occurs at a widespread cultural level because the religious symbols and myths of a culture no longer offer access to active dialogue with the unconscious, the result is a culture suffering from imbalance, carrying along a vast reservoir of unexplored energy which breaks through only in its negative forms such as madness and war (Jung, 1964).

Jung, although sobered by the rarity with which humans seek for wholeness, was relatively optimistic in his analysis of human nature. He argued that the fundamental motivation in human life was a great driving force he called the transcendent function, an urge to fully develop the self in all its functions, to become who we really are as human beings. The transcendent function is the urge to develop a unity, a centeredness in our personalities which can serve as our perpetual guide to unfolding. As human beings we are forward-moving, influenced by the future and our aspirations, not just driven by past experience, as is so often the case in Freudian interpretations.

Jung called this process of becoming increasingly more whole, more centered and balanced, the process of individuation. As Singer (1973) writes, individuation entails a process of reintegrating the entire range of potentiality within the person, restoring harmony from chaos and providing unification of diversity. The path to individuation is a lifetime journey which involves several powerful processes.

At one level, the task of individuation is the task of transcending and integrating all the polarities that lie within our personalities. As we have seen in earlier chapters, most of us grow up disowning many of those potential parts of ourselves which are unacceptable to our parents or our cultures. We develop a persona, a culturally approved role or series of functional masks, to present ourselves to the world. The persona, however helpful and useful it is to give us a sense of needed privacy and ability to move from setting to setting without overidentification with any one part of us, still risks fixating us in only one side of ourselves. The persona in our culture usually draws heavily from only a part of rational, conscious existence, and relegates all other parts of ourselves to unconsciousness. In addition, we tend to specialize in only one mode of taking in information about the world or one way of making judgments about this information and thus we become lopsided in terms of our development of the basic functions of sensing or intuiting, thinking or feeling (von Franz and Hillman, 1971).

For every aspect of ourselves that we have developed, there lies within us the unexpressed opposite, the undeveloped other side of the polarity. The sum total of these undeveloped potentialities is called by Jung the shadow, a powerful concept which has counterparts at the cultural and archetypal level which will be discussed in the last chapter of this book. The shadow represents all those aspects of ourselves which we have neglected in our development—the positives and the negatives, the uninhibited instincts and the unexpressed potential. It is crucial to realize that although the word shadow often carries the connotation of dark, dangerous, and nefarious aspects of the self, this connotation derives more from our schooling under Freudian theory than it does from Jungian thought. To be sure, the journey into the self requires tremendous vigilance and courage and is not undertaken lightly. It is an extremely painful and humbling process to go in search of one's own polarities, to reown the projections one has conveniently seen only in others, to recover the log or beam in one's own eye. It is worth remembering, however, that for every disliked aspect of one's own personality, there is also a shadow of gold to be discovered.

The process of individuation, however, is more than the process of integrating and accepting specific opposites into oneself; on the wider scale, it is a process of developing an active, ongoing dialogue between consciousness and the unconscious. The fundamental polarity that needs balancing is thus the polarity of consciousness and unconscious within the person. Jung felt that the first half of life was devoted largely to the evolution and development of a strong sense of ego, an independent, active, striving, thinking, planning, problem-solving self which functioned largely using the modes of rational, linear logic. The ego gave the person a sense of a personal I, an achieved sense of individuality, and was a crucial partner to the dialogue to be established with the realm of the unconscious. Jung believed, however, that one could become overbalanced in the direction of consciousness, and that the ego needed in the second half of life to surrender to a new center of personality, the Self (Jaffé, 1971; Singer, 1973). The Self is the center of the wider personality formed by the active dialogue of consciousness and unconscious; it is the center of the person living out of wholeness. The Self, unlike the ego, contains all polarities in integration. Imagine the sets of opposites within the total person arranged like the spokes of a wheel; the Self becomes analogous to the circumference or the center, the point from which the entire personality is unified, the point from which is mirrored the wholeness and unity of the universe. To live out of this center point, to live in active dialogue of ego with unconscious, to bring one's consciousness as witness to the broader world of archetypes, is to live in harmony and inner peace yet constant evolution. It is to be open, as we have said, to the gods, and what this openness metaphorically symbolizes. Living from the Self is to hold together, in Rilke's imagery, one's angels and one's devils (May, 1969), the rational and the irrational. It is to witness to wholeness, to recover the resonance of the mandala, that image of unity found recurrently in religions of the world and in the psychological exploration of persons struggling for integration (Argüelles and Argüelles, 1972). It means, in essence, to recover access to the mythical and metaphorical, the only adequate vehicle to an appreciation of the power of wholeness as an image in human life and reality.

INTEGRATING ANIMA AND ANIMUS:
The Image of Androgyny

In the process of individuation and recovering opposites within oneself, an additional aspect of the personality deserves special attention. Jung believed that in addition to those aspects of the personality which he felt were related to biological sex (and one might add to cultural conditioning as a man or a woman), each person carried within himself or herself a contrasexual side which represented all those cross-sex characteristics which one had repressed or not allowed expression in one's dominant personality. The contrasexual side of a man he called the anima; the contrasexual side of the woman he called the animus. Much as Sheehy (1974) illustrates the developmental task of aging in terms of the gradual incorporation of cross-sex traits into one's own personality pattern, Jung articulated this process as perhaps the fundamental challenge of individuation. The effort to become conscious of and reincorporate one's own contrasexual side became symbolic of the whole process of recovering one's opposites and setting up an enduring dialogue with the unconscious.

Jung perceptively argued that many of the fundamental problems of relationships between men and women resulted from a tendency to ignore and repress those aspects of the metaphorical masculine or feminine which were outside our own dominant sex role traits, projecting these traits on the other sex and forcing real women and men to act out or carry the image of our own missing half. The more one repressed the anima or animus and engaged in stereotypic male or female behavior and attitudes, the more the image of the anima or animus would become distorted and occur only in gross or negative terms. Like all aspects of the unconscious, the energies of the anima and animus sought expression in consciousness and if they could not command attention in positive, integrative ways, they might take disruptive and exaggerated forms, thus feeding the cycle of repression and fear. This fear and its accompanying projection would distort, in turn, actual relationships between people. Likewise, a society which represses the metaphorical dimensions of either masculinity or femininity will be out of balance, and the repressed animus or anima characteristics, at the cultural level, will return to haunt and possess the culture.

At the individual level, Jung was concerned that we learn to take back our repressions and projections, to look inside and develop relationships with our contrasexual side and free our friends and loved ones to be themselves rather than serving as the carriers or disappointers of the hopes we embody in our anima or animus. The anima or animus, as the contact point with our vast unconscious, often serves a function as guide to the ego and, as such, becomes tremendously important in the process of individuation. If we ask this guidance of external relationships with men and women, however, we clutter those relationships with aspirations that lie more properly within the self. If we are to become whole, we must accomplish this from inside, not by grafting ourselves onto another person whom we love, marry, or relate to deeply, but by searching within to become all we are capable of being. This process, of course, does not exclude relationships; it simply reminds us that the external process of relating to others can never substitute for the work that must be done within.

Because Jung was especially concerned about the relative neglect in our culture of the unconscious, and because he felt the metaphorically feminine dimension was in closer contact with this dimension of intuitive approaches to reality, he directed far more attention to the development of the anima in men and to the realization of the feminine in culture than he did to the corresponding task of animus-development in women. This task was taken up by his wife, Emma Jung, in her important work, *Animus and Anima* (1957) and in the writings of Esther Harding (1970) and Irene Claremont de Castillejo (1973); however, it remains an important shortcoming of much of the Jungian work that it has focused largely on the evolution of a man's relationship to his anima. The portrayal of the evolution of the anima in terms of its projections in myth and imagery as Eve, Helen, Mary, and Sophia (Lander, 1962) are well known compared to parallel renderings of the evolution of the animus found in the works of female Jungian writers. In light of the dangerous cultural overbalancing in the direction of the metaphorically masculine qualities of Logos, logic, and focused consciousness, Jung's insistence on the resurrection of the metaphorically feminine qualities of Eros, relatedness, and intuitive receptivity seems a crucial corrective. One must note in passing, however, that much work remains to be done in the reciprocal direction for women and the dangers of a swing toward the metaphorical feminine after literally eons of masculine dominance need to be carefully considered. This will, in fact, be among the tasks of the remainder of this book.

With these cautions in mind and with the concepts of anima, animus, myth, and archetype available for speculation, we arrive at last before the image of androgyny, with new possibilities for its understanding at a deeper level. Androgyny becomes not only a useful concept at the level of external sex role behaviors and norms, but a powerful symbol for mediating the process of individuation within the individual and culture. In her beautifully written book on androgyny, June Singer (1976) traces out the significance of this symbol, bringing into our awareness the mythic depths of androgyny as a rich and ancient guiding principle which stands for a healing or making whole of all psychic duality. Androgyny in world traditions symbolizes the experience of polarity inherent in the original unity of the universe, a polarity still held together as a reminder of the truth and necessity of wholeness beyond diversity and of the ultimate transcendence of opposites (Eliade, 1965; Singer 1976). This portrayal of androgyny as the cosmic truth of the "Two in One" takes us out of the framework of a concept only recently emerged from the social psychological laboratory or the therapeutic hour and turns our attention to an image that has inspired humans from the beginning of time and myth. It grounds the image of androgyny in the power of myth to apprehend realities and psychological truths that resist mere linear statements and opens up new meanings and levels of metaphorical significance to the living out of androgyny in daily life.

Throughout human history, cultures have sought to express the concept of a wholeness in the universe and in human experience that lies beyond the beginning duality. This wholeness, in itself inexpressible, comes into human consciousness and experience only through the process of splitting into two halves. It is as though consciousness cannot take in the totality but must conceive of the All as a dynamic interplay between two complementary aspects of reality. This splitting of the two can be seen most readily in the Chinese conception of the intertwined Yin and Yang energies which together comprise the every-changing world. In nearly every religious tradition of the world, before there was a split between feminine and masculine principles of deity, there was a creative matrix or androgynous wholeness which gives rise to the universe. The androgynous nature of the god beyond gods is carefully submerged, suppressed perhaps, in the patriarchal documents of Western religion, as Singer (1976) and others point out, although some passages in the Old Testament, for example, still bear witness to the concepts of God as both masculine and feminine (Christ and Plaskow, 1979). When the image of the Divine Androgyne divides into two principles, it appears that history has deified both the feminine matriarchal and, in turn, the masculine patriarchal alternatives which were once held together in our consciousness. The early periods dominated by the Goddess gave way to the current age of patriarchal religion which overthrew the earlier traditions in the name of the Greek gods, the male deities brought by the Aryans to India, and the Hebrew God, Yahweh. The feminine, even as part of an androgynous ideal, had to be expunged from the record.

The image of the divine androgyous principle had its counterpart in human existence in the initial image of the androgynous being, the original "adham," from whose potentiality both male and female were created and split as part of the fall, the separation of the human from wholeness (Trible, 1979). In this reinterpretation of Genesis, the very creation of male and female as unintegrated polarities is part of the meaning of alienation, not the paradigm for the way things should be. The Judaeo-Christian myth has its parallel also in a Platonic image of original human beings as androgynous, rounded beings who were split by the gods into two parts, each half condemned to search its lifetime for its opposite half (Singer, 1976). The image of twins, such a recurrent symbol in mythology, can likewise be seen as a reminder of the original oneness of human beings and the need to search for one's opposites, one's rejected separate side, in order to become whole (Smith, 1978a).

The symbol of androgyny becomes, then, perhaps the most powerful carrier of the integrative message of all symbols, uniting as it does all that has been identified and metaphorically carried by the fundamental dichotomies of male and female. Throughout time there have been traditions which returned to this image, searching for a way to symbolize the transcendence of these categories and the integration of opposites within the self (Eliade, 1965). Thus, various esoteric traditions and philosophies worked with the image of androgyny, the divine marriage, rex and regina, adam and eve, seeking to release symbolically the power of reunited opposites in what Jung (1963) called the "mysterium coniunctionis." This was the central quest of the alchemists, whose symbols of searching for the philosopher's stone and whose stress on the importance of a man and woman working together in this pursuit carry the androgynous imprint of a struggle to integrate one's opposites, to explore the depths of the self, and to emerge in a new place of inner unity (Singer, 1976; Edinger, 1972). It is to this tradition that we owe the various visual images of androgyny which have tried to capture, in portrayals of the half-man, half-woman king-queen, the metaphorical significance of this quest of wholeness. Our modern age trips over these external images, confusing them for a message of hermaphrodism, however, and it is only with effort that we recapture the eyes of myth and see beyond the literal image into the integrations foreshadowed in the androgynous ideal. Perhaps this path to recover the richness of androgyny via the mythic route is too tortuous in our time for many; however, for those who resonate to the dimensions unveiled in this imagery, androgyny becomes not only an external, pragmatic path but a journey toward inner truths. Androgyny becomes, in fact, a challenge to one's whole concept of ultimate reality and to one's language and metaphors for the divine, calling us to a multifaceted interpretation, beyond goddess and god.

A BRIEF CRITIQUE
AND SOME QUESTIONS

The Jungian approach to androgyny which draws attention to the metaphorical richness of both the traditional masculine and traditional feminine realms of experience and qualities offers a profound complement to the more developmental and social analysis of androgyny found in the first half of this book. The concept of the animus and the anima, as the "inner man" and the "inner woman," when taken symbolically are immensely enriching for a personal journey towards androgyny. They give us words and concepts to hang on to as we carve out new paths through cultural landscapes that offer little support for the goals we seek. In a time of transition, these language cues serve as permission systems for new paths and alert us to the kind of conflicts and awarenesses we are likely to encounter on the way.

The intricacies of the Jungian concepts of anima and animus, however, are not without perils, and rather than carry along more assumptions than I am willing to bear conceptually, I will not be using these concepts explicitly in the following chapters but rather will refer to the metaphorically "masculine" and "feminine" realms of experience in individual experience and culture. I will draw heavily from Jungian writings and insights into these realms, but I do not wish to imply that one must be Jungian to explore these metaphorical dimensions. I, likewise, do not want to be confined within many of the Jungian debates and presuppositions about the nature of people or relationships that are found among many Jungian writers.

In the eyes of many feminists, the attempt to combine Jungian thought and feminist perspectives within one approach to life is almost a contradiction. I am not sure whether the context of androgyny offers a sufficient avenue for working out this confrontation, but it seems the most fruitful image within which to approach this difficult task. The point at which Jungian thought is most vulnerable to a feminist critique appears to lie within Jung's assumption that by virtue of biology, women and men are born basically grounded within either the feminine or masculine realms of consciousness, respectively. Although Jungians acknowledge a role for culture in enhancing these biological predispositions and in cutting people off from their contrasexual sides, this emphasis is by no means primary and the question is not raised as to whether the entire distribution of masculine and feminine orientations might be culturally determined. Thus, in Jungian analysis, women—simply by virtue of being women—have the typical predominant task in their lives of living out this feminine side in increasingly more contact with their developing masculine side. Men, by virtue of being born men, are challenged to live out and develop their masculine side while coming more and more into connection with their feminine side. The starting point for evolution is virtually always from the same-sex side.

I am not convinced, however, that the Jungian insights depend on this necessary assumption that one inherits a predisposition to same-sex traits as a biological extension of male or female gender. In addition, it does not seem necessary to continue to require that literal maleness or female-ness carry our projections of "otherness," felt by Ulanov (1971) to be so crucial to creative integration. It would seem equally plausible that, de-pending on cultural conditioning, one could grow up, for example, as a woman who was trained early to develop her masculine side, and whose task of life would be to recover her feminine side. Especially in today's culture with its emphasis on masculine values as the criteria for success, women are all too likely to identify with this realm of experience rather than feeling comfortable with what Jung would have considered their innate feminine side. I find it more straightforward and less bound to complex assumptions to assume that men and women can be conditioned into either the masculine or feminine realm of dominant values, depending on their environment and the likelihood that in a dichotomous world they will stress one, but not both, of the alternatives. Whatever the starting point the task remains the same, to develop both sides of one's personality, to recover one's nondominant side and to become a fully integrated person.

Several other Jungian assumptions and tendencies deserve notice, critique, and subsequent discussion from the perspective of feminism. Too often, Jungian writings ring with a kind of nostalgia for the "feminine" which, however healthy it may be for men, may mask the innuendo that women would do well not to step too far away from a feminine mode in their relationships with the world. This is especially true in the realm of relationships, which is so often seen as the area of intrinsic talent and creativity for the female by virtue of her link to Eros, the princi-ple of relatedness. Thus the writing of Harding (1970), Ulanov (1971), and de Castillejo (1973) often comes very close to leaving most of the respon-sibility for relatedness in the hands of women, almost absolving men of mutual responsibilities share in initiating this task. The stress on women as the teachers in this area, and on the anima as man's guide, can be dangerously and easily misinterpreted as reasons why women should carry this realm for men and women both, an image curiously parallel but inverted from the blame placed on Eve for the original fall from relatedness to God. Here, in the Jungian version, woman becomes redeemer, rather than sinful one.

The extremely positive stress on the feminine which sometimes pervades Jungian writing, however, is due in part to the association in Jungian thought of the feminine with the realm of the unconscious. One should not suppose that the feminine is to be embraced wholeheartedly; in fact, much Jungian writing is oriented to the struggle of the hero or emerging masculine consciousness against the regressive pull of the unconscious, symbolized as the Great Mother. While Jungian theory goes on, at its best, to argue for the necessity of reconnecting with the feminine, after this process of separation, much of the emphasis on hero imagery and the dangers of the negative mother archetype suggest how easy it is in Jungian thinking to get bogged down in this part of the myth. The result, of course, is not too helpful to women or to relationships with women. Jungians, particularly men, are only all too vigilant to see in women evidences of the negative mother and to feel the necessity of perpetually reclaiming their hero tasks. Likewise, it is easy for Jungians to interpret women's own necessary hero journeys and affirmations into self-consciousness as evidences of animus-possession. Too often consciousness is simply equated to the masculine, and women are thereby double-binded in their struggles for wholenesss. There is not enough writing about the feminine hero journey (Heilbrun, 1979) and its complicated implications for mother-daughter relationships (Chodorow, 1978), nor have we sufficiently begun to question the archetype of the negative mother and its potential rooting in mother-dominated child-rearing patterns (Dinnerstein, 1976), a pattern which might be susceptible to gradual change and evolution. Women too often are urged in the Jungian tradition to work toward relatedness within the realm of home and friendship, saving their more masculine, assertive, goal-oriented strengths for their work, leaving a split between the two realms that contributes to the sex role status quo, rather than a radical transformation of both worlds. And finally, Jungian analysis may, at times, foster a kind of introspective orientation to growth, an inner exploration of metaphorical realms, which however critical this may be, can only be one half of the picture. Inner exploration must be accompanied by outer experimentation, by the kinds of struggles in daily living that characterize the persons speaking out of the first half of this book.

Following the inspiration of the Jungian tradition itself, it is time to "dream the dream onward" (Singer, 1973), "circumambulate" the imagery of masculinity and femininity, familiarize ourselves with the symbols and experiential depths they open to us, and create dialogue in "active imagination" with the intuitions and messages from our own hidden unknowns. In the next two chapters, we will thus take an extended look at the realms of the metaphorical masculine and feminine, within men and women, whatever the starting point of exploration and development. In Chapter 6, we will be exploring ways of strengthening and developing the "inner man," understood as the metaphorically masculine side of ourselves, and in Chapter 7, we will do the same for the "inner woman," seeking ways to nourish and strengthen the metaphorically feminine side of ourselves. Chapter 8 returns from this analysis of personality dimensions to a critique of culture and the role of androgyny as a guiding motif in reaching a creative balance and synthesis of the values and modes of consciousness represented by the traditional masculine and feminine. It brings the hope that at the cultural level we may be able to mirror the opportunity for creativity spoken of in the Tao de Ching (Bynner, 1944, p. 42) that:

> 'One who has a man's wings
> And a woman's also
> Is in himself a womb of the world'
> And, being a womb of the world,
> Continuously, endlessly,
> Gives birth.

6

STRENGTHENING THE INNER MAN

The further we move in our exploration of androgyny and the realms of the metaphorical masculine and feminine, the more important it becomes to stay aware of the danger inherent in this process. It is imperative to recall that we are engaged in a journey of myth, in which we are struggling for insights into what it means to be human and what dimensions of existence seem critical to wholeness. Although the world has represented its sense of the two polar dimensions of existence and value as the "masculine" and the "feminine," and we are continuing this metaphorical portrayal in our search for the deeper meaning of androgyny, it seems crucial to remember that these labels must eventually be shed. The "masculine" and the "feminine" are realms within each individual, male and female, and once they have both been given full expression and integration, it is no longer necessary to retain these labels as clues or guides. We become all that we are; we are a synthesis, a wholeness; we are multifaceted and perhaps no longer need the pull of polarities as a reminder that the task is unfinished.

In discussing the development of the inner metaphorical realms of masculine and feminine in the next two chapters, then, it is important not to get caught in the language. The inner man and the inner woman are images for these metaphorical dimensions and in no way are meant to imply any inherent maleness or femaleness to those two modes of consciousness. It is unmistakable that men have been more supported and encouraged culturally to develop the "inner man" and women have been rewarded for nurturing the "inner woman," but as mentioned in the last chapter, I have chosen not to carry along any of the biological assumptions contained in the Jungian tradition from which much of the guidance in these chapters is drawn. Instead of speaking of the metaphorical masculine or "inner man" we could invent a hyphenated term like assertiveness-discriminative consciousness-rationality to sum up the range of qualities and values found in the traditional rendering of the masculine realm. This would indeed be an advance in the sense of freeing ourselves from concepts dangerously capable of being reified along biological lines, but the result would also be cumbersome and linear, losing much of the richness of the context of imagery and myth from which we will draw in these chapters.

Another caution needs to be voiced at the outset, and this observation involves the necessity of reading the next two chapters as two halves of a very complex whole. In discussing the development of the inner masculine in Chapter 6, it is necessary quite often to speak also of the development of the inner feminine as a crucial part of the process of integration toward wholeness; the same is true in reverse in Chapter 7. Thus, the reader needs to be alert to the simultaneity of these two processes interwoven through the next two chapters and should not be misled by the artificially linear mode of rendering this process, necessitated by the format of two sequential chapters. The development of the inner man and the inner woman go hand in hand within each man and each woman. There is no clear guidance as to the starting point of the journey; the important thing is to begin.

When the metaphorical masculine is given expression in Jungian and other contexts, typically what is meant is the realm of linear, rational logic and objectivity, assertiveness and independence, strength and self-confidence. The masculine is represented as the dimension of "focused consciousness" (de Castillejo, 1973), an ability to direct attention through a narrow beam, aimed at discovery of one particular type of truth. Masculine consciousness is seen as associated with the light, with clarity. It is goal-oriented and intent, represented often by the knife which splits, separates, and discriminates as part of the incisiveness of reason. Masculine consciousness is Logos, the Word, the realm of idea, abstraction, unembodied spirit, and clear transparent ideal. All these qualities recur together so frequently that they all seem a crucial part of the metaphorical masculine, the realm which we will be exploring in this chapter and contrasting with the metaphorically feminine realm of Chapter 7. Although the task of developing the inner man may be different for men and women in the confines of our culture, the task remains crucial for them both.

THE BASIC HERO MOTIF

Perhaps the most far-reaching metaphor and mythical setting for the evolution of the inner masculine is the hero myth, the myth of the development of human consciousness from a state of unconsciousness and the eventual surrender and transformation of that ego consciousness in the development of the wider self and connection with the universe. It is the myth of individuation, and though it is meant for men and women, it is a myth told often in very metaphorically masculine images, a myth of the development of the inner man. As Joseph Campbell writes in his comprehensive book, *The Hero with a Thousand Faces* (1949), the chief role of mythic symbol is to aid the forward movement of the human soul against the regressive tendencies that hold it back. Thus the hero myth pulls us towards the highest development of our capacity for autonomy and individuality, for clarity of consciousness and discrimination, and, if we are listening to the whole myth, suggests that these tools of consciousness must also be surrendered or integrated with another mode of perception involving death and transformation, if we are to have a valid vision of the universe. As we shall see, it is the second half of the hero myth that is at stake today; we have often listened only too well to the first half.

The first half of the hero myth, however, is crucial to consciousness and it is imperative in the development of the inner masculine, especially for women today. It is one of the clear starting places as humans in the call to individuation and we gain much guidance by becoming familiar with its paths. As Teilhard de Chardin writes, we each must create from our own life a self, an "opus" (Sarton, 1973). This is the hero's task, the process of soul-making and its reciprocal side, world-making. Joseph

Campbell (1949) gives us perhaps the most powerful general introduction to the elements of the hero myth, reminding us of the way in which these myth-motifs repeat across cultures and times. The hero myth is always the story of a "call to adventure," a "summons" and "awakening" of the being to a terrifying journey into the realm of the unknown, a journey which can be refused only at the cost of one's integrity and vitality and which leads through danger to the threshold of the world beyond immediate experience. For those who have courage to follow the call, there will be supernatural aid unexpectedly along the path, but the journey is essentially an individual one with no guarantees. The "crossing of the threshold" into a realm of power and unknown dimensions, the necessity of going inward, enduring the "belly of the whale" and the night-sea journey in the darkness of the unconscious, and the "perilous journey" of the spiritual labyrinth through numerous tests and trials serve as the initiation, death, and rebirth of the spiritual hero, a person capable of union with both the metaphorical feminine and masculine, of traversing the realms between the pairs of opposites on which so many of us founder. The "mystical marriage" and "atonement with the father" leave the hero in a new place of wholeness from which he must return if he dares, bringing this wholeness into ordinary reality, a task which is at least as difficult and perhaps more painful than the first crossing of the threshold. Now the challenge is to bring back to one's own culture the insights and visions of wholeness from the realm of the unknown, to live as a "master of two worlds," and to integrate one's ordinary consciousness and independent ego with the vision of the world made possible by immersion in the more total self (Campbell, 1949).

The first half of the hero myth, the call to adventure and the setting out of the individual journey to selfhood, receives even more attention in the work of Jungian writer, Erich Neumann. Although Campbell keeps this individualization process in constant tension with the eventual surrender to a greater whole, Neumann is interested in tracing the evolution of individual ego consciousness in persons and in culture and hence he places far more attention on the initial phases of the hero adventure. In *The Origins and History of Consciousness* (1954), Neumann sets the context for the emerging hero myth in the primeval, metaphorical world of the Uroboros, the snake biting its own tail, the worldwide symbol for the original state of oneness of the world, before the existence of the earth parents or the differentiation into masculine and feminine principles. There is only wholeness, but a wholeness characterized by unconsciousness. The world contains all opposites, but these are not seen by any consciousness or held together in any conscious way.

Out of the uroboric state two processes begin to differentiate, as yet undivided, but holding within them the incipient principles of consciousness and unconsciousness. The Great Mother is the prime symbol of this state of evolution, in which she stands beyond polarity as both good and terrible mother, life-giver and life-destroyer, bountiful and devastating, the symbol of nature's profuse unconsciousness and sheer state of unindividuated being. This is the view of the feminine, seen perhaps from the analogy of the newborn being whose initial immersion in the mother lends her the absolute power of the Great Mother of myth. The newborn has essentially no separate consciousness of its own, and its struggles for a conscious ego are paralleled mythologically by the beginning differentiation of the masculine lover/son from the Uroboros and the Great Goddess. The lover/son is subordinate to her, caught in a cycle of death and rebirth related to her powers of fertility and destruction, and represents the as-yet-unsuccessful emergence of the ego consciousness from the state of unconscious union with the mother world (Neumann, 1954). In light of what happens to this myth in culture, it is perhaps an unfortunate identification which links the metaphors of the Great Mother and the feminine with unconsciousness, and the emerging son, hero, and the masculine, with ego consciousness. It is only too easy to consider women in the light of this identification of feminine and unconsciousness and men in terms of the identification of masculine and consciousness, a danger which even Neumann is prone to suggest. Fortunately, he reminds us periodically that the myth refers to the struggle within both men and women for the separation of ego from unconscious, the first major task of the hero myth, and as Jung argued, the primary task of the first half of life. It is an inward task for us all and has nothing to do with being male or female.

The actual achievement of consciousness is a tremendous feat, worthy of heroic imagery, and for Neumann (1954), this achievement is represented mythologically by the "separation of the world parents" from the original unity of the Uroboros and the Great Mother, the evolution of a separate masculine principle in the image of the Great Father, and the subsequent struggle of the hero against both these feminine and masculine powers. The birth of consciousness has been nearly universally represented in myth as the coming of the light, the splitting of unity into pairs of opposites through conscious discrimination. The original undifferentiated wholeness, filled with meaning, falls apart into its differentiated parts with the rise of ego consciousness: the world is created as we know it, the world of multiplicity, form, and polarity. Seen from the point of view of the ego, this is an important advance.

It seems a crucial recognition in the hero myth that this process of splitting the world parents from the state of wholeness is not without great cost to the emerging hero. Although it constitutes a powerful creative act, the process is inevitably experienced by the hero as a sense of guilt, guilt before the powers of original creation. The hero's act of consciousness abolishes paradise; it is experienced as the original sin, as the fall (Neumann, 1954). There can be no consciousness without this carrying of a profound guilt for one's individual stance, a reminder embedded in so many myths around the world. Likewise, as Neumann (1954) so graphically portrays, loneliness becomes the price paid for the development of the ego. The loss of the "participation mystique" which pervaded and made meaningful the original way of being in the world is perhaps even more painful to carry since it is a self-created loss. The development of consciousness implies a no-saying, a struggle against the regressive forces of the unconscious—whether symbolized in nature as the Great Mother or crystallized in culture as the Great Father—and the process of killing the great parents engenders inevitable guilt (Neumann, 1954).

At times it appears that the parental masculine principle of spirituality and unembodied idea which emerged from the split is perceived as an ally to the developing ego against the realm of the feminine principle and its bodily immersion in organic process. Thus Neumann (1954) argues that the hero can only undertake the "slaying of the Mother" and the dark journey to be freed of the dragon and monster if he is identified with the Great Father and a higher spiritual principle (Neumann, 1954). The assumption is almost made that spiritual means "unembodied" and thus, the Great Mother cannot bear this kind of transcendent dimension of consciousness and must be destroyed. This is, in fact, the energy and innuendo of much of the hero mythology, which focuses on the hero-mother combat and the struggle of emerging consciousness to separate from the Terrible Mother.

However appealing this myth may be to male consciousness, it is nonetheless an oversimplification. Perhaps it is true that the metaphorically feminine, representing the first primal force to which almost all humans are exposed by virtue of our child-rearing patterns, carries with it a real sense of threat to our conscious evolution and growth as separate selves. In this light, the Great Mother as perceived enemy of an adolescent ego-consciousness seems an understandable metaphor. However, it is true that the Great Father also becomes a perceived enemy in this process and likewise must be symbolically slain in the fight with the dragon. The transpersonal parents, these archetypal myth-motifs, are both implicated in the struggle for consciousness, an observation which Neumann (1954) does point out, although the comment may appear buried, relative to his emphasis on the struggle with the Great Mother.

The Terrible Father that must be slain represents the firm grip of culture and forms which imprison and legislate truth, preventing the breakthrough of new forms brought by the returning hero. He is the "devouring father" of the Uranus-Cronus myths, where Father God prevents the birth of his own children, and is slain by his son, who in turn swallows his own sons in fear of their eventual betrayal (Vitale, 1973; Stein, 1973). The Terrible Father is the image of law and order, cut off from the creativity and freshness of the unconscious, and fearful of rebellion in the son who may bring new consciousness to bear on the culture and demand new forms and vehicles of truth. Neumann (1954) adds that those heroes who never face the slaying of the father remain trapped in a kind of "spiritual uterus" that removes them from contact with their own creative feminine side. The Terrible Father represents abstracted reason and spiritual idea, pure ego consciousness, and although that is a crucial trait for the hero to develop in the beginning of the quest, by the end of the quest, by the time of crossing and return, if the hero is not able to open his consciousness to access to the unconscious and return to the metaphorical feminine, he is imprisoned in a fate as detrimental as his initial immersion in the Great Mother. He is trapped in the realm of bodiless spirituality, abstraction, pure idea, and negativity toward the material world (Neumann, 1954).

We arrive, then, at the second half of the hero's journey, the time of transformation, in which the strengthening of ego consciousness through the struggle with the Terrible Mother and Terrible Father has allowed the hero to move forward into the realm of the unknown and recover insights to bring back into consciousness for the good of the culture. Such a journey involves the exploration of the unconscious by a strong and flexible consciousness, and the result is a transformation, a new recognition of the value of the unconscious realm and the mode of the metaphorical feminine within the hero's total self. This new integration of the conscious and unconscious within the totality of the hero is symbolized so often by the mystical marriage with the rescued princess, or the freeing of the positive feminine element as partner to one's own evolution

(Neumann, 1954). What began as a journey to develop the masculine side of oneself, the ego consciousness and independence of the seeker, has now evolved at this point in the myth into a journey which also recovers one's feminine half. Such is the beauty and complexity of myth, for the development of the symbolically masculine and feminine are intertwined. One can see now, too, why it is so crucial to keep reminding ourselves that this journey is all internal and metaphorical; that women as well as men must undertake the hero journey to develop and recover both the masculine and the feminine realms of experience and modes of relating. We have not yet begun an exploration of the feminine dimensions of experience on its own terms, so the stress in the hero myth on the recovery of the feminine can only be a reminder and foreshadowing of an exploration that is to come.

If the ultimate goal of all human life is a flexible synthesis of consciousness and unconscious, represented in an ongoing rich dialogue between the rational and intuitive parts of our beings, it is perhaps unfortunate that the primary emphasis of the hero mythology has been on the first half of the hero legend: the separation from the Great Mother and the development of the ego. As a culture we have apparently become stuck at this point and have seemed to identify ego maturity with the realm of the knife, sword, and laser, rationality and scientific method, aggression and killing, individuality and separateness, guilt and isolation, while the realm of the metaphorical feminine—the intuitive, wholistic, relatedness aspects of ourselves—is denigrated as enemy, or feared and repressed. We are stuck at the point of seeing incest from the point of view of the first half of life where it appears as a regressive pull back toward the parental qualities from which one is only first emerging (Johnson, 1979). Yet as Jung (1956) pointed out, the incest symbol carries a different message for the second half of life where it becomes the task of men and women to "assimilate" into their consciousness those aspects of their contrasexual side they have denied for so long. The symbol of the mother at this point in life beckons toward the creative and future potentiality inherent in the unconscious, not the regressive pull of the past (Jung, 1956), and the hero goes willingly into the labyrinth and the cave, in search of a different connection to the feminine, guided by the slender thread of his own faintly emerging feminine side (Smith, 1975).

It is the forgetting of this second half of the hero myth that is currently being protested by those who criticize our patriarchal culture. The overemphasis on the earlier part of the myth is even receiving attention from within the Jungian tradition itself which was so instrumental in contributing to this emphasis. Thus James Hillman (1973) asks whether it is not possible to evolve toward consciousness via a different myth. Have we perhaps outgrown the hero myth, which fostered and parodies the onesidedness of our contemporary culture, reflecting our alienation from the feminine and portrayal of women as paradoxical enemy and savior?

The hero journey which individuates and develops ego consciousness is a critical step along the path toward wholeness, however. While it must be complemented in the quest for wholeness by the recovery of the more intuitive feminine modes of consciousness which allow access to the unconscious and the total Self, it is a decisive step. It is a step which must be taken. Although those who have been encouraged to develop this ego consciousness to its fullest extent may be ready and perhaps long overdue in their journey to recover the feminine in themselves, this may not be the case for all people. As Saiving (1979) has argued, the sinfulness of an overdeveloped ego and ego-assertion is perhaps a masculine view of sin and does not really apply to the situation more common among those who have never been encouraged to develop their egos in the first place. If anything, the sinfulness of following the more feminine side is the danger of living without self-affirmation or clarity, depending on others for a sense of self. For these persons, often women in our culture, the hero myth is a critical starting point. Women, as well as men, must disengage from the Great Mother and move towards the autonomy of their own egos. It would not be surprising if this process causes a particular challenge to women who must separate themselves from a metaphorical being who resembles them physically. The male hero's task is made easier perhaps in the beginning by his physical difference from "the mother" from which he separates. Although the hero journey is a metaphorical and not a literal, physical one, the danger of the confusion of masculine and feminine with male and female bodies is a recurrent one which is present even in myth. Thus little girls may think the male heroes have different destinies than they can dream of and may not realize they too must and can fight the mother dragon of unconsciousness and dependency.

In our hurry to affirm the second half of the hero myth and its return to the parallel affirmation of the feminine, then, we must not forget that the hero myth offers guidance in the kind of conscious, discriminative qualities needed by women today who are struggling out of traditional roles into the masculine-dominated value system of the world of work. Women need to survive in this field, and if they are to transform it in the direction of greater receptivity to the complementary feminine values, they need full mastery of the assertive, logical skills available in the culture. As Heilbrun (1979) writes, women need new hero images for themselves, or they need to find new ways of identifying with hero imagery. Women writers, she notes, still seem unable to portray the strong, individual and successful woman hero. *Reinventing Womanhood*, the title of her recent book, is a challenge for a new mythology and vision. And perhaps it will be truly the women and other outsiders to our dominant culture who will come into focus in hero roles in our times. As many have speculated, perhaps the only contemporary heroes who are testing and savoring their own power and impact to make a difference in the United States are women and blacks (Axthelm, 1979). Elsewhere the hero quest has grown sour, decaying and stagnating in its initial affirmation of the metaphorical masculine and lacking the guidance to move forward to a recovery of the metaphorical feminine.

VARIATIONS ON THE HERO THEME:
The Myth of Parsifal

The hero myth, for all its shortcomings, is still a powerful guide for the development of those traits we commonly see as metaphorical masculine, and as will be seen, all versions of the myth return in some way to an integration with what was left behind in the metaphorical feminine. Each version captures a slightly different perspective and image to portray this journey, and thus we will explore several other versions of the hero myth than the classical motif articulated by Neumann. We will be exploring variations on the myth of the Holy Grail and the legend of Parsifal, seen from the perspective of both Jungian writer Robert Johnson and mythologist Joseph Campbell, and then we will turn to an examination of a female hero myth, the legend of Psyche, as seen from the varying perspectives of Jungians Betty Smith, Robert Johnson, and Erich Neumann.

There are several versions of the Grail myth, each giving rise to its own form of interpretation. By circumambulating the core meaning via these different approaches and nuances, we gain a range of view points and insights for experiencing the potential guiding reality of the myth. Thus Robert Johnson (1974) draws chiefly from the Grail myth of Chrétien de

Troyes and its rendering of Parsifal; Joseph Campbell (1979) draws his Parzival from Wolfram von Eschenbach.

Both versions present us with a view of the world in which the central force or guiding power, the Fisher King, has been wounded and cannot be healed. The entire kingdom suffers, for its highest principle is wounded. For Johnson (1974) the wound of the Fisher King is the painful recognition of the duality of existence, of separation from a spiritual vision, of being burned by a premature glimpse of wholeness and an early step toward individuation in a man's life that falls short of fruition. The Fisher King's wound came from touching some salmon roasting over a fire, touching something too hot to assimilate, the fish of divine reality. It is a wound carried by all men as part of the development of the masculine, according to Johnson, and sounds very close to the kind of confrontation with the preciousness of life and the horror of war faced by so many of the young men who went to Vietnam. It is a wound that does not heal, that will not be able to heal until some other more innocent part of the person emerges and finds the center spot where the wounded king resides, the Grail castle.

Campbell's (1979) portrayal of the Grail myth begins also with a devastated country suffering from a wounded king, but here the wound seems to represent a dramatic split between nature and spirit. The king has been wounded in the thigh, in his center of vitality, by the lance of a pagan knight he has killed. The highest spiritual ideal lies wounded, maimed by its separation from the world of instinct and nature, the feminine, if you will. It is a fitting commentary on our time, true of European civilization even as far back as the twelfth century when the Grail myth was first written down. Campbell's version opens us up a bit more to the universal implications of the myth for men and women, for he does not share Johnson's insistence that men are the wounded kings in our culture, women having retained some sense of connectedness to a spiritual center. Campbell allows us all to be portrayed as the potential wounded king, wounded in our search for wholeness in a culture where the essential masculine dimension is split from its feminine possibilities.

The Grail myth is a myth of healing, a hero's journey which issues forth in individual spiritual development and a reconnection with the feminine part of existence for the individual and culture. The healing agent—the hero—is Parsifal, a young, innocent, inexperienced boy who stumbles upon the path of spiritual evolution in his meanderings to become a knight. Parsifal stands as the recurrent fool, the innocent, spontaneous, unpremeditated part of the person from whom all real progress and healing occur. In myth and legend, it is so often the least well developed part of us which offers the freshness for new insights (Johnson, 1974).

Parsifal has been sheltered by his mother from the knowledge that his father and brothers were killed as knights; he has been protected by her from even the knowledge of this masculine world of knights, but finally his need to venture into the world takes precedence and reluctantly she consents to his leaving. Johnson's (1974) version of the myth makes much of the role of mother in Parsifal's adventure, and attributes to her a fateful warning to "not ask questions" and follow proper behavior. We can recognize the echoes of Neumann's hero myth in this version of the Grail myth; the hero who does not let go of his connection with the Great Mother, the maternal feminine principle, cannot grow as an individual and when a crucial moment for independent spiritual decision comes, he falls short of the possibility for spiritual evolution. Campbell (1979), too, notes that the hero must be ready to kill his mother in the sense of abandoning her to her grief in letting go of him, and be ready to venture into the world, but Campbell's version does not attribute to her the crippling injunction to hold back all spontaneous questions and thus does not load the myth down unduly with imagery of the negative mother.

As Parsifal makes his way into the world, he encounters a knight whose dazzling manner creates in him an immediate desire to become a knight himself. Making his way with instructions to Arthur's court, Parsifal arrives, an innocent fool, and creates a tremendous impression in Arthur by causing a young woman in the court to smile for the first time in six years. It has been prophesied that this young woman would laugh again when a truly great knight arrived in court, and Arthur takes this as an important sign and knights Parsifal directly, sending him off into the world. Parsifal stumbles from one adventure to another, challenges and slays the dazzling Red Knight, and incorporates through this process, according to Johnson (1974), the shadow side of the masculine, the strong, violent, aggressive, potentially destructive side that needs to be mastered in the evolution of the masculine. The whole episode of challenging the Red Knight, putting on the conquered Red Knight's armor over homemade clothing, trying to control the Red Knight's runaway horse—all conjure up the image of the adolescent masculine hero, struggling to prove his manhood, a phase which Johnson notes is sometimes never outgrown in people who go on "Red Knighting," as he calls it, all their adult lives. There is far more to the masculine hero journey than the struggle with the Red Knight, although that is an important option along the way for the more extroverted persons who need to work out their heroism in external imagery.

Not long after the encounter with the Red Knight, Parsifal encounters an older man Gournamond who helps him assimilate the experience and turns him into a real knight. Johnson sees Gournamond as a necessary transition away from the negative feminine influence of his mother, for Gournamond gives him instructions for his quest and tells him the right question to ask if he ever happens upon the Grail castle in his adventures. He warns Parsifal not to seduce or be seduced by a woman during his journey, an instruction which Johnson (1974) interprets as applying to Parsifal's relationship to his own internal feminine side. In the fragile beginning of his own discovery of the internal feminine, he must be very careful to treat her with full respect and not demand of her immediate gifts nor be seduced by the waves of mood she may show him in the period of their becoming acquainted. So, too, if he does gain access to the Grail castle, he must ask the wounded king, whom does the Grail serve? Gournamond is also a key figure in Campbell's portrayal of the myth, yet serves more as the agent of cultural rule and order; he socializes Parsifal, in a sense, and is the one to warn Parsifal that a true knight asks no questions. In any case, whether the prohibition comes from the Mother or the Father, however well-meaning, the masculine hero myth involves somehow the danger of this prohibition against spontaneity and the challenge of working this through to a reincorporation of one's natural impulses and feeling. Perhaps the biggest obstacle to growth we give the adolescent male in us is the prescription to live life and face our woundedness without asking questions.

Somewhere in his wanderings, Parsifal now comes across a woman who wins his loyalty and offer of help. Whether her name is Blanche Fleur as in Johnson's (1974) version or Condwiramurs as in the text followed by Campbell (1979), she represents for both perhaps the realm of the inner feminine and the possibility of a lifetime marriage and love, brought together for the first time at this point in European consciousness. Parsifal does not stay with her, but is bonded by an inner loyalty which accompanies all his subsequent adventures. The inner feminine appears perhaps only after the hero has left the parent and gained control of his own aggressive, combative side.

Access to the Grail castle has, of course, been the dream and quest of every knight, every hero throughout the myth, but it is only at this time, having met the inner feminine, that Parsifal stumbles upon the actual castle itself, crosses the drawbridge, and is entertained before the wounded king. It is a crucial moment in the myth, the long awaited moment of healing, the opportunity for the asking of the question that will restore unity, but the chance is missed. Parsifal holds back; he dares not ask the question, either question: the abstract one voiced in Johnson's (1974) version, "Whom does the Grail serve?", which is a question of spiritual priorities and of the surrender of the ego before the higher self, or the simple, spontaneous, compassionate question, "What ails you?" which Campbell (1979) points to as the only way in which the rigidity of form and protocol can be healed by the influx of true love and caring between humans. The opportunity is missed, Parsifal hesitates, and the next morning he leaves. All is as before, except that he must bear the burden now not only of the wounded king, the split in his own inner nature, but he must also carry the vision of the incredible beauty of the Grail castle and the glimpse of the spiritual realm it implies, knowing that he has failed and that the opportunity may never return again. The agony of the missed dream beckoning is the pain that must be carried by the hero, who through his own hesitation has brought about his own destiny and lost a chance to restore harmony in the world.

Johnson (1974) argues that the agony of glimpsing the Grail castle accompanies the male throughout his life. The opportunities for glimpsing its riches are rare, aside from the fleeting moments that are too short to really enter. Perhaps they only come twice a lifetime: adolescence and middle age, the crises of spiritual hunger, the times of restlessness which can give momentum to a life. Parsifal continues his quests, the sword and the image of the Grail accompany him, but it is a painful time. Victories mount up; he sends so many knights back to Arthur that he is summoned to appear. At the banquet of honor, however, a "hideous damsel" appears, recounting his failures, raging at the lost opportunity and the failure of the ultimate quest and, at a very important moment, she sends forth all the knights once more on a renewed quest. As Johnson (1974) notes, the "hideous damsel" is perhaps the inner feminine who has been forgotten and left behind in the frenzy of world-striving and success-seeking that hides the disappointment and pain of the failed earlier quest. She is a critical inner messenger, for she reinstitutes the individual quest, taking each person out of the collective paths where they have gravitated and setting each one forth alone to enter the darkest part of the forest to clear his own path (Campbell, 1979).

Parsifal wanders again from adventure to adventure; he vows to not rest until he has found the Grail. Although there is little hope to find the Grail again, he chooses to search and, in that way, makes it possible. He becomes so involved in the process, however, that he forgets his overall orientation. One day he stumbles on pilgrims and, finding out it is Good Friday, he remembers again the woman, his love whom he left behind so long ago. Chrétien de Troyes, from whom Johnson (1974) draws, ends the myth here. This is as far as we have gone as a culture, argues Johnson; we have just now remembered the missing feminine, we have been reminded of the spiritual nature of the quest, but we have not yet come upon the Grail castle the second time, able to ask the critical question of whom does the Grail serve. We have not yet discovered that the Grail serves the Grail king, the highest center of the self and world, not the selfish aims of the ego who squanders the world and leaves it wounded.

Campbell (1979), following Wolfram von Eschenbach, is willing to take the vision further. His Parsifal encounters in his journeys a dark Moor whom he fights, not knowing that the two are brothers, sons of the same father who went east with the Crusades. In discovering this and reuniting, the opposites within one whole, ego and shadow, Parsifal gains access once more to the Grail castle. The two enter together and Parsifal, in real compassion and surrender to the moment's needs against all rules, asks the King, "What ails you?" The healing comes, to the king, to the country, and to Parsifal who is reunited with the woman he has been loyal to all these years. The hero has reunited his masculine questing and his feminine compassion and caring, his individuality and his relatedness, his assertiveness and his feeling. He is whole; Grail and sword stand together, the wound is healed.

THE FEMININE HERO JOURNEY:
The Myth of Psyche

Although the hero journey, as it has been portrayed thus far, carries a message for both men and women in the development of the metaphorically masculine potentiality within us all, the imagery at times seems overbearingly masculine and it is easy to confuse the outer male with the concept of the "inner man." It is instructive, therefore, to take a close look at another type of hero journey, a journey formulated in the imagery of a female hero, the myth of Psyche. Psyche represents a rare phenomenon in myth, the portrayal of the evolution of the hero in terms of a female protagonist. As such the myth is of special interest to us: Will it uncover any other useful dimensions and guides for the development of the inner masculine? How will this myth, in the context of a female outer figure, portray the intertwined evolution of the inner masculine and the inner feminine? Will different nuances appear, different insights and emphases, that might be useful to both men and women? After centuries and millenia of dominance by masculine values and visions, in which the male hero myth often becomes the norm for measuring all inner growth, will the image of a female hero myth offer new ideas especially for women setting off today on their quests? Will the myth offer today's men insights into the interwoven development of masculine and feminine that will allow new access to the inner feminine in ways not hinted at in previous imagery?

Again, with the myth of Psyche, there are many versions and many voices of interpretation. I shall be drawing from the amplification largely of Betty Smith (1978b), introducing also at points the emphases of Johnson (1976) and Neumann (1956), who have each directed attention to this myth. Again, the goal of this portrayal is not a simple recounting of the external tale, but an attempt to suggest imagery rich in implications for inner development. There are few images of the female hero: Psyche is one of the richest, not only in her struggle to develop contact with her masculine side, but also in the critical evolution of her feminine side. She never leaves either side out of balance; as such it is a hero journey that proceeds in two dimensions, suggesting that the "hero" quality is the quality of movement, of individuation in a life, and that it can occur within masculine and feminine realms. Dichotomies begin to break down; we are at the threshold of wholeness.

Psyche was the youngest daughter of the king and was worshipped as if on a pedestal, by all around, for her great beauty. As such, Smith (1978b) notes, she is the newest principle of feminine development which has emerged, promising a new beauty and quality of personhood which will be a threat to Aphrodite, the archetype which carried the feminine until that time. By the time we arrive at the Aphrodite of this myth, she has fallen already from her place as the binding power of the universe and been represented in partriarchal imagery as the vengeful, vain, and blindly clinging maternal principle of the archetype of love and passion. This is the Aphrodite we find in Neumann's (1956) and Johnson's (1976) versions; Smith (1978b) is gentler in her understanding of the great goddess who must begin to give way before a new dimension of the feminine: the concept of an awakened feminine sensitivity and ego consciousness that rests no longer in the dark of unconsciousness. Psyche is the female hero who must break with the Great Mother. Her beauty is our earliest clue, a clue that a new force is evolving that will threaten the connection to the old.

Psyche, however, leads a lonely, solitary life upon her pedestal, cut off from human contact by her great beauty, and succeeds only in rousing the jealousy and anger of Aphrodite. Perhaps, as Johnson (1976) writes, she is the untouched, unmarried soul deep within, too perfect for the ordinary world, a soul that exists in us all, delicate and lonely. Meanwhile Aphrodite aims to send her son Eros, the God of Love, to make Psyche fell in love with a dark and loathsome dragon, and when the king seeks out an oracle for guidance, he learns that his daughter is to be taken to the pinnacle and crags outside the city to await her marriage with the dragon bridegroom, the "dark spouse," as Smith (1978b) portrays him. Psyche's first act of independence and movement from her pedestal to a new existence comes through this funeral marriage which she greets nobly, actively surrendering to her destiny, awaiting on the solitary crag for an unknown transformation and death. It is interesting, as Johnson (1976) points out, that for Psyche, the hero's journey in a sense at least begins with marriage, a process of transformation from which we have all too often hidden the pain, fear, and terror of the unknown that lie ahead for the bride, particularly in ages past. That marriage too, in the tension between maiden and matron, can be a call to evolution is an important reminder. We should probably not make too much of this point, however, because Psyche moves still in concert with her destiny; she has not challenged it nor does she seek more consciousness. She surrenders an ego not yet developed, hinted at only in the lonely vigil of her life, and on the crag she waits.

Unknown to Aphrodite and, of course, to Psyche, the God Eros came to cause Psyche to fall in love with a dragon, but seeing her great beauty, he decides to disobey his mother in secrecy and live with Psyche himself. Thus as Psyche waits upon the crags, Eros calls upon a gentle wind to float her down to his palace and there she is cared for by disembodied voices which meet all her needs. Every night he comes to her in darkness and in darkness they remain, enjoying blissful, consuming love. It seems very important that this phase of nourishment and gentleness in the dark, of baths and food and music and love occur for Psyche at this point, argues Smith (1978b). The hero journey of the feminine, the evolution of ego consciousness in the woman must take place without losing touch with the deep nourishment of the feminine side, a process so neglected in this culture. We will see this repeatedly in the myth of Psyche; it marks perhaps the chief contrast with the masculine hero myth where the male hero often unites with the evolving feminine side of himself only towards the end of his evolution as hero. The myth suggests that the woman starting on the hero's path must never lose touch with her feminine side. Perhaps we have reached this stage too as a culture; male or female, we must begin the journey of consciousness with simultaneous attention to the nourishment of the feminine intuition and the natural bodily embeddedness of us all. We can no longer careen for years searching the Holy Grail via the adventure of the sword, hoping we will stumble upon the feminine dimension when the time is right and we have been successful in other ways.

The tension of the myth has been building to this period in which Psyche and Eros live in mutual ecstasy, unrevealed to each other, meeting only in the dark, a kind of paradise that conjures up the earliest stages of being in love with all its unconsciousness and passion. Psyche does not know her lover, and though she is drawn to him, she begins to question, to wonder who he is. As Smith (1978b) notes, Psyche is able to carry in this feeling-toned mystery of their relatedness the qualities of the moon goddess and the deeper feminine which only trust expression when they are unexposed, but to be asked to carry this beyond a certain point begins to feel like an obstacle to her further evolution. Perhaps Psyche would not have grown as restless so fast if she had not begun to miss her sisters and long for human company, imploring her husband for permission to bring the sisters to the palace. Against his advice and warning, she invites them and listens to their words. The sisters, roused by jealousy, fear, and the other shadow qualities of her other side, work away on Psyche until, in fear and curiosity she decides that she must discover who she has married and whether he is perhaps a dragon-serpent and all has been deceit. Armed with a razor and a lamp, knowing that what she seeks has been forbidden her, she comes upon her husband at night. Seeing that he is, in fact, the great god Eros, she lets fall her knife and pricks herself on one of his arrows, falling in love with him for the first time in full consciousness of who he is. A drop of oil, however, falls from the lamp, burning Eros who wakens, leaps from the bed, and flies away. As he flies upward, Psyche clings to his thigh until she begins to fall; he follows her back down to earth to remind her that he must leave if she should once disobey his wish to be unseen, and saying that, he leaves her there and disappears.

Psyche's decision to seek to see her husband, to become conscious of her existence and love, is the moment signaled out as the central pivot of the myth. All else has been preparation for this first full act of consciousness, in which Psyche awakens from her state of unconscious darkness. By her courage to develop her independent capacity to see, Psyche forces both herself and Eros into a rupture and separation from their original unconscious union, which however painful, marks the beginning of her evolving individual "destiny" (Neumann, 1956). It is an awesome and terrible reminder to an emerging consciousness that the birth of the ego spells the beginning of isolation and the loss of the loved one. To only begin to see as we stand on the chasm of separateness, to only know god on the edge of the receding, to discover the lover only to lose him—it is a painful price to pay for consciousness. Psyche, in her own way, in her decision to take action into her own hands and armed with the knife and lamp of discriminative consciousness, plunges into the development of her other side. It is the great act of heroic disobedience, without which evolution of the hero does not seem possible, but she feels her loss as the loss of the external masculine, a loss of relatedness, and it will only be through an inward-turning journey to develop her own masculine side that she will arrive at the ultimate reunion with the other, a joyous marriage of her two fully developed sides.

Discouraged, in pain, seeking to end her life, Psyche throws herself in the river, only to be tossed back up on the bank where she encounters the god Pan, who encourages her to try to win Eros by her promise of service. Though not so dramatic as her moment of raising the lamp to see, what occurs between Pan and Psyche has tremendous implications for her journey, argues Smith (1978b). Just as the long period of darkness and protection was necessary to nourish her feminine side in preparation for the ultimate movement toward consciousness, Pan reconnects her via his advice and encouragement to the deep parts of her own inner nature. Psyche returns to the basic life-affirming energy of her instincts and makes space in her life, in the despair of her heightened consciousness, for her feminine side. Always, this return to the bodily, nourishing part of herself provides the healing and balance that is necessary for the next step. It is remarkable how much this aspect was missing from the early hero journeys, where the endless push, without a stop for water or air or feeling, was all too reminiscent of the driven quality of what we have considered the masculine destiny and price of consciousness. Psyche and Pan have much to say to our times, though their message necessitates a new type of hero, a hero who acknowledges his or her own needs for nurturance and rest.

As Psyche resumes her wandering, she seeks the temples of Demeter and Hera, two great goddesses whom we will encounter in the next chapter. In this conscious search to connect with the greater feminine principle, we again see Psyche strengthening herself for her encounter with Aphrodite, who represents in this myth, perhaps, the Terrible Mother of the hero myth. By now it should not be surprising to see this tendency of Psyche to stay connected to her feminine side, even as she ventures forth into tasks requiring conscious articulation and independence. There is throughout the myth of Psyche a paradoxical turning to fate, a sense of active surrender that gives us another new insight into a different dimension of the hero journey. While the emphasis earlier in the chapter was on defying fate, and to some extent this emphasis is still true in Psyche's searching for Eros despite his command and disappearance, there is still an element in which Psyche waits before each new venture, gathering in energy, following the paths of energy that exist rather than wrestling against nature. This, too, is a form of heroism which has its place in human experience and should not be confused with passivity.

Demeter and Hera, while wishing her well, do not want to go against the commands of Aphrodite, so it remains for Psyche to continue her journey by deciding to face Aphrodite herself. In going to Aphrodite and engaging in the tasks set before her, Psyche undertakes a heroic quest that develops her masculine side, but keeps it inextricably moving forward in rhythm to the harmony of her feminine side. In Aphrodite, Psyche confronts the jealous, regressive earth mother who clings to her unindividuated son Eros and resists, as Neumann (1956) and Johnson (1976) point out, the evolution of a new way of conscious relatedness in the feminine, an ability to relate person-to-person in full individuality rather than to follow the necessity of blind passion and fertility of the original matriarchal feminine. In a sense, in Psyche's willingness to confront the Terrible Mother, she also makes it easier for Eros to do the same, to move himself on his own evolution toward greater ability for conscious relatedness.

Aphrodite imposes four tasks on Psyche, each demanding a balance of her feminine and masculine sides. The tasks suggest the kinds of challenges that accompany the female hero journey and the kind of skills and precautions she must take on her path. At each point Psyche is ready to give up and although her surrender may be seen as a lack of confidence, it places her in positions to gain help from resources in her environment and herself and allows her a period of waiting, consolidation, and ego-surrender before the tasks that lie ahead. The first task challenges her to sort an entire mound of seeds into their separate piles, and with the aid of the ants and that part of her being which is developing this skill, the task is successfully completed. As Smith (1978b) reminds us, the task of sorting seeds, of distinguishing the future potentiality within the small beginning, of setting priorities, of putting one's house in order are tremendously important starting places for any quest. The second task, that of retrieving some of the golden fleece from the fierce rams, is also successfully accomplished by Psyche herself by following the advice of a reed, who cautions her to stay in the shade rather than confront the rams in the full daylight and later, after they have moved off, to collect some of their fleece left on the branches of the bushes where they had been grazing. Again, Smith (1978b) suggests the importance of learning to wait for the right time, to not dive head first into the Apollonian realm of clarity, dramatic form, and intense light, but to gather a kind of warmth and protection from the wool of one's own instinctual self and save the great encounter for when it is necessary. This insight seems far more clarifying than the efforts taken by Neumann (1956) and especially Johnson (1976) to portray this task as some confirmation of the necessity for a woman not to stray too far into the masculine realm except in balance with the feminine, to make a peaceful "contact" between the masculine and feminine rather than present a "struggle" or threat (Neumann, 1956).

In either interpretation, however, the successful contact of masculine and feminine appears to prepare Psyche for her next and third task, to bring back a little crystal bottle filled with the water from the high, rocky source of the river Styx. As Betty Smith (1978b) reminds us, Psyche dies a little before each task, surrendering to the impossibility, and this time her help comes through an eagle from Zeus, a keenly perceptive, high-flying, emerging spiritual sense of herself which allows her to contain a small measure of the powers of the unconscious, underworld waters and return the beautiful crystal to Aphrodite. The fourth and final task, made possible by her previous preparation and the guidance of a tower who speaks with the wisdom of human questing through history, involves her descent into the underworld to bring back a box of Persephone's beauty mixture for

Aphrodite. The tower is very specific about the risks: she must go with hands and mouth full of money and food for the ferryman and the dog which guard the various thresholds of Hades, and she must resist the calls for help of a lame man and donkey, a drowning man, and the women who weave the fates and call for her help. This challenge is decisive for the feminine hero journey, for here more than anywhere else she must suspend her well-developed feminine side of relatedness and say no to those who seek her help. This is the task that demands her full energies (Johnson, 1976) and requires resisting the claims of others' needs which threaten to distract her from her task (Neumann, 1956). As Betty Smith (1978b) adds, at this highly developed moment in her journey, she must learn to discriminate those things worth saving, she must restrain her own tendency to rescue, she must hasten to the task that only she can do, the task of her own individuation. It is an ironic and powerful insight that the feminine hero must always keep the realm of the feminine within reach, but that she cannot afford to succumb to its timelessness, to the endless qualities of weaving and relatedness, if she is to reach a balance in her individual life.

Psyche does not make it back to earth without yielding to the temptation of opening the box she bears for Aphrodite; perhaps, as Smith (1978b) suggests, it is a statement and recognition of herself, transformed as Aphrodite's equal, a new image of the feminine for our time. Perhaps, as Johnson (1976) suggests, even the experience of failure belongs to the hero's task of individuation and wholeness, the Jungian ideal which replaces a vision of perfection with a vision of completeness as the goal towards which we strive. Whatever the interpretation, it is a sleep of transformation from which she is awakened by her own other side in Eros, whose own growth has allowed him to break free of his mother and seek his father's consent for their marriage. Their marriage leads to Psyche's divinization and echoes the mystical marriage of previous male hero myths. Here, in both Psyche and Eros, the masculine and feminine principles of consciousness and relatedness are brought together in new birth, a mortal child named Pleasure. Perhaps she is mortal because the enduring marriage of masculine and feminine within each life, within each hero journey, must always be created anew. The hero, male or female, must always break from the gods and return to them only when he or she is whole.

NOURISHING THE INNER MAN

Despite the existence of the myth of Psyche, so much of the imagery associated with the hero myth, the development of the metaphorical masculine and its ultimate reunification with the metaphorical feminine, has focused on the male figure that it seems especially necessary to direct attention to the development of the "inner man" in women today. In contrast, men seem at least at one level to resonate to the hero myth, although many cling tenaciously to the first half of the myth, especially in this time in which the long neglected feminine principle in our culture is rising and many men seem to see it only in its feared, negative dimensions. These persons rally back to the dragon fight and the slaying of the Terrible Mother, and are ever alert to detecting her form in each woman they meet, seeing her all too readily, they think, in today's more assertive, independent woman. Those men who have seen ahead to the second part of the myth have a hard time not returning to the security of the first half of the myth in which it is clearer to be all-male. For men today, then, the development of the "inner man" includes the reminder that the hero myth moves on to an integration with the feminine. It is the time to move to the next chapter, so to speak, to rediscover the inner woman.

Women today, in contrast, need the encouragement of remembering that the hero myth belongs to them too; that its messages of separation and return, of the individual journey, are part of the female quest also. They seek a way to discover and nurture the "inner man" in themselves without doing violence to the integration with the feminine which they know is an important part of the hero journey. Many women have moved far towards this reincorporation of the inner masculine; some have lost sight of or never envisioned the parallel nourishment of the feminine which seems such an important part of the hero's search. In the remainder of this chapter, then, we will explore some of the many, more concrete, ways of developing the "inner man" that women, no matter where their starting place, may find relevant to the journey. Again, although this concept of the inner man resembles the Jungian concept of the animus, recall that we will be exploring this metaphor without the assumptions that each woman starts with a basically feminine self and only gradually builds up the masculine. Some women, in our time and age, may well be more grounded in the masculine. Likewise, we will not be carrying the typical wariness of so many Jungians that a woman must be especially alert to the dangers of overdevelopment of her masculine side, a wariness that seems to dampen self-confidence in exploring these dimensions for fear of being labeled animus-possessed. The danger of imbalance and overdevelopment of the masculine is, of course, real in today's culture, but the risk must be taken if we are to complete the entire hero cycle. One cannot have a completely developed feminine side without a parallel development of the masculine. Finally, if the image of nourishing the "inner man" is offensive in the context of women developing a part of themselves, retranslate freely, finding your own personal metaphor for the dimensions we will be exploring. Although the image of the inner man is useful because it serves to reinforce the idea of being dependent on one's own internal, metaphorically masculine, resources rather than turning to the external male for these qualities, it is an image that also must be surrendered, for once it is part of oneself it is simply that—another part—not needing to be given the label male or female. It is perhaps only from the standpoint of androgyny, in fact, that one can begin to let fall the labels, for only then can one trust that in affirmed wholeness, no part will be ignored.

Who, then, is the "inner man?" To the woman who has been trained to seek the fulfillment of life in relatedness to another, as has been the most common cultural message to all women, the inner man comes first of all, perhaps, to her as the soulmate, the "ghostly lover," as Harding (1970) calls this powerful image. The inner man in this form calls out to the woman as her perfect equal and complement, as perfectly evolved as she is in her own integrations of masculine and feminine, a being who is most like her in her full individuality, a spiritual partner who is able to love and be loved in a harmony of body, mind, and soul. The longing for this lover, friend, companion, soulmate is easily projected upon the men that women love, and long after the projection has slipped to the side, the "ghostly lover" haunts the mind and soul of the woman searching always for this other perfect mate.

It is a seductive image, a desperate image, however, this longing for the soulmate, as long as it remains unrecognized as a part of ourselves. To seek the ghostly lover externally is a doomed quest; no mortal person can bear or be asked to reflect indefinitely the image of divinity and perfection for us. The soulmate will never exist "out there" except in fleeting moments when we all carry the image of gods and goddesses, when we ·tap into our archetypal depths and witness the energies coming from another source than our own—those moments when we appear truly beautiful, or are carried outside ourselves in excitement at an idea, or are touched deeply by compassion or despair. We can only broaden the space inside to be witness to these visitations, we can only enlarge the container of ourselves, as the Jungians say; we can not ask these moments to stay with us as our captives.

Yet the seductive image of the ghostly lover may offer guidance too. The solution to the longing is not a stoical renunciation of this kind of connectedness, but the possibility that the transformative experiences which women have been encouraged to seek externally may instead be deeply interior experiences. In the discovery of one's own internal complementarity, one's own soulmate within, one begins to build inside the scaffolding of a new wholeness. Perhaps the skeleton of our own less developed side will make us pine away for the full fleshly encounter with that which we are not yet fully in ourselves, but gradually we come closer to nourishing a new birth within ourselves. The skeleton takes form, and flesh, and substance from within ourselves. We give birth to our other half, and find him within us. What appears to be a turning-in process is really a turning out: a movement to a new center of gravity within, which allows, for the first time, a freer encounter with the other from the fullness of myself. It is the first time a woman is capable of moving beyond the idolatry of love, in which outer persons remain only carriers and vehicles to the marriage within. For the first time she can be truly present to another.

Finding the soulmate within carries some of the transformative imagery of becoming husband to oneself. This image, despite its heterosexual loadings, releases the power of the inner marriage with whatever strength of ritual and enduringness that ceremony brings forth in human community. Becoming husband to oneself is an image which so uproots the expectations that the solutions to life's problems are external and male-oriented, that it becomes a powerful and liberating image. In finding the inner man, a woman finds herself, the divine lover, husband, and companion within. In finding "him," she launches herself toward the only true base of security: the strength one gives oneself from within in the form of self-nourishment, self-security, and self-support. Discovering, developing, reincorporating the inner man is thus—for a woman—a way toward feeling more able to take care of herself. It is a way of rediscovering one's own psychical and physical strength, the kind of self-confidence and sense of autonomy that allow one to enter into work and relatedness with the capacity for real interaction and mutuality, not one-sided need and dependency based on being half a person. The inner marriage is the reminder to women that they cannot afford to continue to let men be their sole-supporters or their soul supporters.

Recovering the inner man is turning to oneself for approval and valuing that voice within. It is learning to recognize what "I want" and "I feel," rather than screening everything through a filter of second-guessing what the other person wants and would approve. Discovering the inner man is learning to give compliments to the self, to not discount the positives from others as if they were fooled by some warped vision that fails to see the wretched, undeserving creature we carry around inside. It is learning to exorcise this inner image or nourish it to wholeness, daring to affirm new self-images rather than carry around the well-practiced ones that hook our pain. Recovering the inner man is daring to feel strong and vital, tough and resilient, to walk with big strides and wear clothes that allow movement and shoes that support confidence. It is daring to breathe in air and stand up tall, to take up space in the world and be seen and heard. It is reowning our own sexual vitality from its incarceration as the "female eunuch" (Greer, 1970) or man-created woman, daring to "unpaint" ourselves (Daly, 1978) and please our own standards rather than those taken from the media. It is realizing that the love, the attraction, the sensations, and feelings I feel toward others are *my* creation; they are not given to me by another except as I give myself permission to express those parts of myself. Therefore they cannot be taken from me in loss. I remain whole; a lost love does not mean the inability to love; unexpressed sexuality does not mean the loss of my own vitality. Externality proves nothing; the source of selfhood lies within.

The overcoming of a lack of self-confidence and the creation of an independent identity, a sense of knowing who one is, are perhaps the first and most basic steps in developing the inner man for women. As Emma Jung (1957) warned, one has to develop confidence not only with respect to the external world but with respect to one's own developing masculine side. One must find ways to beware putting oneself down for supposedly feminine traits, for thinking that what one has done with one's life is in any way inferior, for affirming one's own motherhood, daughterhood, sisterhood, or capacity for relatedness. Women must not discount their intuition as fuzzy, their warmth as sentimentality, or their compassion as smothering, although they must, of course, be alert to these dangers. They must not consider their skills in mediation and communication as wishy-washy middle-of-the-road thinking, or their concerns for process as regressive in the pull to real revolution. Thus, even as they listen to and enhance the inner masculine, women must be wary of selling out to its dominant voice in our culture, a voice which characterizes often not only the general culture but the feminist environment as well.

Developing the inner masculine involves the creation of a new kind of assertiveness, an ability to affirm one's rights in ways that are neither aggressive nor self-effacing (Jakubowski-Spector, 1973). It is defusing the word assertive from its imagery of the battle-axe or the castrating woman, to reclaim the powers of expression and clarity of intent. Assertiveness is the ability to say no without excuses, to make mistakes without obsessive guilt and self-recrimination for our lack of perfection, to say yes even if it means we might be happy, joyful, or non-suffering without justification. Being assertive is learning how to own our own anger and find ways to express it from its own source as "my anger" rather than as a dumping in exhaustion and rage on the other person. Being assertive is daring to confront, to see difference as opportunity rather than confirmation of unlove, to ask for things of another while realizing they may not wish to agree. Being assertive is knowing when to resist the lure of the helper role, when one is at the fourth task of Psyche and cannot afford to "rescue." Being assertive is refusing to allow negative thoughts about oneself to become addictive; it is banishing self-discounts and self-punishments of compulsive eating, regretting, or fearing. Assertiveness is learning how to fix and take care of things in one's life, mastering machines, asking questions at the gas station, the doctor's office, even going into a hardware store or a lumber yard without feeling like a trespasser. Assertiveness is daring to carve out the lifestyle one can live with, to create one's own inner morality and spirituality that is based on individuation rather than the collective solutions (Harding, 1970). Assertiveness is feeling good about being single in a world of married people, being married in a world of feminists, or being whoever one is in a world only too prone to be suspicious of uniqueness.

If self-confidence, inner independence, and assertiveness are part of the path to the inner masculine, a second major area deserving attention is the world of work and the skills and dimensions it offers for the developing woman. Emma Jung (1957) mentions it second as part of the critical factors in developing the inner man: work that demands the use of one's mental energies. Not all work in the external world fits this requirement nor is all valuable work salaried; meaningful work includes any long range project, any creativity that extends the self. Still, one can make a strong case for the role of almost any kind of creative, externally-oriented work in the world as a context for developing one's metaphorically masculine skills. Jobs, professions, and careers offer women increasingly demanding environments for the development of their rational, ordering, goal-setting sides. The ability to make decisions and stay with them, to hold responsibility in this daily accountable way, to plan and forecast, to anticipate and follow-through are not skills absent from the home and world of relationships, but they are brought into special focus and rewarded by the business and professional world in such a way that a woman can give full voice to this side of herself and her intellectual creativity without constant fear that these skills will be threatening or abrasive to her home environment.

Work offers an environment for getting in touch with the god Apollo, the god of form and balance and reason reigning in our culture, to open up to these dimensions without the preoccupation of competing loyalties. Work offers to women a way of tangibly increasing their power and decision-making in marriage and society (Bird, 1979), the modern parallel to the increased status of women in societies where women contribute to the highly scarce and valuable commodity of protein in the diet of the tribe (Tavris and Offir, 1977). In the effort to develop her masculine side but not overdose in its seductiveness, work offers an environment in which a woman can express her creativity in a disciplined way (Harding, 1970), where she has avenues through which she can be tangibly appreciated for her intellectual side and does not have to pour forth in constant demonstration of her cognitive worth. She is valued by her peers and colleagues; she is confident of her abilities; she can relate without a need to prove her incisiveness at all times. It is not so much that women who remain in careers in the home cannot develop their intellectual, leadership, decision-making skills; rather the risk is simply that she will not be rewarded for these consistently and that she will use these skills as a weapon for recognition in precisely the environment where she is least likely to be affirmed for these qualities. Thus spinning her wheels, she does not move on into a genuine flowing creativity that might follow if she had one foot at least in another world or minimally, a "room of her own" (Wolfe, 1929). Work offers, finally, a means to take initiative toward some non-interpersonal goal where her energies can be released in the service of the goal in itself without the justification of personal relatedness (E. Jung, 1957).

The danger with this discussion of work, however, is its seductiveness. It is so easy to turn in this direction as to a panacea, and get trapped instead in the all-too-frequent male pattern of a work-dominated life. The danger for the professional woman is not so much even the danger of a work-dominated life, for who is to say that such creativity is not truly the path for some women as it is for some men. Rather the danger is that the focus on work is lived out under the exclusive shadow of the masculine values and modes of consciousness, under the first half of the hero myth mentality, and one forgets to temper, to blend the insights of the masculine with those of the feminine realms. It is perhaps naive to think that the entry of women in full force into positions of power and influence would bring about this automatic tempering; it is too easy to identify with the dominant masculine values and get stuck in the aggressive power of early developments of the masculine. However, work does offer an excellent training ground in the masculine skills and resources of will, deed, word, and meaning (E. Jung, 1957) which can be assets in the translation of feminine values into the external world. Thus, as Harding (1970) points out, the mental capacities for judgment and organization from the Logos realm can be brought to bear in the interest of Eros and relatedness, if they can only be held together by some more encompassing "superordinate" value. Women must bring this harmonization into their external work, not only for the sake of their own inner development, as the Jungians often seem to argue, but for the sake of transforming the world. New possibilities in all fields of work might follow from a more integrated base in the traditional masculine and feminine: new modes of collaborative leadership, new approaches to the discovery of knowledge, and new styles of cognitive skill that include both the verbal and the visual, word and image. So, too, the newfound masculine skills of women can be brought back into relationships, the realm of the traditional feminine. How to do this is a tremendous challenge, for Jungian tradition suggests that planning and goal-setting are best left out of the realm of relatedness. Perhaps, however, there is a role for clarifying, discriminating, and negotiating in carving out new interpersonal lifestyles in an age of chance. If new integrations of masculine and feminine can be visualized in the realm of work, one would hope there might be new possibilities for analogous integrations in the realm of home and relationship.

A third and critical reminder to the woman who seeks to develop her masculine side is the message of Emma Jung (1957) and Harding (1970) that at this point, more than ever, a woman needs the nourishment of the feminine, the valuing and legitimization of the dimensions of relatedness which she can find so often in her friendships with other women.

In relationships to men it frequently seems that her interests in the nuances of feeling and relatedness are resented as intrusions rather than as the pleasurable exploration of the complexities of feeling; it is with her women friends that she confirms this critical part of being human. As she reaches new integrations of the masculine and feminine within her, it is her hope that men too will move toward similar integrations, in order to meet some-day as more fully individuated human beings enjoying each other's rich-ness. However, in this age of dominant masculine styles in work and male fear of relatedness in the home, professional women and women whose commitment is to the family and the home are both starving for the nourishment they need. They turn to each other, sisters in the same quest, garbed in different clothes and daily tasks, but facing the same journey of integration. If they can affirm the feminine for themselves and each other, perhaps the overflow of this vitalization can carry into the culture. Perhaps it is enough that they are beginning to feel again and celebrate this access to the feminine, that they are recovering Psyche and her reminder that the hero's quest must stay attuned to the deep feminine depths as well, the depths we will begin to explore in the next chapter.

Though she has the friendship and nourishment of other women on the way, the female journey to discover the masculine inside herself and integrate it with the feminine is basically a hero's path. There is no way around the necessity of standing alone, and learning to deal with the loneliness of the journey is perhaps the most important learning for the person who would set out. In our culture, neither men or women have been encouraged to learn how to live with solitude. Women, ironically, by staying closer to their feelings may even do somewhat better at this task, for they have access to their inner depths through centuries of training. In contrast, our culture has trained men to be unaware of how dependent they become on women to live out their emotional side for them, and in situations of loss, men turn quickly to a desperate loneliness, seeking re-placements for companionship (Goldberg, 1976). Women become at those times more transparently what they have always been, stopgaps against solitude, carriers of feeling, vicarious alter egos through which men can vent their tears, tenderness, or dependency. It is ironic, however: men say they are unafraid of being alone, yet they rarely allow themselves to be alone; women are trained to be desperately afraid of being alone, and they actually thrive and evolve from solitude.

Cultivating one's own aloneness, developing one's own ability to go through the loneliness into the joy of being enough unto oneself, these are the real challenges of the hero journey. Treasuring one's aloneness means freeing oneself from the ability to be scared by words like spinster (Daly, 1978), old maid, or nun. It means affirming one's aloneness even in relatedness, not being thrown off base into ruminations and fantasied preoccupations by relationships in one's life. It means discovering, with Sarton (1973), that solitude can be an entry to relatedness and sharing despite its pain, that isolation and living without a family can lead to openness to a greater world in which one's energies are available to and touched by many people rather than encapsulated in a few.

Living with aloneness is recognizing, however, when one needs companionship, treasuring the intimacy of a moment rather than clinging to a desired pattern (Lindbergh, 1955), turning to others and to activity, not as a frenzied attempt to suppress ache but as the full expression of articulated wish. Aloneness is not deprivation, or self-imposed punishment for one's unacceptableness; aloneness is a preference that sometimes does not mean being alone. Solitude is not the fetish of the liberated woman, but a quality necessary to us all, to the hero of whatever form, to Parsifal and Psyche. Imposed or sought out, welcomed or protested, loneliness is a great teacher. To enlarge the container of our being leaves us with as much room for emptiness as joy, for the great void is the potential other side of presence. Loneliness is related to the great thresholds, the edges of new discovery; it is present at new birth (Frantz, 1977), in the acute destiny of the solitary mother (Harding, 1970) and, as we have seen, in the journey of the hero away from the gods.

It is with this message that the hero myth speaks to the quest for the inner masculine, reminding us of the solitude of the path and the uniqueness of the particular integrations of masculine and feminine which will be found. The hero myth can only be a beginning, a beginning which turns back in fullness to a recognition that neither half of the journey—the going out in individual, assertive clarity and consciousness or the return in union with the intuitive side of ourselves—is complete in itself. We are caught today midway in the hero myth, beginning to see that there is a second half to our journey, but blinded by the fear that comes with great repression or neglect. The feminine is rising and we see it only with the eyes of a child's memory if we see it at all. It is time to welcome back the great goddess with open eyes and present meanings, to take the heroism of our adulthood into new confrontations and mutual nourishments with the feminine within ourselves. It is time to dream the dream onward, to write a new myth for our time.

7

NOURISHING
THE INNER WOMAN

In the journey toward wholeness in contemporary culture and personality development, the realm of the metaphorical feminine stands out as the dimension most in need of exploration and affirmation. The hero's vision has only too often fallen short of the envisioned reunion of masculine and feminine sides and become entrapped in external assertions of ego and individualistic will. The disrupted result of this alienation between ego and world, mind and body, has created a mindset unheeding of the interconnectedness of life and prone to exaggerated thrustings of technology into ecological patterns. We have forgotten to search for the missing treasure and balance point to this disorder wtihin our own beings, to discover with the rabbi in the paradoxical tale told by Heinrich Zimmer (1946), that the treasure sought in long external journeys into distant lands is to be found after all in the corner of one's own kitchen back at home. As Irene Claremont de Castillejo writes, it is time to turn from the explorer of outer space to a new type of explorer: the "inner hero," the journeyer into the recesses of the self, into the realm of the feminine. If the feminine as a metaphorical dimension of human experience is to be given nourishment in our time, there must first be a recognition of the importance of this dimension, a feel for its qualities and nuances, its contribution to consciousness and wholeness. It is only then that the myth of Psyche as an integration of the masculine and feminine developmental journeys can take on significance as a myth for our time. We can only nourish that which is capable of reverberating in full awareness at many levels of our beings. Such is the intention of this chapter: to bring into awareness and familiarity the metaphorically feminine realm of existence and to reaffirm its relevance as the missing half of the dominant cultural affirmations of the metaphorical masculine.

What, then, has the realm of the metaphorical feminine represented in human experience and how can we understand its significance? Bearing in mind the great danger of oversimplification, we can point to a cluster of qualities which together convey some of the spirit of the feminine dimension of experience. Perhaps the most frequently chosen association to the feminine, at least in Jungian writings, is the quality of relatedness carried by the powerful image of Eros, which as Harding (1971) cautions, is not the "sentimentalized" Cupid of everyday romance, but the god Eros who represents a force beyond the pull of personal relationships. Eros as relatedness speaks of a dedication and grounding in the interrelatedness of the entire universe, in the interconnectedness of all action, in an urge toward participation in being which is as deep as the biological need for reproduction (Harding, 1970) and complementary to the need for full consciousness in a relationship of all kinds. Eros represents the passion of connection and union not only between persons, but between persons and ideas, thought and feeling. Eros stands in contrast but not in necessary opposition to Logos, the masculine spirit of disembodied idea, thought, and linear form. Eros forms a bridge to Logos, an access point, a matrix of meaning. The feminine, as the principle of Eros, offers an openness to meeting, as de Castillejo (1973) writes, or as Ann Belford Ulanov (1971) adds, an openness "to presence," to the mystery of coming into contact with an otherness, an acceptance of a new meeting between beings.

As the vehicle and carrier of relatedness, the feminine gives voice also to a kind of vague "stirring" of feelings, a "yearning" for freshness that pulls the individual toward wholeness (E. Jung, 1957). In this way, the feminine urges us towards completion and individuation, encouraging us in the "embrace" of the unknown (Ulanov, 1971). The feminine mode of consciousness is very close to what we mean by intuition, the function which de Castillejo (1973) calls "diffuse awareness," to contrast it with "focused consciousness." This is the realm of a very subtle form of consciousness tuned in to multiple sources of information and holistic processing, which grasps a sense of the entire spectrum of events and conveys information about dimensions others might dismiss as unduly shadowy or intangible. The feminine mode of vision is more spatial, more like the image of seeing in the dark through accommodation and patience in the light of the moon and stars, rather than through the narrow-beam of the flashlight which cuts a clear path but distorts at the edges of the path of light. It is not so much that consciousness is missing from the feminine experience as that the type of consciousness is different from the rational mode of thought processing that we have been trained to associate with the scientific method and logic. Feminine consciousness has a distinctive light of its own: a light more like the light of the moon (Harding, 1971) which illuminates the world of the night and reveals ways of seeing that would be inaccessible via the light of the sun. These two modes of consciousness are crucial to each other, and as Guggenbühl-Craig (1977) cautions, we must beware an easy simplification which locks us into the equation of Eros as feminine and Logos as masculine, as if they were fixed and unrelated opposites.

The feminine mode of consciousness can also be described as a kind of non-goal oriented "image thinking" (Ulanov, 1971) and as such bears a remarkable resemblance to the kind of orientation necessary for a full understanding of the mythic and symbolic dimensions of human experience. To lose touch with this feminine mode is to neglect and lose access to the nonrational, symbolic dimension of life (Ulanov, 1971). Rediscovering the feminine means revalidating the "symbolic modes of perception" (Ulanov, 1971) in both religious and scientific searches to approximate that which lies beyond words and can only be grasped by metaphor, symbol, or image.

The Jungian approach to the feminine, in its emphasis on recovering this dimension of Eros in the context of a dominant masculine culture, has tended to place stress on the concept of the anima, the contrasexual part within each man which draws him toward the wisdom carried in the unconscious and mediated by this feminine side. The central emphasis in Harding (1970) and de Castillejo (1973), following the work of Carl and

Emma Jung, is thus on the role of the anima as mediator of the feminine dimension and guide to one's own inner depths and resources. As Lander (1962) argues, the feminine principle in man nourishes the connection with one's own unconscious and becomes a "bridge" or "guide." The anima is the "femme inspiratrice" (E. Jung, 1957), easily projected onto concrete women in one's daily life, and undergoing an evolution of imagery related to progressively more spiritual images from Eve to Helen to Mary to Sophia, the incarnation of divine wisdom (Lander, 1962). One of the most powerful images of this role of the feminine in mythology is the image of Ariadne, daughter of the king Minos of Crete, who aids Theseus in his journey into the labyrinth to slay the Minotaur by providing him with a thread by which he can trace his path. As Betty Smith (1975) describes, the journey into the transforming center of the Self necessitates a connection with the "vital thread" of feminine consciousness, for a map will not help in the darkened paths of the spiritual labyrinth. As de Castillejo (1973) writes, the greatest striving is to stay "on one's thread," to be tuned in to one's own inner truths.

While this imagery of the anima, the feminine side of man, is extremely useful in the context of male development, it is unfortunately true that the same Jungian writers who assert this role for the feminine in man also tend to exhort concrete external women to play this role for the individual men in their lives. In other words, they often assume that a woman by virtue of her biological sex is more in touch with the feminine and connected with the principle of relatedness, and thus can be a powerful guide to men in their inner evolution. While it is true that women may indeed by training and encouragement be more aware and committed to the intuitive and relatedness dimensions in life and thus be able to model and encourage this mode in others, it seems dangerous to urge them to carry the role of guide to male evolution. In fact, as long as women are willing to carry the image of "femme inspiratrice," one might question whether men will learn to take back their projections and turn to their own inner anima for guidance. In addition, modern women who have been encouraged to join the masculine-dominated world of work and education have often lost touch with their own inner feminine guidance and can hardly be expected to provide the authority in this area for men as well. In light of these problems and observations, we might do well to avoid such Jungian language as the "anima" and speak instead of the "feminine" within us all, male or female, and the necessity of connecting with this inner guide to the intuitive realms, this midwife of the soul. The danger is always to literalize, to mistake gender for metaphor. The feminine is a dimension of human existence, not the special province of the female, however much it has been assigned, allowed, or left by default to her as her special province and area of training.

The special significance of the recovery of the feminine in culture and personality today is testified to by the range of writers who emphasize the dangerous overdevelopment of one-sided masculine value systems in Western culture. Neumann (1955), in the spirit of Jung's own writing, emphasizes this exaggeration of consciousness and neglect of the whole person, arguing for the necessity of regaining access to the archetype of the feminine. Von Franz (1974), in her careful analysis of fairy tales as clues to individuation, traces the effects of the Christian value system on European consciousness which witnessed the repression not only of the shadow sides of God but of the feminine, creating an exclusive emphasis on the light side of the feminine in Mary and a concurrent return of the excluded shadow in the images of the witch. This was especially true of Protestant imagery, which even excluded the image of Mary. Von Franz (1972) turns to the fairy tale images of the repression of the feminine in our time: the destiny of Sleeping Beauty, the sleeping feminine, or of the miller, first agent of modern technology, who sold his daughter to the devil. Such is the predicament of the feminine today, trapped or sleeping, her energies unavailable to a world suffering from her absence. The need to connect again with this feminine principle, Harding (1971) argues, is an especially poignant one for modern woman who has ironically lost her grounding in the heritage that was hers for millenia as she struggles to join the dominant culture. Only with the recovery of the feminine and its acceptance and revaluation will culture be radically transformed in the interests of wholeness. Only at this point, writes Hillman (1972) will we be able to move "psyche into life," to transcend even the "myth of analysis" and all therapeutic modes based on a dichotomous separation of life and analysis, relatedness and reason. Only then does the androgynous image become an actuality.

Whenever any major archetype of human experience is denied access to consciousness and valuation, it is likely to erupt into consciousness with the force of its negative shadow side and be represented solely in destructive imagery. Thus, the images of the feminine which appear in modern culture are only too often the images of the Terrible Mother, the avenging Goddess and the witch, the hurricane, the harpy and Medusa, the Gorgon's Head and the spider. These images frighten and drive us further from an openness to the feminine, contributing to the general

American trend toward portrayal of Momism, oedipal themes, and "Portnoy's Complaint" as the key images of woman in our culture. The continued repression of the full faces of the feminine is a dangerous delay. The plundering of her domain, the earth and the seas, can only breed revenge (Graves, 1948). Harding (1971) urges us to become aware of this great force within us, to become reconciled to what she calls the "barbarian" within, rather than go the way of past cultures which were overthrown externally by the excluded, barbarian elements neglected by that culture. As de Castillejo (1973) adds, we must become aware of the danger to culture from the overdevelopment of thinking and the repression of feeling, a situation remedied only through a rebalancing of masculine and feminine modes in our consciousness and civilization.

RECOVERING THE GREAT GODDESS

The recovering of the feminine requires a journey into metaphor, a search for missing symbols of the feminine, a recovery of "herstory" from the records of history, a study and reconstruction of "thealogy" based on the image of the goddess (Thea) rather than a reiteration of theology, the study of god (Christ, 1979). The search for symbols to mediate our awareness of the feminine dimension is even more important in light of the fact that the feminine dimension, in itself, speaks in imagery and feeling-toned metaphors. We must be alert to the quality of presence that is being conveyed in the images and not get trapped into literal debates or portrayals of concrete external beings or deities in the name of the feminine. The gods and goddesses are carriers of the qualities we find within, clues to an awesome presence and ways of relating to the world that cannot be forgotten. The symbols of this chapter will be explored in order to direct attention inward, to lead us to the edge of the unknown, not to coerce belief or prove existence. Imagery is a clue to that which cannot be spoken clearly, which needs articulation but defies the current cultural modalities. If we seek the goddess, it is as a witness and symbol of the feminine within ourselves and the world. We turn to the images of the goddess because these images carry the most powerful, unarticulated assumptions about the nature of ultimate reality, and it is precisely the feminine as divine, as inherently valuable and primary in the universe, that is most in need of affirmation in our time.

One of the most important contributions of feminist scholarship today has been the reminder that before the rise of partriarchal religions reigned a vast period of matriarchal worship dating back to the neolithic period of 7000 B.C. and the agricultural revolution and beyond (Rich, 1976; Stone, 1976). Whether or not there were in fact women with real power in those times, the matriarchal values were clearly affirmed in the worship of the great goddess, the earth mother, powerful not only in her awesome capacities for birth and connection with nature, but devastating in her negative side, her destructiveness, and her connection with death. Goddess of mystery and transformation, life and death, time and eternity, she gave birth to the universe through union with the male consort created also from her womb. Her body was the source of all being: her nourishment extended to all her offspring who sought her for protection and affirmation of life as well as meaning in death. It is to this great goddess that we turn, now, in her multiple images and facets of being which reflect and release her great archetypal power.

The Mother

The image of the Great Mother, while it represents the most well-known of the renderings of this great feminine archetype (Jung, 1959), is actually a derivation from an earlier and perhaps even more powerful symbol of oneness. This primordial symbol has been represented in a variety of images witnessing to the original unity of all created being, the ground of all existence. In the Eastern traditions of Hinduism, the goddess emerges from this unity beyond duality, beyond male and female, beyond creation. She is "primordial energy," Maya, the dynamic expression through the multitude and diversity of creation of the essential oneness and identity of all beings and things in the world (Zimmer, 1946). The goddess gives birth to being, yet she represents the energy which precedes being. She carries in her own power the transcendence of duality, or being and non-being. The image of the great goddess lies at the threshold of this polarity: she is mother of the world, yet she is also potentiality and energy before there is form. Different traditions place emphasis on one perspective or the other, and sometimes on both. The Taoist image of the "uncarved block" is closest to the image of the great mother as the container of the unborn, of nonduality, of the birthplace of polarity, of emptiness and potentiality (Argüelles, 1977). Here the feminine is formless, the gateway to form, the image of "impermanence" and change, of flow and process (Argüelles,

1977). She is the Uroboros, the snake eating its own tail, the great round, the images of wholeness and completeness of a universe before the split of consciousness and unconsciousness (Neumann, 1955).

The further the mother archetype differentiates itself from the formless images of the Uroboros, however, the more the archetype tends to fall into duality, to become split into two distinctly positive and negative aspects which are given expression as the Good Mother and the Terrible Mother (Neumann, 1955). Not only is the Great Mother the image of abundant life and exuberant creation, providing sustenance for the created world, but she is the agent of death, the other side of the murderous process which is life, which feeds on itself, as Joseph Campbell (1962) so powerfully portrays, and which must cause death in order to open the way for new birth. The West may have forgotten the images of Isis, of Gaea, and Demeter, the great goddesses of vegetation and creativity, but it has repressed almost completely the image of Kali, the dark Goddess of Hinduism, whose mouth flows with blood and whose neck and waist are garlanded with human skulls and hands (Campbell, 1962). She is India's powerful "symbolization" of the cycle of birth and degeneration, beauty and horror, the devouring and sustaining mother of time (Zimmer, 1946). As the Argüelles (1977) perceptively note, the Great Mother contains both Eros and Thanatos, love and death, those two powerful forces which even Freud confronted in his search for an understanding of human nature.

The symbol of the Great Mother is also further split not only into positive and negative aspects, but into two qualitatively different modes of feminine experience which Neumann (1955) labels the elementary and the transformative. In an insightful analysis, he portrays the ease with which these different modes interpenetrate and give birth to each other and reverberate with the multiple images of the feminine. The great symbols of the feminine, the vessel, the womb, the cave and sphere, the egg and tomb, receive emphasis in one context or another, carrying the image, for example, of the nourishing container that protects and feeds, or the image of the vessel as place and vehicle of initiation and transformation into the mysteries of life and death.

It is perhaps in the elementary mode of the Great Goddess that the human first encounters the feminine. This is the dimension of the feminine which Neumann (1955) emphasized in his insistence on the need to break free from this unconscious, powerful obstacle to the growth of the conscious ego. As Neumann (1955) writes, it is the maternal, elementary force of the feminine, immersed in the imagery of feeding, nurturing, and protecting, which is most likely to show up as both the positive Good Mother, Demeter, Isis, and even Mary, and as the negative Terrible Mother, Kali, Hecate (the dark goddess of the moon), and the Gorgon. Here lies the polarity of the vegetation mysteries of birth and immortality as well as the death mysteries with their emphasis on death, dismemberment, and sickness. The challenge of human life is to first encounter the feminine in the guise of the maternal and work through the ambivalence of this experience to an understanding of the transformative feminine.

The ambivalence portrayed in the imagery of the elementary aspect of the Great Mother is noteworthy in several ways. As Dinnerstein (1976) writes in her profound analysis of the implications of mother-dominated child-rearing practices, the ambivalent needs, loves, and hates that characterize the early years of dependency on one's caretaker are all later projected onto women in ways destructive of equality in the world. For example, since women were perceived as all-powerful as mothers, they are to be feared and deprived of real power in other avenues in the world. This process of projection onto females of the negative elementary goddess imagery has characterized not only the fears of so many male writers throughout time, as Simone de Beauvoir (1953) has written, but it has probably influenced the writing even of those psychologists most concerned with recontacting the feminine. In Neumann (1954; 1955), for example, we discover the feminine often along with a fear of being engulfed by the negative imagery, a feeling not uncommon among men today who are encountering the feminine rising in our culture after years of repression and finding that the first forms to appear are often indeed the negative ones. Our first human experiences of rejection and loss, of not being totally understood or met in our needs, are often felt within the context of the mother, and however important this separation may be to the evolving independent ego, the loss and expulsion from unity and bliss are easily blamed on the maternal force, the earliest way in which we know the feminine (Neumann, 1955).

A complete encounter with the feminine cannot stop with these portrayals of the negative elementary feminine, however, despite their importance as a reminder of the repressed dark side of the Goddess who hovers close in our time. The negative maternal metaphor cannot carry the entire image of the Great Mother. It seems important in contemporary society that women are going beyond this negativity and fear and finding new meaning in the symbol of motherhood. It seems especially significant that many voices active in the early feminist writings of the 1970s are now affirming the importance of motherhood, and are feeling a need to reconnect, if only symbolically, with this process of giving birth and what that conveys about a way of being in the world (Chesler, 1979; Fallaci, 1978; Rich, 1976). Mothers are claiming their rights to be totally human, to acknowledge their hopes and fears, their doubts and disgust, to develop trust in their own processes and reactions, rather than bounce off their own and others' projections of what the perfect mother should be. Women are recovering their insistence on a life-affirming world that sustains the beings they have nourished for nine months, and they are raging at the life-destroying practices of rape and war and ecological pillage that characterize modern society (Daly, 1978; de Castillejo, 1973). They are affirming with Tillie Olsen (1979) that the oral language they have woven around their children as they taught them to speak is a language worthy of being heard. They are affirming the validity of their own feminine experience, joining in the timeless worlds of an Abyssinian woman that woman's life has had a transformative dimension that is qualitatively different than a man's, altering her forever with her first love from maiden to mother, offering her a knowledge outside the experience of man (Kerényi, 1949).

The important dimension of this reaffirmation of a woman's experience as mother is not the literal participation in this powerful event, however important this may be to many of the older women who are turning to childbirth past the age of thirty-five and discovering in this experience a rebalancing of themselves in many ways. Again, the perpetual temptation to confuse the literal with the symbolic is always present. What seems important in these rediscoveries is the symbolic reconnection with the metaphorical feminine. Whether or not one has a child in reality, the reconnection with pregnancy and childbirth as human experiences is part of the reaffirmation of the feminine in culture today. We can see this in the increased participation of men in the birth process and in childrearing, and in both men and women in their exploration of the creative process, whatever the vehicle of the "birth"—whether art, writing, science, or any form of long, disciplined, and loving work. The processes of gestation and birth are transformative experiences which take us far beyond the purely elementary mode of the feminine; they are creative of both child and mother. Both beings are affected forever by the transition. In the pain and letting go, the ambivalence and intensity, the fear and doubt and joy, the solitary endurance (Chesler, 1979; Harding, 1970) and celebration of the separation of the one into two, lie the archetypes of all creative experience, all letting-go, all surrender to a new unknown. In recovering birth, and in recovering the elementary feminine, we simultaneously move toward the awareness of the transformative feminine, that image of change, rebirth, and renewal which has spoken to us of possibility throughout time. The birth process is another kind of hero's journey which thrusts us into our aloneness in the world and bears the pain of all transformation, yet does so in an interwoven pattern of pushing and letting go, guided by the breath of our awareness and the surrender to time.

The transformative aspect of motherhood is only one illustration, however, of the general transformative character of the feminine which Neumann (1955) outlines. In this dimension, the feminine is related to transitions, movement, change, evolution, and growth. As was true of the elementary aspects of the feminine, the transformative potential of the feminine can be experienced in either negative or positive dimensions. Thus, not only is the feminine given symbolic form in the imagery of the anima (soul-guide), muse, virgin, or Sophia—all of whom are associated with the inspiration mysteries of vision, ecstasy, and wisdom, but the darker sides of the transformative feminine shade into the images of Lilith, Circe, temptresses of madness, stupor and drunken ecstasy. The powerful kinds of knowing associated with the feminine, the intuitive insights that give birth to prophecy have been both revered and feared throughout history. Janeway (1975) suggests that women who have survived past childbearing years, protected by their exclusion from the male-dominated hunt, may indeed have developed the capacity for great memory, enabling them to predict the future on the basis of their larger time perspective. Whatever the precise reason, the image of the wise old woman exists in many cultures despite the tendency to project onto such women the negatives of the feminine powers feared by a culture.

Perhaps the most tumultuous reaffirmation of the feminine in today's post-feminism is a recovery of the transformative feminine dimension and the refusal to be silenced by the negative imagery associated with the Witch and Spinster. Rather than shun the concepts in fear, women are being urged to reaffirm the witch in each of us, to celebrate the spinning and weaving of our own fate and destiny, to recover our "cronology," as Mary Daly writes (1978), our heritage as strong, single women, hags, harpies, and crones. It is women who hold the key to the mystery of life and living, argues this new wave of voices who speak not only in words, but in anger and joy and ritual. Recovering the Great Mother and Goddess is to recover a process of initiation, a training ground in a new way of being

(Harding, 1971). This initiation, however, is again a metaphor. Just as giving birth is to be celebrated as a symbolic way of being in the world that draws energy from the elementary feminine, so too the initiation and incantation of the witch is meant as a way of recontacting the symbolic transformative feminine. To literalize ourselves as either mother or witch is to stop short of the mythic exploration of our full potential as humans who transcend male or female imagery.

Body, Sexuality, Mortality

It was the goddess as body, as vessel, as womb who became the first image to contain our sense of universe (Neumann, 1955). The goddess gave birth to the world of form from her own body—not, as Carol Ochs (1977) points out, as a patriarchal creation by the word of God alone, but from her very being. As such, she is connected to her creation, she is her creation: the world participates in her being in a way unrecognized and unfelt in patriarchal alternatives. The implications of this difference in world view are tremendous, for as Ochs (1977) continues, God the Father creates the world with the distance of an artist who can evaluate and judge his creation as good or bad, whereas God the Mother gives birth in continuity and bondedness with herself and is inextricably linked to her creation in a way incompatible with a harsh distancing morality. Creation is; it is neither good nor bad. It is both or neither.

It is difficult for modern persons to recapture the significance of this shift in world view. We have become so alienated from our bodies that the idea of the world as the body of the divine, as the expression and symbolization of the universe can scarcely be assimilated. The idea that our own bodies are images and reflections of wholeness, sanctified in their very being with no need for appeal to an animating spirit or soul separate from the body, is an unusual one. We have become accustomed to thinking of ourselves as disembodied beings in our essence, with physical shells added on during earth existence, to be transcended and shed upon final enlightenment.

But suppose the Goddess is body, too; that is, suppose the divine is fully corporeal and immanent, as well as transcending form. Suppose the physical dimension of experience is not separate from the spiritual, but an integral part of the whole process of growing in awareness. The heritage of the great goddess to our time lies precisely in this reaffirmation of the divine in matter, the overcoming of the projection of evil onto the flesh of Eve and the supposed insatiable sexuality of woman asserted by the early patristic fathers.

The "resacralization" of the body (Orenstein, 1978) implies the ability to develop a new relationship with the physical, to learn the language of the body. As Sanford (1979) argues, the rediscovery of the feminine, of the mode of relatedness and real contact in this case with the body, is crucial for the release of healing. It is central to a renewed self-confidence as women in ourselves, in our bodies, so often the carriers of a sense of self and self-esteem. The recovery of the body lies behind the anger and efforts to wrest back from the medical professions control over our own bodies—in health care, in contraception, in pregnancy, in abortion, in the birth process. Rather than being self-conscious, embarrassed, disgusted, hassled, or alienated from our bodies, women are celebrating a new type of grounding in physical form and acceptance of those special potentialities and rhythms, the patterns and shapes inherent in being female. We do not have to be bodiless, a secondary substitute for lacking a male body, to be let into the Kingdom of Heaven. The Goddess is already within.

Closely related to the reaffirmation of the body implicit in the return to the Goddess imagery is the rediscovery and resacralization of sexuality. The denigration of women and sexuality has permeated most of Western culture, and will continue to do so, argues Ruether (1973) as long as men fear the deep vulnerability that comes through intimacy with another being. As long as women can be perceived as merely body, and an inferior one in addition, she does not require a real confrontation and encounter as another real being. Our fear and distrust of sexuality as somehow incompatible with spirituality can be projected onto women by both women and men. The recovery of our own sexuality and our own validity as fully human, spiritual, sexual beings is a celebration of wholeness, of the divine dimension within all union, sexual or otherwise. It is a refusal to dichotomize body and spirit, sexuality and spirituality. Awareness can belong to the whole spectrum of human experience; all is a vehicle for growing. At a more pragmatic level, the surfacing of the sexuality issue, writes Friday (1977), is crucial to the unraveling of the mother-daughter relationship, to honesty between human beings, and to building new ways of being adult and sexual.

Where the body and sexuality are held sacred, a new relationship with death can and perhaps must evolve. The Goddess as a symbol of birth and death thrusts into our awareness the ever presence of death. As such she frightens and overwhelms, and typically elicits a response of repression, described by such writers as Ernest Becker in *The Denial of Death* (1973). Yet this response of fear and avoidance is only one alternative to the appearance of the Goddess; if she is welcomed in her fullness, death can become a part of life, a visitor and reminder of the preciousness of each passing, a preparation for the continual letting-go that is life. If we are truly alive in form, then we are not just inhabiting our bodies on the hope of ultimate release; death is not just an entry into a longed-for goal and culmination of striving. Instead, as Carol Ochs (1977) writes, if we are at home in the world as in matriarchal awareness, we long for awareness and fullness in the whole cyclical process that is. The recovery of the feminine is movement toward the center of the wheel of life, not escape from the rim. Death is a reality that leads to rebirth; life and death are seasons of continuity, not dichotomous events to be feared. It is the ego personality that fears death, not the soul for whom death comes as a completion and transformation, a part of life (de Castillejo, 1973). This affirmation is much closer, as we shall see many times, to the wisdom of Eastern religions and their teachings of the transcendence of dualities, including the duality of enlightenment and being in this world, and ultimately of life and death.

Nature

Woman as nature has been an association frequent in Western and Eastern culture, stemming perhaps from the same observations which gave rise to the original power of the goddess. The connection of women with childbirth, with the cycles of menstruation, and with the process of nursing gave her a kind of built-in readiness to be likened to the mysteries and rhythms of other growth processes in nature. The connection with nature can be seen as either benevolent or destructive, depending on which natural processes one chooses to focus on as analogies. Whichever focus dominates, the tendency has typically been, however, to link woman with matter and man with spirit and to render the former subservient or inferior to the latter. This becomes the central point of leverage in the new affirmations of the feminine metaphor.

Susan Griffin (1978) is among the many women now giving embodiment to "the roaring inside" of the female voices buried deep in the experience of the earth. In her powerful book, *Women and Nature,* Griffin contrasts the taming, measuring, numbering, excavating, plundering, controlling, and studying of nature undertaken from a separate patriarchal perspective with the rich, labyrinthine, patient, connectedness of the experience of the feminine, at home and participating in the land, the trees, the body of daily life. It is a powerful voice, this voice that speaks from within a new space and "revisits" matter with a newly embodied vision. What is important, again, is not any sentimentalized connection of women and the earth or the moon, for the symbols elude each other and reverse in many cultural traditions (Ferro-Luzzi, 1980; von Franz, 1972); what is crucial is the reawakening of a new mode of relating to the earth, a process in which we are deeply rooted in an awareness of our interconnectedness, our mutual fragility. What is carried in the image of the feminine is a rediscovery of "gyn/ecology," as Mary Daly (1978) calls it, of our oneness and responsibility for mutual nourishment as plants, soil, animals, and humans on this earth. This is not just a woman's issue; it is a human one. If the reaffirmation of the goddess ends only in a celebration of the concrete female body and her connection to nature, we have failed to move mythically into the symbolic possibilities of this way of being for us all. We will have succeeded only in introducing a new and frozen metaphor.

The general qualities of the metaphorically feminine consciousness which are associated with the great goddess are likewise in need of application and development in all human beings, not just women. When Neumann (1973) writes "On the Moon and Matriarchal Consciousness," the intent is not to reify these concepts into a female duty but to legitimize this way of being in our world which has lost touch with this awareness. Moon consciousness, writes Neumann (1973) in this essay, corresponds to a totally different apprehension of time; its imagery and metaphors stem from the natural world, rather than the planned, controlling, logical, forceful realm of doing and thinking. Feminine consciousness proceeds by qualitative time, a recognition that time is not an abstract, equally divisible substance that moves in metered linear fashion. Time ebbs and flows, has rhythms and periods, cycles of change, intensity and uniqueness, waxing and waning. There are favorable times and unfavorable times for certain events; periodicity is built into being.

In feminine consciousness, there are occasions when time cannot be hurried or forced, where creativity has the nature of a conception as opposed to an intentional act (Neumann, 1973). As Neumann adds, the person's ego can only turn to waiting, to giving forth its whole being in the process of gestation; there is a time for "ripening" which must be respected. This quality of being able to "do nothing" but only to "let happen" is a terribly difficult process for modern humans, male or female. We are taught that to do nothing is to be idle and ineffective. Receptivity and passivity are disparaged by our active, striving culture, with little awareness that waiting is a kind of activity in itself.

As Neumann (1973) and von Franz (1972) reiterate, most of the deep processes of creativity and growth require long periods of waiting, of preparation, of incubation. The image of returning to the forest, to silence, to the importance of secrecy and discretion are important images in fairy tales and in the feminine hero journey, writes von Franz (1972). The writer knows the danger of revealing the created word too soon (von Franz, 1972); so too in all creation there is a delicacy that must be respected. The process of individuation, of growing a soul, takes time; one cannot constantly uproot a growing plant to check on its progress any more than one can expose the self at all moments to the harsh glare of public light. To learn to "let things happen," to allow for the fruit to form and ripen—this is the modality of the feminine. As de Castillejo (1973) reminds us in the image of Penelope who weaves and unweaves her tapestry as she waits for Ulysses' return, waiting is fundamental to feminine experience.

Wisdom, in this way of being, is concerned not with the learning of truth externally but the experience of inner transformation (Neumann, 1973). Knowledge grows out of one's whole being by a process of organic growth, an unfolding of a right relationship with one's surroundings, an acceptance which embraces and shapes experience into new creation (Neumann, 1973). In the urgency of joining the male-dominated world, of affirming women as equals with men, often this valuation of the quality of waiting and patience has been denigrated by feminists as another form of the oppression of women or as a failure of "existential transcendence," as even de Beauvoir (1953) seems to suggest. However, to insist on the primacy of self-affirmation and expression, or on the efficacy of carrying out all intents assertively despite possible ignorance of the full complexity of the situation, is in itself, perhaps, a kind of oppression which the reaffirmation of the feminine may help to remedy. To learn to differentiate the moment for action from that of "letting things happen" is perhaps the greatest paradox we face as humans (von Franz, 1974). In ethical conflict and in all complex decision-making, we must be prepared, writes von Franz (1974), to sustain the conflict until the unexpected solution emerges, to surrender our ego wishes and intentions to the perception of the greater self, to know how to blend the special tools of discrimination and conscious attention (Psyche's sorting of the seeds) with the willingness to follow feeling and intuition. "Letting happen" is finally the message of the old tale of the Rainmaker, told by de Castillejo (1973) and von Franz (1972) who describe the situation of a town suffering from drought and an old man, whose withdrawal into a state of oneness with himself is enough to return the environment to harmony and release the rain. "Letting happen" is part of the Taoist active nonaction, part of entering the Creative Void; it is a way of contacting and being nourished by the feminine in ourselves.

DEPATRIARCHIZING MYTH:
Restoring the Goddesses
to their Origins

According to recent anthropological understandings, the great goddess is believed to have dominated the great matriarchal cultures of the neolithic age and ruled over a fertile, stable, agrarian society and the first settlements and cities. As men became more confident of their power, control, and consciousness over against nature, however, a new wave of religious upheaval began to spread over much of the world. In Greece, in India, and in the Middle East, there arose a warlike, aggressive, masculine culture which worshipped gods or a god and which took over and dethroned the goddess. Judaism, and with it Christianity and Islam, epitomized this trend in that the new masculine, patriarchal awareness was crystallized around one male deity, Yahweh. The same tendency was occurring in India, where the great goddess was replaced with such gods as Indra and Agni, and in Greece, where the great goddess gave way to the Olympian gods and to goddesses who represented only pale representations of their former selves (Rich, 1976; Spretnak, 1978).

The long eras of patriarchal imagery have deprived women and men not only of images of the divine within feminine experience but have alienated us from the power and potency inherent in the archetypal feminine. Without strong affirming images, the feminine rising in our consciousness must turn to negative forms for expression. It is not enough to reaffirm the imagery of the Great Goddess, however, for the feminine must be given further differentiated expression in our awareness and culture. As Guggenbühl-Craig (1977) cautions us, there are numerous archetypes of the feminine available to us, and now that less energy is bound up in the maternal archetypes through the advent of birth control and the new choices opened up to women as a result, the energy of the feminine archetype can find renewed expression in many forms beyond the Great Mother. Some of these forms need bear no relationship to men whatsoever, as the images of the Amazon, Artemis, and the Vestal Virgin testify, and must be freed of their pathological connotations if the full range of feminine experience is to become accessible to us as men and women (Guggenbühl-Craig, 1977). The traditional Jungian imagery of the feminine expressed in the images of mother, heteira, amazon, and medium (Ulanov, 1971), can open up into innumerable combinations and images relevant to our time. The task of this section, then, is to delineate a few of these possibilities, to restore to consciousness some of the archetypes that speak especially to contemporary society, to remythologize the goddesses to their original power as mediators of certain dimensions of experience struggling for expression today. We must reach beyond the familiar patriarchal renderings of these mythic beings, and in the process, hopefully release in ourselves an appreciation of the energies they represent.

Aphrodite: Connectedness

It is difficult to recognize in the vain, jealous, and controlling image of patriarchal Aphrodite the original power of this great goddess of connectedness. To restore Aphrodite to her essence is to remember her as the binder of all things (Smith, 1977). She is the great earth goddess who surrounds and sustains all beings in connectedness—not just through the power of human love but through the pull of cosmic attraction at least as powerful as the forces of gravity. As Betty Smith (1977) argues, she was the first god to disappear in the shadow cast by Christianity, rendering her part of the general denigration of womanhood, sexuality, the body, and passionate relationships. To recover Aphrodite is to bring back the dignity of the body; it is to see further than the preoccupation of women with romance and love relationships and to unleash the passion of connectedness and union into all our relationships, with people and with objects of creation. To restore Aphrodite is to live in a translucent world where meaning holds together the entire matrix, where passion disrupts yet empowers, uniting disparate concepts and implausible dualities. Aphrodite is the wife of Hephaestus, the least attractive of the gods; the least congruent image finds a place within her universe. To know Aphrodite is to love ideas with the same connectedness as people; to demand the intensity and radical presentness of intense love of all one's relatedness; to know the dark and the light side of union and separation; to bring feeling to rationality. To recognize Aphrodite is to connect with all of life, not just a husband, wife, or child but to relate in mutuality to all creative acts.

Artemis: Virginity and the Wild

Artemis, the twin sister of Apollo, provides a powerful metaphor for the mode of being in the world that contrasts so well with contemporary affirmations of the Apollonian virtues of Logos, form, balance, and lucidity. Artemis is the goddess of the hunt, the goddess of the wilds, whose connection with nature, the forest, and the instinctual world is affirmed in a kind of delicate power that speaks of the freshness of wild things (Harrison, 1924). Artemis is the goddess of "untamed nature," who is associated with the light and mystery of the moon; she attends at the birth of animals and humans, assisted by the power of the night and the ecstasy of the dance (Spretnak, 1978). She is the mediator of new things, of the transition, present at the beginnings, possessing a grace and elusive beauty in connecting with her environment (Smith, 1978a).

Above all, Artemis is the Virgin and it is in this image that she must be restored. Contemporary society has lost a sense of the power of this metaphor, confusing it with a simple statement of biological or sexual fact. To recover Artemis is to regain a sense of the energy of this archetype, to recover the virgin within ourselves. To the early Greeks, the virgin is she who is "one-in-herself" (Spretnak, 1978), defined by herself alone and not by any connection to a man. Virginity in the great goddesses had nothing to do with their sexuality so much as it represented an affirmation of their independence and self-sufficiency as beings and incarnations of the divine. As Neumann (1954) writes, virginity implies a freedom from possession by any man and an experience of openness to the divine. Virginity is not asceticism or chastity but an allegiance to the wild, to the state of being untamed, as Mary Daly (1978) outlines. Artemis energy is a celebration of this self-possession and freedom to define the self in connectedness with one's inner intuition.

Artemis is poised, too, on the boundary between the potentiality of maidenhood and the fullness of motherhood (Kerényi, 1949). Guarding the region where something fresh and new may come into being, she stands between the world of form and intuition/instinct, the mediator of the new potentiality in each creative act (Smith, 1978a). It is this metaphor for the virginal aspect of our creativity which we have lost in losing Artemis.

Celibacy, as part of the imagery of the virgin archetype, is even more profoundly misunderstood by our culture. As Layard (1972) argues, celibacy is actually a transformation rather than negation of sexuality, aiming at a higher union with God. Virginity in this view is a "spiritual pregnancy," a return to the sanctity of one's own inner being as the vehicle and womb of one's transformation and growth. As a metaphor for the sacred and inviolable, virginity represents the intensification of self-growth, the transformation of energy toward soul-making.

Artemis as a goddess stands in most dramatic contrast to Athene, goddess of wisdom, the arts, and protector of the city of Athens (Harrison, 1924). Athene is the epitome of the patriarchal goddess, deprived of her own independent birth from the great goddess by a mythology that sees her spring full-grown from the head of Zeus. She is the goddess with a father but not a mother. For Daly (1978), she is the classic "token woman," and as such her independent heritage is so lost to time that she lies almost beyond the possibility of reclamation.

Demeter and Persephone:
The Mother-Daughter Celebration

The goddess who seems to be undergoing the most profound reaffirmation process in our culture today is actually a dual goddess, present in both her maternal form as Demeter, the Corn goddess, nurturer of grain and agriculture, and her daughter, the maiden Kore or Persephone, goddess of the underworld. In the unity of her two forms, the Eleusinian goddess provided the focus of the ancient mysteries at the heart of Greek religious life for nearly 2000 years (Kerényi, 1977). As Kerényi (1949) writes, daughter and mother stand together in living continuity at the threshold between these two experiences of being a woman. The Eleusinian mysteries allowed anyone, male or female, to participate in the deeper meaning of this connection, and as such the mysteries form a powerful spiritual expression of the feminine that is still masked in mystery due to the long years of secrecy characterizing the tradition.

The myth of Demeter and Persephone is a powerful one for our time which is suffering from the separation of mother and daughter of which the myth speaks. In the myth, the close relationship which prevailed between Demeter and Persephone is interrupted one day when they are out in the fields delighting in the flowers and Persephone is stolen by the god of the underworld, raped, and taken into the earth as his bride. There are many versions of the myth, but the essence is this abrupt and painful separation of the beloved daughter from her mother. Demeter, overcome with grief, wanders the earth, unable to be consoled, refusing to nourish the growth of plants and other living things. The earth too mourns, until the conditions of drought and famine drive the other gods to intervene; Persephone is allowed to return to her mother on the condition that she has not eaten anything in the underworld; her husband, however, has deceived her into eating some pomegranate seeds, and thus she will always need to return to the darkness of the land of death for at least three months out of each year. The separation of mother and daughter will always reverberate throughout the world in the passing of the seasons.

The important aspect of this myth for our time, however, is perhaps not the separation in itself, but the emerging joy of the rejoining of mother and daughter. Charlene Spretnak (1978, p. 110) speaks so poignantly of this moment, when Demeter, after months of waiting and despair, first hears the sounds of the crocus and animals heralding the message that "Persephone returns! Persephone returns!"

> When Persephone ascended from a dark chasm, there was Demeter with a cape of white crocus for Her Daughter. They ran to each other and hugged and cried and laughed and hugged and danced and danced and danced.

In a world dominated by the imagery of Father and Son and the fears of Mother and Son, the mother-daughter relationship has slipped from consciousness as a point of celebration and often taken on the malevolence of its shadow side. The rediscovery and reforging of this connection between mothers and daughters that is surfacing into public consciousness with the popularity of such books as *My Mother, Myself* by Nancy Friday and *Of Woman Born* by Adrienne Rich carries the force of a neglected archetype. There is much healing to be done, much work of listening and relistening to each other's stories to help to reunite the long years of alienation. The increased feminist tendency to turn to other women for nourishment and support is finally including the mother-daughter bond within this possibility, renewing a heritage of love, support, and affirmation that characterized the life of women on the American frontier, who through the passion and sharing of their letters were able to bridge their loneliness and alienation from a community of sisters, mothers and friends (Smith-Rosenberg, 1975).

The separation from the mother is a painfully necessary experience in the life of every human, yet it has often been neglected as a source of ambivalence and estrangement between mother and daughter. So alike in body and destiny, mother and daughter have been able to project upon each other their unmet needs, desires, expectations, and fears, and often never ventured to explore the chasm of distance that split between them. Terrified and determined to prevent the painful symbolic rape of the daughter, mothers have protected their daughters from this threat of sexuality and the separateness it implies. A situation of symbiosis is often created which, as Nancy Friday (1977) recounts, triggers the daughter's necessary rebellion yet subtly leads her to seek to recapture in a relationship with a man a similar situation of total dependency on another person.

The separation from the mother is crucial for the daughter's growth in autonomy; like the little boy, she must push toward her own independence. As Chodorow so perceptively argues (1978a, 1978b), the little girl turns to her father not only because she is pushed to find a male love object in our culture but also, at least partly, as a way of dealing with the sense of rejection she experiences from her mother, her first love relationship. Her early needs and longing focused on the mother and her need to also separate from the mother create an ambivalence in the relationship between daughter and mother that colors all her relationships with women. Since men have not been trained to be as deeply involved in the early nurturance of relatedness, she never can get the kind of warmth and love in the context of a relationship with a man which she longs for, yet she is barred from friendship and love from her mother whom she must leave behind in order to grow up. This developmental situation creates a poignant bind that characterizes women today: a longing yet frustrated search for a close love relationship with a man, and an ambivalent relationship with women and especially mothers with whom one has the potential for closeness but the fear of engulfment.

The central struggle between mothers and daughters, writes Flax (1978), is to integrate both the needs for nurturance and autonomy within one relationship. It has seldom been possible for women to offer both to each other, for a mother to love her daughter passionately and also participate in nourishing her independence. Rich (1976) speaks of the need for "courageous" mothers who struggle themselves and do not resign themselves to the female condition of oppression, who model for their daughters the possibility of strength and mothering. In a particularly insightful analogy, Flax (1978) illustrates the way in which this conflict between the norms of nurturance and autonomy has plagued the relationship between feminists and women advocating traditional motherhood, between the "right-to-lifers" (nurturing) and the "right-to-choice" (autonomy) advocates in the empassioned debate over abortion. To overcome the division between these two basic needs for warmth and independence is what the separation and reunion of Demeter and Persephone is all about.

The Eleusinian mysteries which involved purification rites, a journey through the night to Eleusis, and secret ceremonies which released the experience of inner knowledge for those who were prepared to "see" are the sacred rites of the joining of the mother and daughter in ourselves. They are the affirmation both of the pain of the separation and loss of the fragile, youthful, virginal part of ourselves and of the joyous refinding.

The mysteries witness to the passage and growth of the spirit with its confrontation with loss, the splitting that allows for reunion (Kerényi, 1977), and the death necessary to rebirth. The moment of revelation in the mysteries, marked by the holding up of an ear of grain, speaks in image of the cycle of life and death and the ultimate transcendence of all separateness by the reunion with the life flow of mother to daughter, the circle of immortal life (Kerényi, 1949). As Jung (1949) adds in his analysis of the Kore archetype, the Demeter-Persephone myth is the archetypal expression of female life, extending backwards and forwards in mother and daughter, witnessing to the continuity of life across generations and seemingly "outside time."

The joy and insights accompanying the Eleusinian mysteries, when the early delights with Susan Griffin (1978) in the restoration of daughters to mothers, is not only a joy for women but for all humans who have lost their experience of the feminine. As Nor Hall (1976) asserts, the healing of feminine emptiness in our time requires the reconnection of mother and daughter in full embodiment within ourselves, not a search for completion via the external male. We must mourn with Demeter, enter into the bleak, sterile period of "incubation" before any creative experience (Hall, 1976), follow the loss of the daughter into the unconscious, and we must be willing to wait actively and search the earth for her return. The love that surges from the reunited "house" of mothers and daughters promises the nourishment so long missing for women today (Barreno,

Horta, and da Costa, 1975). We are all mothers who have lost our daughters, daughters who have lost our mothers, until that time when the metaphorical feminine returns to consciousness and unity in our culture.

Beyond God and Goddess

It is not surprising that the process of recovering the Great Goddess and of restoring the goddesses to their origins would carry profound implications for the emerging field of feminist theology, one of the most vital and creative areas to emerge out of the recent feminist movement. It is fascinating to note that the Death-of-God theology of past decades may indeed have witnessed to the closing of an era of consciousness, and that soon a whole new generation of feminist theologians would begin to speak of a new vision of the divine and tesify to new modes of religious consciousness that transcended old dualities. If God was dead, perhaps the Goddess lived. If Judaeo-Christian patriarchal religion of the past four-thousand years could look to Moses and Jesus as guides to spiritual experience, perhaps a new wisdom might emerge by recovering Mary and even Eve, symbols of a feminine heritage left dormant for millenia since the age of matriarchal values and the Great Goddess.

The feminist critique of the Judaeo-Christian heritage builds on the discovery of the patriarchal reversals and "appropriated" symbols from the earlier goddess imagery found in the Greek religion. This patriarchal overthrow, for example, reduced such great earth goddesses as Hera to a quarrelsome wife of Zeus, although the constant marital strife of Hera and Zeus witnesses to a goddess tradition that is never entirely subdued by the incoming patriarchal invasions (Harrison, 1924). In this process, the entire classical world gave rise to a philosophical dualism which split reason from emotion, spirit from body, intellect from relatedness, and laid the groundwork for a further denigration of woman and related feminine values (Ruether, 1979).

In Judaism, Sophia, the feminine side of god and embodiment of wisdom, is expunged from the Bible to be replaced by an exclusively male God, a warrior god, a jealous god who repeatedly urges his people away from the worship of deities who are not even identified within the texts in their actual identity as goddesses. In the classical patriarchal reversal described by Mary Daly (1978), God creates woman out of man, and Eve is assigned the role of ritual scapegoat, responsible for expulsion from the garden and carrier of the female curse of uncleanliness and inferiority.

Matriarchal values of bondedness with creation from the body of the goddess are replaced, as Ochs (1977) persuasively portrays, by the patriarchal ethics of a creator god who can judge and condemn creation, a shift in consciousness reflected so dramatically in the story of Abraham and Isaac. In his willingness to slay Isaac, Abraham asserts a loyalty to an abstract principle and judgment above the loyalty and love of offspring which would follow from the ethics of the goddess, who defends her creation against all violation of the natural order. Expelled from the garden and an experience of being at home in the world and connected to the soil, patriarchal religion wanders with Moses, affirming a religion of the nomad and exile, of the wasteland and the desert, avenging the evilness of cities and the realms of the feminine (Ochs, 1977).

The repression of the feminine side of the divine is expressed in Christianity even more clearly in the very person of Jesus Christ, as the male incarnation of God the Father. Whatever his personal qualities or teachings of the valuation of woman and androgynous qualities may have been, the male imagery of Jesus is a powerful carrier of unconscious messages to women about their inability to reflect the divine (Daly, 1973). The trinity likewise excludes the feminine in an ironic reversal of the "triple Goddess" imagery from which the Christian trinity may be derived (Daly, 1978). In addition, argues Daly (1973, 1978), the war, genocide, and witchburning which plague Christian history are direct consequences of "phallic morality" under God the Father, and of the patriarchal transformation of the affirming tree of life, legacy of the great goddess, into a tree of death, a crucifixion.

Depatriarchizing Judaeo-Christian myth means a return to a careful analysis of the ancient texts, to a recovery of the traces in Genesis of a plural mother-father god who creates, not man first and woman second, but man and woman equally and simultaneously, and in which the separating of the primal Adham of humanity into Adam and Eve, male and female, marks the beginning of alienation from the godhead for which Adam is as equally responsible as Eve (Christ and Plaskow, 1979). Depatriarchizing Christian myth goes much further, argue feminist theologians, than recovering the androgynous message and model of Jesus; the challenge is to move beyond Christocentric symbols altogether, beyond God the Father and the Son to new images and words for the God experience that can bear witness to the feminine dimensions of spirituality, for women as well as men. To affirm a mother-father god, to speak of the divine with feminine and masculine pronouns and imagery is intended not to encapsulate the divine in any sexual or anthropomorphic parameters, but to stretch and break our attachment to imagery, all of which is ultimately inadequate and can only serve as metaphor for the unknown (Christ and Plaskow, 1979).

The power and courage of new naming of the divine calls further, in Mary Daly's (1978) words, for the "re-membering" of the Goddess, gathering her together and taking her back in the full richness of her positive and negative forms as Isis and Artemis, Demeter and Persephone, Aphrodite and Kali, and her human expressions as Lilith and Eve. It is the Protestant tradition, in particular, which must face this task, for the Roman Catholic tradition was able—in fact was forced by popular pressure—to reincorporate the heritage of the goddess cults, the dimension of nurturance, mercy, and wisdom into their tradition in the person of Mary (Ashe, 1976; Ruether, 1977). As Tillich, Jung, and others have pointed out so often, the Protestant tradition has insisted on a very masculine interpretation of the Godhead, and given almost single-minded affirmation to the masculine values of reason, competition, and linear progress (Romero, 1974).

Yet Mary too needs liberation, as Daly (1978) argues; to rediscover Mary would only take us as far as an image of the conquered Goddess, a man-made woman, a double-binded woman caught between virginity and motherhood whose submission to Father and Son has none of the power and affirmation of the original goddess. The Catholic Church has at least offered women the images of virgin and nun as models of the independent, striving, autonomous woman, whereas Protestantism offers only the model of the minister's wife (Daly, 1973); still, the image of Mary is one of subordination to her son rather than an affirmation of Mary and Jesus as the "twin souls" of God (Jarvis, 1979). Thus, despite the advantages of having a goddess image of any kind, the figure of Mary continues to be inadequate as a complete expression of the feminine today (Warner, 1976).

Depatriarchizing religious experience means, finally, a reaffirmation and celebration of the individual and collective experience of women as the ground and source of spiritual insight equal to any other dimension of word and spirit. It is the reclaiming of our own daily lives, the richness of this world and its passion, its relationships, its life, and its death as a nexus of reality at least as spiritually significant as the rarefied abstract realm of heavenly spirit. It is saying yes to the body, to the experiences of menstruation, childbirth, sexuality, and aging as essential parts of our souls, of our religious consciousness, not as sinful additions. Recovering feminine spirituality means the affirmation of power that promotes life, that takes in order to give, that balances waiting with action in a spiral of change. Perhaps above all, reclaiming the feminine inspiration in religion may allow us to go beyond conceptualizations of the divine that lean on either god or goddess metaphors, to discover with Daly (1973) God the Verb or, in her even more radical image, to transcend the whole concept of God versus human, creator versus creature, the pattern of all dualistic religion (Christ and Plaskow, 1979).

To move beyond God and Goddess is to affirm both the metaphorically masculine and feminine realms of values and consciousness, to affirm rational linear thought and intuition, to affirm spirit and body, to discover the simultaneity of the divine as both a transcendent experience and an immanent reality present in every act. It is to experience surrender not just to patriarchal authority and law but to the process and flow of life, including death; to find meaning here and in the beyond, to live in two worlds at once and know that they are one. Whether one calls this an androgynous vision, an integration of masculine and feminine world views, or whether one feels even this image is limiting, the emphasis is on recovering wholeness—for women as well as men—and on breaking through to new visions of reality in which these dimensions of experience, masculine and feminine, Moses and Mary, are transcended altogether.

NOURISHING THE FEMININE IN DAILY LIFE

One of the dangers of an extended abstract portrayal of the metaphorically feminine dimension is the tendency to lose touch with the immediate qualitative feel of the very dimension we seek to describe. This is particularly true of the feminine which defies the linear mode and is only too often squeezed dry by the attempt to communicate in words the impact of its power. One of the key reasons we have turned so extensively to images of the goddess in this chapter is in the hopes of bypassing the insufficiency of language and of capturing some glimpses of the feminine by metaphor and analogy.

The remainder of this chapter attempts to take this pursuit of imagery and concreteness even further into direct application to struggles in the life of men and women to nourish and embody the feminine dimension within ourselves. We shall examine five different dimensions: the necessity of recovering and revalidating the supposedly weak and unbeneficial traditional feminine qualities, the recovery of the body and ways of nourishing it, the importance of women friends, the art of living relationships without planning, and the danger of the traps of literalizing the feminine into concrete acts of childbirth and marriage.

Recovering Feminine Values

The nourishment of the feminine must begin with a revaluation of the contribution and importance of the traditional feminine values in our daily lives. Women are so used to second-class status that without realizing it, we claim our feminine heritage out of a kind of inferiority position which must be corrected before a true affirmation can proceed. We have been so ready to eagerly seek out the supposedly superior male qualities of assertiveness and individuality that we have rarely guessed that our own heritage might provide an important corrective balance to these dominant qualities in our culture.

Jean Baker Miller's book, *Toward a New Psychology of Women,* was one of the crucial turning-points in this revaluation process. She calls attention to the way in which women become the "carriers" for society of those qualities of human experience which are problematic or unacceptable within the dominant norm. It is time, she argues, for these qualities to enter the mainstream of culture, and for men as well as women to recover the wisdom of these dimensions rather than relegating them to only a part of the human species. That which we have been taught to see as weakness is really hidden potential and strength. Even the traditional feminine quality of vulnerability and helplessness is crucial to the process of living, allowing one to turn for help when needed, to acknowledge the reality of the tenuousness of human existence without which we deny and repress our fears and emotions.

Men need to realize, writes Miller, what women have been experiencing all along, that the subtleties of day-to-day nourishment of the well-being of others is not ultimately incompatible with self-growth; that responding to the needs of others need not be a necessary detraction of one's own self-assertiveness. The relationship between self and other is not intrinsically competitive. The Hobbesian view of human nature in which man aggresses inevitably against his neighbor may indeed reflect what the male of the species has been doing, but is no commentary on the years of giving and serving contributed by the female of the species. As anthropologists are asserting, our species may have evolved so quickly largely because of its capacity for cooperation and sharing, not because of its skill in bearing arms (Leakey and Lewin, 1977). It is women, affirms Miller, who are most in touch with creative possibility, for as persons without power, they have less investment in the status quo and are more able to envision new alternatives. Living outside the "real world" as defined by men, women have access to another mode of being and intuiting which may, in fact, be more real and encompassing than the linear, rational preoccupations of the dominant class. Miller is not arguing that women should stay separate in this world, however, but take this heritage into the culture, refuse to carry it for others, and side by side with men, struggle to develop both the powers of conflict and assertiveness as well as the readiness to give and receive.

If a woman will take an inner stand in defense of these feminine values, argues de Castillejo (1973), then her masculine side can collaborate in a constructive rather than a dominating way in her evolution toward wholeness. The assertion of will and power is not incompatible with caring and connectedness, reminds Carol Christ (1979), and the concept of mutuality is the most affirming expression for the ideal meeting ground of masculine assertiveness and feminine concern (Bianchi and Ruether, 1976). Anaïs Nin (1975) urges us finally, to a new appreciation of the power of inward change as a first and powerful step toward external change in the world. The ability to surrender, yield, to be dependent, to care for bodily needs, to cry, and to ask for help are part of what it is to be deeply human. They are strengths, not weaknesses, and the journey to this affirmation is often an inner one. Meditation, working in one's own garden, the quiet tending of daily needs and inner secrets is the context in which the feminine can give birth. We cannot legislate this transition in any direct sense, whether as a personal plan of self-improvement or a plan of social action. The revolution is an inner evolution within us all, nourished by the most intimate of nuances and appreciations, as the long neglected feminine begins to grow roots in the soul.

Recovering the Art
of Self-Nourishment

The recognition of the need for self-nourishment does not translate directly into action without much work and practice. In a culture which neglects the body and its care, which exhorts us through a work ethic that perceives quiet time as wasteful idleness, it is difficult for men and women to find time and courage to care for themselves. We rarely remember that we *are* our bodies, we are not just minds which trail our bodies as necessary inconveniences. Starting with the body means learning to pay attention to its messages of pain and tension, to stop and stretch and breathe, to give it rest and time for transition and recuperation at the end of a hard day. Ironically, it is often the woman in the home who may even be less likely to find time for self-restoration than the person who works in an external job and has a culturally understood grievance against the rat race.

Learning to tune in to the body is training for care-giving to the whole self; it is learning with Psyche, to ask for help when one is exhausted and stressed beyond alertness; it is learning the wisdom of waiting and not pushing for some issues to emerge. Self-nourishment is learning to give gifts to the self: a long, languishing bath or shower, a period of time alone, an hour to curl up and read or to wander outside without agenda. Self-nourishment is especially tied to learning to say no without guilt or a long series of excuses, to defend our space as worthy of our own choices and orchestration.

Finally self-nourishment is learning how to soften the "Amazon armors" we have developed as a result of success in the masculine world, learning, as Linda Leonard writes (1979), to welcome weakness, the image of the fool, as opportunities for new creativity and reorganization of ourselves. We must learn to step out of professional personas and our working roles when we return home, to know how to reach out in softness and intimacy toward ourselves and others and not consider this a waste of time. It takes courage to go into this tenderness, the courage of releasing the dominant masculine values we may live in the external world and learning to be at home in the feminine, a process which is the only real preparation for the day when we can more strongly integrate masculine and feminine both within the home and the outer world.

Reclaiming Women as Friends

As we saw in the last chapter, a powerful resource to a woman trying to integrate her masculine and feminine sides in the shadow of a masculine-dominated culture is her ability to find and nourish her friendships with other women. Here, as Harding (1970) describes, she can give voice to the full passion of her interest and caring about the nuances and subtleties of the relationships in her lives without being made defensive about their importance. Here she is neither frightening nor boring to those male others in her life who so often, through their own conditioning, are not at home in the world of the feminine, and who prefer to dodge the issues of conscious relatedness. This need for the nourishment of the feminine is especially a strong need for the professional woman, but as mentioned before, she meets a sister in the woman immersed in the life of home and family, for each is eager for the affirmation of connection with the world they intuit but rarely can occupy in the external world.

It is interesting that the more one develops one's masculine side through some kind of external work and creativity in the world, the more the corresponding desire for high conscious intimacy and relatedness seems to emerge as a need among professional women. It is Harding's (1970) hope that this evolution toward wholeness on the part of women will open up the possibilities of new types of conscious relatedness between men and women and a parallel evolution among men of their feminine and relatedness sides. This possibility, however, seems very remote to other radical feminists who instead celebrate the "sparking" of female bonding and friendship (Daly, 1978). This feminist separatism is perhaps a strong testimony to how alienated from the total fabric of society the feminine experience has become; so deep a gap is envisioned from patriarchal society that no valid expression of the feminine can escape co-optation by the masculine except through isolation. Feminists are reminding themselves that the first menstrual taboos may have been self-imposed periods of female self-affirmation and protection from male demands (Harding, 1971). Although it represents only one possibility, there is power in this separation. Without the female to carry the dimension of feeling and intimacy in his life, the male may have to face the collapse of his own resources, the void which Mary Daly (1973) describes, and turn instead to the cultivation within himself of those qualities he left for women and considered beneath his own self-image.

Surrendering to Relationship

One of the most difficult challenges we face in a culture which places its emphasis on planning and goal-setting is to learn how to allow relationships to happen in our lives. This is a particularly difficult struggle for professional women who have received considerable training in delay of gratification, long-range planning, and problem-solving in their work and yet who have deep longings for a complementary intimacy in their daily lives.

The temptation of the masculine orientation is to launch into relationship very much like a contractual negotiation where each spells out what he or she wants in the relationship, the odds of certain future developments are calculated, and each decides whether or not to invest in the risk of such a situation. Although we rarely actually become so pragmatic in such situations, much inner fear and self-searching is often devoted to lengthy variations of the theme: "where is this relationship going." To recover the feminine in every day experience is to be willing to take the risk of letting relationships evolve in their own time-frame, to let the probabilities of continuation emerge out of the context of shared joys or meaningful struggles rather than out of a cost-benefit analysis of the pros and cons of being in this particular situation. This is not to suggest that one throws out the mind and one's full awareness in staying close to the present. Instead we are being asked to discover that the relationship one has with another is not something abstract one decides to have one day, but that the whole nebulous struggle of being with another is already the relationship. One does not start living tomorrow. Life has already begun; it is already what we are making of it.

Translating this attitude into action is a difficult one, for the very eagerness of professional women for relatedness often traps them into preoccupation and vacillation about whether to continue in a friendship, for example. It is difficult to let go of the desire to analyze and process the relationship one has and values, and the result, as von Franz (1972) outlines, is often an escalation and entanglement of the inner turmoil one hoped to escape through rational deliberation. What is happening in these situations, writes von Franz (1972) is that the ego's attempts to salvage and clarify the situation result only in closing out the spontaneous emerging of the present. Thus, ironically, new data is lost, the present is embroiled in self-doubt and preoccupation, and one protects oneself from the unexpected risks of surprise endings or happenings by keeping a daily ledger of plans and promises. Willingness to surrender to the present is an issue of living with the feminine; this process is not devoid of awareness but rather represents a responsive, sensitive, tuning-in to what is happening in this moment and seeking the seeds of the entire situation there, not in the fears and fantasies of the projected future or remembered past.

Avoiding the Traps of Metaphor

The final issue in this discussion of ways of nourishing the feminine involves the dangers inherent in the process of confusing metaphor for literal reality. This has been a danger throughout this analysis of the metaphorical masculine and feminine, and must be stressed once again as a crucial reminder. However much the feminine may be associated with the realms of relationship and mothering, the implication of this connection is *not* to urge women to become mothers and marriage partners, but to find ways to incorporate the inner qualities of these experiences in their relationship to all experience. This reminder is especially important if we are to consider the realm of the feminine relevant to the lives of both men and women in their androgynous searches for wholeness.

The real temptation for a woman, a temptation that has so often obscured her search for wholeness, has been this very ease of taking the feminine literally, living the feminine in outward form but neglecting the inner expression (Neumann, 1973). In contemporary society, marrying and having children are not the only avenues of expressing the feminine in our awareness, however. The task of cultural childbirth, the labor to bring forth new forms for our time, may, in fact, fall precisely on those women who choose to forego the path of literal childbearing (Hall, 1976). The task of the integration of the feminine into our culture must become a symbolic task, capable of being carried by us all. It is undoubtedly true that the echoes of the unborn child or the home and family not chosen may call out to those who choose the metaphorical path like the voices of the weaving women who try to tempt Psyche to join them as she goes into the underworld. Spinning symbolic children which carry the breath of metaphor, we each pursue the pathless way to the feminine, warmed by the paths of others while we walk alone. How precious that the feminine is not contained in form and so can clothe us on whatever path we choose.

8

INTEGRATING INNER
AND OUTER
The Problem of Culture

The challenge of androgynous personality development that we have been exploring throughout this book always occurs within a broader cultural context. The way in which the general culture dichotomizes or integrates traditional masculine and feminine values provides a backdrop for understanding the challenge of individual androgynous growth within that particular culture. In a culture such as ours, which has been shown to esteem "masculine" characteristics more highly than "feminine" qualities (Deaux, 1976), the search for individual androgyny is a more difficult task than it would be if these individuals received the support of a more generally androgynous culture. It is important, then, to explore the possibilities for androgynous integrations at the cultural level and to anticipate some of the enhancements and risks that may accompany any movement toward an androgynous cultural consciousness. What is happening at the inner level of personality development has its parallels in the external realm of cultural values, norms, and modes of consciousness; movement in one dimension is enhanced or diminished by what is happening at the other level. Personality and culture are two sides of an evolving network of mutual influence, and it is as important for psychologists to direct attention to the larger issues of androgyny for our times as it is to elaborate the process of individual movement in that direction.

EXPLORING THE CULTURAL SHADOW

The question of androgynous development within our culture raises immediately the issue of how we will begin to deal with the collective shadow, the aspects of human development that have been considered unacceptable within the dominant cultural environment. Returning to Jungian conceptualizations of the shadow, we can speak metaphorically of a culture's shadow, which corresponds to the dark side of a culture's aspirations and ideals, to those qualities which do not find a place within the dominant ideology or tone of that culture. If the culture as a whole, as well as the individuals within that culture, are to move toward a greater state of wholeness and a more developed capacity for completeness, attention must be directed to the shadow and toward the capacity for containing and embracing greater polarities and dissonance peacefully within the whole. Typically, our culture has been motivated by the Judaeo-Christian emphasis on perfection, a value system which pushes people toward an often one-sided emphasis on a few carefully designated ideal virtues, rather than advocating the more Jungian goal of completeness (Jung, 1958). If perfection is the aim of life, certain qualities not deemed perfect will be excluded and the creation and maintenance of a very large shadow system is guaranteed. This shadow then pushes at our awareness, ready to erupt into negative forms directly proportional to the force needed to exclude these dimensions. What might turn out to be positive undeveloped potential in a culture thus becomes, through repression in the shadow, a source of energy which is more likely to show itself only in its feared, demonic, or uncontrollable forms. As is true at the individual personality level, the shadow must be confronted, not only because this may prevent such negative eruptions in the culture, but because the shadow qualities, when raised to consciousness, may have much vitality to offer to the dominant value system.

In directing attention to the level of the collective shadow, we must face not only the challenge of integrating what we individually have left in darkness but what our entire Western civilization has left in darkness. As has been suggested in past chapters, our dominant culture is still rooted rather firmly on the foundation of the hero myth, a myth which corresponds to the struggle of evolving consciousness to separate itself from the darkness of unconsciousness, of an unreflective relationship to nature from which humans emerged. It is the myth of the son separating from the Great Mother and allying himself with the Father—the realm of Platonic ideal, thought, spirit, and reason. Western culture, as James Hillman points out in *The Myth of Analysis* (1972), has become the expression of an Apollonian consciousness, dedicated to the values of rationality, objectivity, balanced form, logic, linear thought, and mathematical reasoning. This is a scientifically-oriented culture, a left-brained/right-handed culture as Robert Ornstein (1972) points out, a culture of individuality, competition, and heroism as in Philip Slater's (1970; 1974) portrayal. As has been pointed out by Mary Daly (1973; 1978), Ann Belford Ulanov (1971), Susan Griffin (1978) and others, we have come to consider all these very Western qualities "masculine."

According to this analysis we live in a metaphorically Apollonian-masculine culture and consciousness, in which the characteristic modes of right-handed/left-cortical consciousness dominate. We value rational, linear, analytic, logical, scientific ways of knowing. We process information quantitatively where possible and have confidence in numbers and abstractions. The cultural emphasis is on action and doing, power and competition. We have evolved a society dominated by individualistic striving, agentic self-assertion, violence and aggression, being right, and being strong. We see this in Western culture at large, in science, and in academia. Social prophets of both sexes (Slater, 1974; de Castillejo, 1973) have even begun to suggest that the ecological crises of our planet are a direct consequence of our one-sided emphasis on individual striving and other traditional masculine, technological values. Mary Daly (1978) takes her critique of patriarchal culture even further, seeing it as a generation of life-denying necrophilia, living out its phallic morality to its inevitable issue in war, rape, genocide, and the patriarchal atrocities of footbinding, suttee, genital mutilation, witchburning, and gynecological experimentation. The atrocities, however, are not only directed against women but against earth, against ecology, against planetary wholeness. As Rosemary Ruether (1979) writes, the modern exaggerations and dominance of masculine values is lived out under the images of "Mother Earth and the Megamachine."

How then does the collective shadow appear to this type of civilization? What archetypal energies lie unnamed, unrecognized to our culture? What images draw to them the specter of darkness, of danger, of threat or inferiority? What values are relegated to silence in our culture?

Two images emerge immediately; they are interwoven yet they deserve separate attention in the confrontation of the collective shadow of our time. The first image comes from Dionysus, the powerful Greek dying and rising God, and the second image comes from the metaphor of the feminine, which we explored so extensively in Chapter 7. It is fascinating that each image carries us into the realm of darkness and bears within its symbolism already a connection and affinity for the shadow dimension we are exploring. Western traditions have associated the sun, the spirit, fire, the day, and light not only with the divine but with the masculine, and it seems somehow appropriate that in entering the shadow of this culture, one finds a realm in which the metaphorically Dionysian and feminine modes of consciousness are comfortable and at home. This is precisely why these dimensions are so neglected, for one must overcome great fear to relinquish the clarity of day and enter into the dark, earthy realm of unconscious and long-forgotten resonances.

The cultural journey of completeness, like its individual counterpart, leads always into the shadows, into the darkness itself, into the labyrinth and the dark night of the soul. To learn to see in the dark, we must enter into the darkness, let our eyes get used to the dark and leave behind our reliance on customary tools. A narrow flashlight beam will only create even more frightening shadows, capricious monsters, and caricatures. We must learn a new way of seeing, a new way of valuing. We must be open to the possibility that darkness, too, has its mystery, its holiness, its potential; it has something worth seeing, something to offer us. It is not just a pale shadow of our reflected light, but rather a richness that is part of reality, that needs to be recovered, to be integrated if we are ever to speak of wholeness. It will be an awesome journey, however, which leads us close to the edge of terror, madness, and a sense of lostness without which new discoveries will be merely grafts onto basic patriarchal, masculine vision rather than new, genuinely androgynous possibilities. In this delicately balanced search, it is important to remember with Ursula Le Guin

(1968) that we are the source of our shadows; we cast them. In a sense then they are *our* shadows, bearing our shape, our form, and our name. If we can own them as connected to ourselves, we can recognize them and move beyond our fear.

Dionysian Consciousness

In the movement into the collective shadow, then, perhaps the first shadow image is that of Dionysus. In contrast to the Olympian God Apollo, Dionysus is the God of paradox, born of human and divine origin, whose existence and appearance compel attention to the dichotomies of existence. As Walter Otto (1965) describes, Dionysus is the god whose appearance marks the shattering of traditional form and order, who transforms the snug secure world of thought and social form. Dionysus is the god who is himself mad, who sets before us the fullness of life and violence of death, the closeness of creativity and destructiveness, the unity of the paradoxical, the vitality of emotion and sexuality, the energy of life complete with its suffering, ecstasy, sorrow, and destructiveness—the truth which can make one mad but without which one also cannot live. Dionysus, the god whose followers were women, who himself united the masculine and the feminine is the god who carries, as Hillman (1972) points out, the archetypal image for a kind of consciousness to balance our Apollonian consciousness. It is a consciousness which reaffirms the realm of paradox, of mystery, of emotion, of death and suffering, of the body, birth, and creativity. The Greeks did not separate Apollo and Dionysus: they knew the two belonged together, as the heavens must be grounded in the depths below (Otto, 1965). It was those who cling only to Dionysus or ignored him completely who went mad; the path to wisdom lay in integration.

Although the reintroduction of Dionysian consciousness into our Apollonian culture is critical, and its importance is testified to by the amount of fear which labels this possibility as dangerous, orgiastic, or even evil, Dionysian consciousness alone is not powerful enough to correct the dangerous imbalance in the masculine direction which our culture has taken. As Mary Daly argues (1978), Dionysian versions of feminine values are still largely within the masculine province; they are not healing to women but, in fact, unleash madness, for they are not grounded basically within the life-affirming potentiality of the goddess, of feminine experience, but are the exaggerated attempts to attach feminine inspiration to a largely masculine godhead. No wonder the result is painfully out of balance. Daly directs us instead to the need to turn toward uncorrupted, woman-created visions of the feminine experience so needed in our culture, the kinds of images leading to the affirmations of the great goddess in our time.

The Metaphorical Feminine

When we turn, then, to the second dimension of the shadow most preva-lent in contemporary culture, we enter into a metaphorical realm of the traditional feminine and all those characteristics and values associated in its symbolism: the mystery of life, birth, the body, and nature; a feeling ap-proach to life; intuitive and receptive approaches to knowing; and the values of relatedness, community, and thus wholeness itself. We enter also into the metaphor of left-handed/right-cortical modes of consciousness which process information in holistic, intuitive, spatial, and nonverbal ways, a consciousness that often bears more resemblance to insights and modalities common in Eastern philosophical and spiritual traditions than to our own Western masculine emphasis (Ornstein, 1972; 1973). This cluster of characteristics emphasizes the intuitive, the mystical, the emotional, the passive-receptive ways of understanding the world as well as the value of interrelatedness, the letting-go of individualistic ego-striving, and the im-portance of holistic concerns, community, and caring. Missing from our dominant value system, these feminine characteristics instead find expres-sion in countercultural movements (Marcuse, 1964; Roszak, 1969), in the popularity of Eastern religious movements or practices (Cox, 1977a, b), in the growing emphasis on ecology, holistic health, and transpersonal psy-chology, in our oppressed groups, in our homes, in our women, and sometimes in the mystical trends of religious teachings of the West. But we find them only rarely in the masculine marketplace that shapes our main-stream culture.

As Jung and such important Jungian analysts as Marie-Louise von Franz (1974) have written, patriarchal Christianity, the foundation of Western culture, has excluded these feminine values from formative action in the world, despite their partial affirmation in the teachings of Jesus, and has largely relegated the feminine to the shadow realm, to an association with evil and darkness. The extent to which the Christian and Western consciousness is alienated from its own undeveloped feminine values at a deeper level, is the extent to which it will link Eve and the Devil, will exclude the feminine from the trinity, and continue to dichotomize spirit and nature as a contrast of good and evil. Jung, himself a deeply spiritual person, wrote in his powerful book, *Answer to Job* (1958), that the most significant event in post-reformation religious history was the papal decision in the early 1950s to declare the new Dogma of the Assumption of the Virgin Mary. At the level of metaphor and symbol, this decision—which so often outrages Protestant rational thought—brings for the first time in Christian history a metaphysical representation of the feminine principle into Heaven in a position of full, bodily, and archetypal power. Jung was very concerned that Protestantism, currently so allied with the rational Apollonian consciousness, would neglect to see that it was in grave danger of losing any connection with the feminine. Tillich too draws our attention to the overwhelmingly masculine tone of Protestant theology and a critical need for a recovering of the feminine, mothering, nurturing, intuitive sides of divinity represented, at least to some extent, in his concept of the ground of being (Romero, 1974).

The greatest danger of long-term relegation of powerful dimensions of existence to the realm of the shadow is the tendency of those dimensions to become associated with fear and evil. Lying within the cultural shadow, the Dionysian and the feminine have received attention mostly in their negative forms as they pushed for recognition against the dominant values of a culture, and it is in this form that they often return to our resisting consciousness. Thus the values of nurturance or relatedness, when repressed, become the image of the suffocating Negative Mother; nature ignored becomes Hurricane; body ignored becomes disease; intuition ignored becomes witchcraft and the occult; emotions ignored become madness or war; community ignored gives rise to allegiance to any group which can offer relatedness and a sense of belonging. We are surrounded by the signs of such eruptions, yet they speak of an imbalance that has come close to the edge of change. The feminine and the Dionysian are calling for a place in our conception of value and reality.

Our Western culture thus stands in need of an androgynous balancing. Deeply embedded in individualistic, rational, technological, competitive values, our society would benefit greatly from the reaffirmation of the traditional feminine metaphor: a revaluation of interpersonal sensitivity, holistic perception, the values of relatedness, responsiveness, and love. These values can no longer be ignored as irrelevant or overly idealistic, nor can they continue to be relegated to the home as the special province for recuperation from a world in disequilibrium. The insights of the feminine mode of consciousness need to find expression and inform action in the external world as well.

The truly-needed cultural revolution of our time in the sex role area is thus not merely a feminist revolution in which women gain equal power and positions with men, but a revolution in which the traditional feminine values of nurturance, interrelatedness, and intuitive modes of knowing stand as legitimate alternatives to traditional masculine values, blended perhaps in new and creative syntheses that can energize new solutions to world problems. The real revolution would be an androgynous revolution, a revolution not only in terms of individual behavior, but in terms of values and modes of consciousness in which both men and women would value masculine and feminine modes of being in the world. The goal is balance and wholeness, an integration of traditional masculine and feminine qualities in an androgynous ideal for personality development, values, and consciousness. The ultimate form of revolution, in fact, might be a kind of revolution in consciousness and spirituality involving the transcendence of duality and dichotomous thinking in all spheres, unleashing tremendous cultural crossbreeding, synthesis, and integration. The revaluation of the feminine mode of consciousness as part of an androgynous goal augurs well for both scientific renewal and spiritual evolution, broadening the parameters of each pursuit and enlarging the scope of our inquiry.

What is at stake in the metaphor of the androgyne is not just the opportunity for human wholeness at the personality level but a chance for an integrated cultural consciousness that heals the most flagrant dichotomies and imbalances of our times. We are being asked to move beyond the hero myth with its stress on separation from the feminine and the feminine as enemy (Hillman, 1973) toward a new affirmation of the feminine and the ultimate transcendence of both masculine and feminine imagery in a new vision of wholeness. As Jung writes about the process of incorporating the shadow, we are asked to move through a narrow opening into an unbounded territory of "unprecedented" ambiguity, beyond all distinctions and opposites (Sarton, 1973).

The other side of the entry into the shadow is the opportunity for living beyond cultural dualities, for returning to the hieroglyphic unity of the "heart-soul" (Neumann, 1954), the joining of thought and feeling in one lived reality and inspiration. The welcoming back of the shadow is the celebration of images of wholeness yet unknown, of mythologies yet unwritten, of symbols still unshared.

MOVING TOWARD BALANCE:
Risks and Pitfalls

The search for wholeness contains many risks and pitfalls, however, and in the meantime, the guiding image of an androgynous goal and balance point must be continuously kept in mind. In a time of transition we can so easily err in overemphasizing either the masculine or the feminine to the exclusion of the other. Although the ultimate goal may be the reaffirmation of the feminine mode of consciousness into a genuinely androgynous cultural ideal, the process of arriving at this goal poses dilemmas and challenges to an evolving culture. These challenges can be explored in terms of two major dangers of emphasis. Since we represent a culture which currently overvalues the masculine, the first and greatest danger is that in liberating ourselves from traditional sex roles we will do so in ways which continue to affirm the masculine value system of our dominant culture. Accordingly, our concern must be with whether the insights of the feminine mode can be voiced in a language and metaphor that is true to the feminine, without dominant masculine metaphors and methodology from the culture intruding and distorting the message. The second and opposite danger lies in forgetting that the revaluation of the feminine is a means, not an end in itself. Overlooking this, we may flip over and embrace the traditional feminine system without seeking to relate it to our masculine values. Here the concern is with whether the feminine mode can be developed and explored without raising it to the status of a new false absolute, as onesided as the dominant masculine mode has been.

Both of these dangers seem to be present in two modern social change movements: the feminist movement and the consciousness-exploration movement. Although not often compared in this way, these two movements raise in different forms the potential for some kind of androgynous rebalancing, whether in bringing women and men into greater equality and balance in the world, as with the feminist movement, or in revalidating the more Eastern, intuitive approach to knowledge on an equal footing with Western rational-logical approaches, as advocated by the consciousness movement which has explored the avenues of Eastern thought and meditation. Both movements have aimed for integration but have been equally susceptible to exaggerations which focused on only one side of the polarities. These two cultural movements then offer helpful clues and warnings about the risks of any one-sided search for androgyny.

The Feminist Movement

The evolution of the feminist movement alerts us to perhaps the most pressing risk facing androgynous development in our time: the danger that we cannot really escape the shaping assumptions of our dominant masculine value system. It is a sad irony, in fact, that the women's movement, which wanted so desperately to reaffirm the value and role of women in our culture, came dangerously close to simply striving for equality within a male-dominated value system. Feminism was long overdue and provided a powerful first step for women toward their androgynous possibilities. Feminism brought women back in touch with their disowned personhood and legitimized for them the search for identity and consciousness. As we have seen, the myth of Psyche and her quest for selfhood was rediscovered, and Simone de Beauvoir (1953) wrote that women must claim their transcendent rights as subjects and creators of their own destinies. Stressing the values of confidence, independence, assertiveness, and choice, feminism restored to women access to those psychological characteristics previously regarded as exclusively masculine and to those domains of power, achievement, and self-actualization formerly reserved to men.

The femininst movement, however, largely failed to move beyond this affirmation of the "masculine" for women into an equal reaffirmation of the traditional "feminine" qualities and characteristics that were its heritage. Subtly and insidiously, early feminism took on the trappings of its environment, a culture dominated by the traditional masculine values of individuality, egotistic striving, ambition, violence, and analytic rationality. In an effort to avoid masculine hierarchical structures, early feminist groups often ironically unleased some of the worst of individualistic power battles and psychological violence. It is perhaps even symptomatic of feminist preoccupation with masculine values today that we stress assertiveness training for women, power issues related to affirmative action, or research on achievement motivation and issues in sexism rather than on the simultaneous cultivation of intuitive insights, inner experience, cooperativeness, love, and sensitivity. It is perhaps also symptomatic of our overvaluation of male norms that we have been extolling independent, self-actualizing life-styles for the new woman as superior to lives interwoven with commit-ments and responsibilities to and with others, a trend that Bardwick (1977) identifies as "narcissistic hedonism," echoing the individualistic norms of our masculine society.

It is not surprising that feminism, in coming so close to copying male versions of power and meaning, alienated so many women in the country whose lives were closer to the traditional feminine values. Focus-ing their highest values on equality rather than wholeness and awareness, early feminists seemed to overlook the implications for a real cultural, androgynous revolution which lay within their own potential. Even Simone de Beauvoir (1953), a powerful energizer of women's transcendent striv-ings, lacked an appreciation for what she called the "immanent," the receptive, the Yin power of woman's psyche. It took a long time for women to emerge who could write with the power and scale of de Beauvoir and move us closer to a reminder of the feminine heritage and clues for a transition to an androgynous consciousness for women and men. Included among those women are Mary Daly (1973, 1978), Anaïs Nin (1975), Irene Claremont de Castillejo (1973), Susan Griffin (1978), and June Singer (1976). Writers like Jean Baker Miller (1976) whose work is focused on a reaffirmation of traditional feminine characteristics as strengths instead of weaknesses, appeared relatively late in the second feminist renewal of the 1960s and 1970s.

The recovery of the authentically feminine has taken so long, even among feminists, that we are currently witnessing a powerful wave of feminine revivalism that threatens to err in the opposite direction, drawing us into new feminine idolatries in contrast to the previously alluring pa-triarchal themes. The beauty and power of a reawakened feminine aware-ness has captured the longings and imagination of many modern women and some embrace the rediscovery of this long neglected force with a near-cultic celebration of Woman as the expression of nature's harmony and rhythm, of oneness with the life force. The enthusiasm is the overflow-ing energy of a remembered destiny, the excitement of inner affirmation, the healing of a neglected identity. There is little writing that compares in impact and power to this affirmation and "re-membering of the Goddess," of the woman who spins her own destiny, of the independent woman, the wise one, the witch who dares to be wild and untamed in her affirmation of herself and her sisterhood of creative discovering selves (Daly, 1978). Yet, this immersion in the feminine experience, in the telling of our tales, tempts also in the direction of imbalance, and while the path into the labyrinth must be a priority in our time, the path back out requires the effort of communication with our other sides, if only for the eventual transcendence of even that androgynous image which serves as a temporary guide. We cannot afford to linger in the nostalgia of the rediscovered intuitive mode of consciousness any more than we can cling to its opposite. We must nourish ourselves continually from this source without building new shrines to guard the comings and goings of this search into ourselves.

The Consciousness-Exploration Movement

It is tempting to turn to the consciousness-exploration movement as a kind of analogue to the early feminist movement and draw some ironic parallels between a female-dominated feminist movement which advocated masculine values and a male-dominated consciousness movement which advocates feminine values. Despite this oversimplification, the emerging consciousness-exploration movement may well be a counterpoint to the early feminist movement. As the feminist movement urged women to turn outward with assertiveness in the world, the consciousness movement has encouraged men (and women) to let go of status-striving and learn to turn inward, to meditate, and to feel. Both movements raise, at different levels and in different forms, an androgynous ideal of wholeness, balance, and the integration of polarities. Both movements, too, are susceptible to exaggerations which focus on only one end of the polarity, whether in sex roles or modes of consciousness.

As in the feminist movement, the greatest risk in the consciousness movement involves the danger that we may carry our Western, individualistic, masculine metaphors into our very search for holistic, Eastern, feminine ways of knowing. The risk of carrying over these masculine metaphors can be heard in our language and tone, even in the writings of such interpreters of the new consciousness as Castaneda (1972) with his metaphor of the warrior. Ernest Becker, in *The Denial of Death* (1973), portrays the "hero" at the spiritual edge of paradox and assertive surrender to the greater whole, but his thoroughly masculine imagery and tone underscores the terror of this encounter. There is no glimpse of the feminine heritage which sees receptivity and surrender as sources of tranquility and peace. There is very little sense that surrender to the flow of the universe, which draws from a feminine metaphor, might be a very different and far less terrifying experience than surrender to some authority or absence of authority, an image which draws from a more masculine, even patriarchal, conceptualization. Existentialism, too, with its nearly total affirmation of transcendence is a masculine approach to consciousness, crucial in its understanding of the self-creative human, but only partially adequate to a comprehension of human life in all its androgynous potential.

One of the greatest risks in the pursuit of holistic philosophies and modes of consciousness is the danger that we will lapse into spiritual individualism even in the process of seeking wholeness. Eastern approaches to perceiving reality require relinquishing the personal ego and the illusion of the individual as separate from the universe. Yet how tempting and dangerously easy to pursue the Eastern path with all the energy and personal ambition of the Western personality in a kind of spiritual egotism or "spiritual materialism" as Chögyam Trungpa (1973) calls this process. In the West there has existed—and there continues to exist—a heavy focus on the individual self. As Tom Wolfe (1976) writes in "The Me Decade," we place our highest value on personal fulfillment Now. The whole thrust of psychological narcissism that characterizes contemporary culture, the compulsive focus on the self that testifies to our lack of security, has received increasing attention not only in Christopher Lasch's The Culture of Narcissism (1979) but in numerous popular sources as well.

Self-actualization has long been a psychological goal in the West, and it would be surprising if the growing consciousness-exploration movement did not take on the individualistic trappings of the humanistic psychology movement from which it has evolved. Ego appears to reside quite comfortably within the psychic-exploration movement also, somehow oblivious to the caution from Eastern writers that psychic phenomena are tempting but distracting powers along the path to spiritual realization. The West has a fascination with power and individual achievement; we might have predicted, then, the tendency for consciousness-expanding programs to claim to enhance their students' "personal power" and to offer them modes of dress or symbols which set them apart from their culture. In the West when we put on robes and beads we stand out, our spiritual quest "shows" and becomes a form of display. This is a long way from the spiritual attainments of the Zen masters which are said to resemble the "tracks" birds leave in the sky (Watts, 1965).

The spiritual achiever runs several other risks in dragging along his or her Western, masculine consciousness into the search for intuitive modes of knowing. Idries Shah (1976) has commented that it is easy to become a "spiritual technician," caught up in the technologies and techniques of consciousness-expansion. We inherit this tendency from our Western linear schedules which lead us to believe that twenty minutes of meditation upon rising, followed by fifteen minutes of yoga, a special Hindu prayer at lunch, a T'ai Chi lesson in the evening, and a round of chanting before bedtime will somehow add up to a transformed life. We carry no sense of wholeness into this search, and certainly not of surrender, which as Peter Brent (1976) argues, is an alien and pejorative concept in our culture. We would rather stay in control, stay "masculine" in our orientation, and package our "feminine" explorations in bite-sized chunks which can be more comfortably contained in our dominant system.

In the search for an androgynous consciousness, a member of Western culture who has avoided contaminating this search by an overindulgence in masculine habit patterns still faces a second major hazard. This risk consists of flip-flopping over into the opposite polarity, submerging oneself in the intuitive, Eastern, feminine approaches, and losing perspective on the androgynous goal. Peter Brent (1976), in his study of the Indian guru, cautions us about the danger of engaging in a wholesale "cultural piracy," indiscriminately importing the symbols of an Eastern tradition— guru, mantra, and ashram—without the cultural basis for understanding these traditions. Idries Shah (1976) adds that in these indulgent imitations, we mistake external appearance for inner reality. This confusion of the "container and the contents" (Ornstein, 1976), the phenomena of "recreational spirituality" (Sudano, 1980) and "Karma Cola" (Mehta, 1979) are the pitfalls of a culture hungry for the embrace of the missing feminine in Western culture, yet starving and unable to discriminate in its search for nourishment. The tendency to fall in love with symbols of Eastern consciousness illustrates, at least in part, the process of cultural projection. Having disowned the feminine mode of consciousness in our culture, we project it outwards, and fall in love with our projections rather than develop our own unused potential. Theologian Harvey Cox (1977a) argues that we created the mythical East and will have to give up these illusions if we are to discover the insights of the true "East" within our own traditions.

One of those aspects of Eastern modes of consciousness which is perhaps most tantalizing to the Westerner is the mystical experience of satori or nirvana. The Westerner, who receives little education in experiencing and working with emotion in his or her masculine culture, may easily become addicted to the pleasure of rediscovering his or her emotional, intuitive side. There is a real danger of mistaking an emotional high for spirituality. We are cautioned by Shah (1976), for example, against the "sentimentality of the emotional junkie," which we might interpret as someone who has become lost in the feminine side of the consciousness polarity and forgotten the demands of an androgynous ideal. Ram Dass (1974, 1977), Sri Aurobindo (1956), and Trungpa (1969, 1973) are among the writers and teachers who speak to this dilemma of integrating the newfound feminine consciousness and receptiveness into masculine action patterns in this world. They remind us of the dangers of ignoring our masculine heritage. They are to the consciousness movement what an earlier Mary Daly (1973) had been to the feminist movement: reminders of the androgynous ideal and the need for integrating the legacies of both masculine and feminine.

As we have seen, this integration is the goal for an androgynous culture as well as an androgynous person. The goals are complementary and mutually facilitating, but all persons face the challenge of determining for themselves where they are in this integrative process. It may well be that this is a time when most men can benefit from the emphasis on emotions and intuition found in the sensitivity, humanistic, and conscious- ness movements. A word of caution to women, however, is given by such writers as Williams (1976) and Kanter (1977): in their eagerness to redis- cover the feminine, women may overindulge in these movements and would do well to look toward cultivating masculine skills in action, plan- ning, and decision-making and to bring their intuitions into disciplined expression and evaluation in the world. For both men and women, the central challenge is to stay tuned in to the integration of masculine and feminine in their own lives and to seek experiences which will lead to greater balance. The nature of these experiences will thus shift through life, spiraling towards ever more encompassing integrations.

OPPORTUNITY FOR NEW INTEGRATIONS

At both the individual and cultural levels, there are real pitfalls and tempta- tions that accompany the "return of the repressed" and the rediscovery of the shadow in a culture which has lived out of balance for so long. The other side of the danger, however, is the opportunity for totally new ways of conceptualizing and relating to reality: new possibilities for creative styles of leadership that are both confrontive and collaborative, which carry power yet are embedded in a consciousness of interrelatedness and cooperation; new opportunities for teaching styles that integrate the academic and the personal, the cognitive and the affective; new approaches to scientific research which combine the traditional quantitative, mathematical, linear, rational-logical approaches of the experimental method with the naturalistic, holistic, qualitative richness of the case study or naturalistic change study.

Ornstein (1972) is only one of many who are calling our academic community to what is basically an androgynous revolution, a broader perspective which would revalue and legitimize "feminine" modes of knowing in active complementarity with the "masculine" approaches, enlarging both the methodology and the scope of that which is considered worthy of attention. Blackburn (1971) argues, for example, on behalf of a "sensuous-intellectual complementarity" in scientific pursuits which would reaffirm both approaches to knowledge. Feminist writers and thinkers tire of the impoverishment of logic, of the swordplay of intellectual exhibitionism, of mind-molesting in the selling, pushing, and production of the factual or what one can touch, see, count, measure, and thus claim to be real. It is not so much that intellectual machismo is powerful and envied; rather it is boring, decaying, degenerating, and doing violence to the birth of new possibility in the realm of ideas and intellectual discovery.

The possibility that the West must develop its own metaphors for the recovery of the feminine dimension of experience and consciousness was suggested by Shah (1976) who calls attention to some of the parallels discussed in Chapter 5 between modern theoretical physics and new modes of consciousness. Modern science, by backing into an appreciation of mythic and metaphorical modes of exploring the world may well offer us new symbols for androgynous perception, a wedding of quantitative rigor with qualitative insight, and a reminder that both paths are ultimately inadequate in apprehending reality in itself. The metaphor must always be transcended, even the metaphor of androgyny. As the physicist Pauli writes, the "tacit myth" for our times rests precisely in moving beyond the opposites of rationally versus mystically-derived knowledge (Jaffé, 1971). Campbell (1972), too, looks to modern science and its unexpected openness to the insights of religious perspectives as a hopeful sign of the new myths being born in our times. It is a myth which needs the guiding reminder of androgyny in order to avoid either the powerful pull of the traditional masculine scientific ethic or the tantalizing beckoning of a one-sided glorification of the feminine intuitive modes which we have only recently been willing to acknowledge.

The opportunities for new integrations and the transcendence of the polarization of masculine and feminine metaphors are particularly dramatic, however, within the field of religion and spiritual experience. Reclaiming the image of androgyny for the Judaeo-Christian perspective means recovering the missing feminine side of the divine and of human experience, suppressed within patriarchal religious traditions in Old and New Testaments. It means daring to name the divine by new names, to venture beyond the Christocentric idolatries carried by God the Father and the trinity (Daly, 1978), where spirit is male and all that is female is excluded as bodily and earthy. Feminist theology is calling us to a recognition of the mother-father god, images and language which can enable women, too, to carry the image of the divine in their very being (Christ and Plaskow, 1979). We are challenged to rediscover the image of Mary and then push it backwards into its pre-patriarchal guise to a new recognition of the power of the Goddess in all her rich manifestations and implications for life-affirming energy and "gyn/ecology" (Daly, 1978; Ruether, 1977). Feminist theology means the recovery of our feminine experience as the ground of a new "thealogy," the telling of the stories of women by ourselves as legitimate source of transformative spiritual experience (Christ and Plaskow, 1979).

To some of the feminist theologians who voice and celebrate these new visions, the concept of androgyny has grown lifeless compared to the richness of new "be-ing" that flows from the spinning of the selfhood inspired by the goddess (Daly, 1978). To Mary Daly (1978), androgyny risks becoming merely a fastening together of two essentially opposite modalities, fused in a kind of static balance that continues to encapsulate the destructive seeds of patriarchal consciousness and its perceived opposite. Starting from this duality, she argues, there can be no hope for genuine birth of wholeness. Carol Ochs (1977) likewise calls us beyond the androgynous vision, fearing that androgyny will merely mean a static stalemate rather than a total transcendence of either side of the polarity into new realms of possibility.

This danger of reifying the masculine and feminine metaphors even within the concept of androgyny has, of course, been a concern raised throughout this entire book, and we return now to its reaffirmation. Simply by the use of the concepts "masculine" and "feminine" we risk being stuck in duality. The dominance of masculine modes of consciousness is so strong and the temptations to either avoid or throw oneself into unbalanced affirmation of the feminine are so persuasive, that the image of androgyny has been proposed as an important reminder of the need for balance and integration in the search for wholeness. It is an image like all metaphors which risks distortion even while aiming at the truth, and must in the end be surrendered.

However the time for this surrender can only happen in the emerging affirmation of new forms. The search for integration of the masculine and feminine in our times is still too tenuous, too fragile before the dualistic and dichotomous concepts and norms that dominate our consciousness. It is indeed time to look beyond polarity towards the affirmation of spirit and body in a new religious consciousness (Ruether, 1979); to envision the multifaceted divine, beyond goddess and god; to affirm both the transcendent power of divinity beyond all forms and the immanent richness of divine presence in all creation; to celebrate the person who is at home in the world of passion and relatedness as well as the wandering exile searching for abstract, spiritual principles (Ochs, 1977). It is time to push beyond duality in all dimensions of culture and to be ready to receive new possibilities; it is time to carve out new roles and recognize new qualities within ourselves that emerge from the shadow of our non-dominant sides. It is time to hold before us the image of androgyny, and someday, it will be time to surrender that image too in the affirmation and living-out of a vision of wholeness yet unknown.

REFERENCES

ALLEN, M. J. "Locus of Control and Anxiety as Functions of Sex and Sex Role Identity." Paper presented at Western Psychological Association, Seattle, Washington, April 1977.

ANGYAL, A. *Foundations for a Science of Personality*. New York: Commonwealth Fund, 1941.

ANGYAL, *Neurosis and Treatment: A Holistic Theory*. Edited by E. Haufmann and R. M. Jones. New York: John Wiley, 1965.

ARGÜELLES, J. and M. *Mandala*. Berkeley: Shambhala, 1972.

ARGÜELLES, M. and J. *The Feminine*. Boulder, Colorado: Shambhala, 1977.

ASHE, G. *The Virgin*. London: Routledge & Kegan Paul, 1976.

ASSAGIOLI, R. *Psychosynthesis: A Manual of Principles and Techniques*. New York: Hobbs, Dorman & Company, Inc., 1965.

AUROBINDO, S. *The Future Evolution of Man*. Pondicherry, India: Sri Aurobindo Ashram, 1956.

AXTHELM, P. "Where Have All the Heroes Gone?" *Newsweek 94* (1979): 46.

BAKAN, D. *The Duality of Human Existence*. Chicago: Rand McNally, 1966.

BAKAN, D. "Psychology Can Now Kick the Science Habit." *Psychology Today* 5 (1972): 26, 28, 86—88.

BARDWICK, J. M. Lectures on the Psychology of Women, presented at National Science Foundation Chautauqua-Type Short Course for College Teachers, Oregon Graduate Center, Beaverton, Oregon, October, 1976 and March, 1977.

BARNETT, L. *The Universe and Dr. Einstein.* New York: Morrow, 1957.

BARRENO, M. I., HORTA, M. T., and DA COSTA, M. V. *The Three Marias: New Portuguese Letters.* Garden City, New York: Doubleday, Inc., 1975.

BARRON, F. "Originality in Relation to Personality and Intellect." *Journal of Personality* 25 (1957): 730–742.

BARRY, H., BACON, M. K., and CHILD, I. L. "A Cross-Cultural Survey of Some Sex Differences in Socialization." *Journal of Abnormal and Social Psychology* 55 (1957): 327–332.

BECKER, E. *The Denial of Death.* New York: The Free Press, 1973.

BEM, S. L. "Psychology Looks at Sex Roles: Where Have All the Androgynous People Gone?" Unpublished paper presented at UCLA Symposium on Women, 1972.

BEM, S. L. "The Measurement of Psychological Androgyny." *Journal of Consulting and Clinical Psychology* 42 (1974): 155–162.

BEM, S. L. "Sex-Role Adaptability: One Consequence of Psychological Androgyny." *Journal of Personality and Social Psychology* 31 (1975a): 634–643.

BEM, S. L. "Androgyny Vs. the Tight Little Lives of Fluffy Women and Chesty Men." *Psychology Today* 9 (1975b): 58–62.

BEM, S. L. "On the Utility of Alternative Procedures for Assessing Psychological Androgyny." *Journal of Consulting and Clinical Psychology* 45(2) (1977): 196–205.

BEM, S. L. and KORULA, C. W. Scoring packet for the Bem Sex Role Inventory. Unpublished manuscript, 1974.

BEM, S. L. and LENNEY, E. "Sex Typing and the Avoidance of Cross-Sex Behavior." *Journal of Personality and Social Psychology* 33(1) (1976): 48–54.

BEM, S. L., MARTYNA, W., and WATSON, C. "Sex Typing and Androgyny: Further Explorations of the Expressive Domain." *Journal of Personality and Social Psychology* 34(5) (1976): 1016–1023.

BERGIN, A. E. and STRUPP, H. H. "New Directions in Psychotherapy Research." *Journal of Abnormal Psychology* 76 (1970): 13–26.

BEZDEK, W. and STRODTBECK, F. L. "Sex Role Identity and Pragmatic Action." *American Sociological Review* 35 (1970): 491–502.

BIANCHI, E. C. and RUETHER, R. R. *From Machismo to Mutuality: Essays on Sexism and Woman-Man Liberation.* New York: Paulist Press, 1976.

BIERI, J. "Cognitive-simplicity as a Personality Variable in Cognitive and Preferential Behavior." In *Functions of Varied Experience,* edited by D. W. Fiske and S. R. Maddi. Homewood, Illinois: Dorsey Press, 1961.

BIRD, C. *The Two Paycheck Marriage.* New York: Rawson, Wade Publishers, Inc., 1979.

BLACKBURN, T. R. "Sensuous-intellectual Complementarity in Science." *Science 172* (1971): 1003–1007.

BLOCK, J. H. "Conceptions of Sex Role: Some Cross-Cultural and Longitudinal Perspectives." *American Psychologist 28* (1973): 512–526.

BORUN, M., McLAUGHLIN, M., OBOLER, G., PERCHONOCK, N., and SEXTON, L. "Women's Liberation: An Anthropological View." Pittsburgh, Pennsylvania: KNOW, Inc., 1971.

BRENT, P. "The Gurus: For Us and For Them." Presentation given at the Psychologies East and West Symposium, sponsored by the Institute for the Study of Human Knowledge and the University of California, San Francisco, November 13-14, 1976.

BRENTON, M. *The American Male.* Greenwich, Connecticut: Fawcett Books Group-CBS, 1966.

BROVERMAN, I., BROVERMAN, D., CLARKSON, F., ROSENKRANTZ, P., and VOGEL, S. "Sex Role Stereotypes and Clinical Judgments of Mental Health." *Journal of Consulting and Clinical Psychology 34* (1970): 1–7.

BYNNER, W. (translator). *The Way of Life According to Laotzu.* New York: John Day Company, 1944.

CAMPBELL, J. "Arthurian Romance: The Holy Grail and the Medieval Tarot." Conference seminar sponsored by Westerbeke Ranch, Sonoma, California, March 16-18, 1979.

CAMPBELL, J. *The Flight of the Wild Gander.* South Bend, Indiana: Gateway Editions, 1951.

CAMPBELL, J. *The Hero With a Thousand Faces.* Princeton, New Jersey: Princeton University Press, 1949.

CAMPBELL, J. *Myths to Live By.* New York: Bantam, 1972.

CAMPBELL. J. (ed.). *Myths, Dreams, and Religion.* New York: Dutton, 1970.

CAPRA, F. *The Tao of Physics.* Berkeley: Shambhala, 1975.

CARLSON, R. "Sex Differences in Ego Functioning: Exploratory Studies of Agency and Communion." *Journal of Consulting and Clinical Psychology, 37* (1971): 267–277.

CARLSON, R. "Understanding Women: Implications for Personality Theory and Research," *Journal of Social Issues 28* (1972): 17–32.

CARLSON, R. and LEVY, N. "Self, Values and Affects: Derivations from Tomkins' Polarity Theory." *Journal of Personality and Social Psychology 16* (1970): 338–345.

CASSIRER, E. *Language and Myth.* New York: Dover, 1946.

CASTANEDA, C. *The Teachings of Don Juan: A Yaqui Way of Knowledge.* New York: Ballantine, 1968.

CASTANEDA, C. *A Separate Reality.* New York: Simon & Schuster, 1971.

CASTANEDA. C. *Journey to Ixtlan.* New York: Simon & Schuster. 1972.

CHESLER, P. *With Child: A Diary of Motherhood.* New York: Thomas Y. Crowell, 1979.

CHODOROW. N. "Mothering, Object-Relations, and the Female Oedipal Configuration." *Feminist Studies 4*(1) (1978a): 137–158.

CHODOROW, N. *The Reproduction of Mothering.* Berkeley: University of California Press, 1978b.

CHRIST, C. P. "Why Women Need the Goddess: Phenomenological, Psychological, and Political Reflections." In *Womanspirit Rising: A Feminist Reader in Religion,* edited by C. P. Christ and J. Plaskow. San Francisco: Harper & Row, 1979.

CHRIST, C. P. and PLASKOW, J., eds. *Womanspirit Rising: A Feminist Reader in Religion.* San Francisco: Harper & Row, 1979.

COHEN, M. B. "Personal Identity and Sexual Identity." *Psychiatry 29* (1966): 1–14.

CONSTANTINOPLE, A. "Masculinity-Femininity: An Exception to a Famous Dictum?" *Psychological Bulletin 80* (1973): 389–407.

COTTLE, T. J., EDWARDS, C. N., and PLECK, J. "The Relationship of Sex Role Identity and Social and Political Attitudes." *Journal of Personality 38* (1970): 435–452.

COX, H. "Eastern Cults and Western Culture: Why Young Americans are Buying Oriental Religions." *Psychology Today 11* (1977a): 36—42.

COX, H. *Turning East.* New York: Simon & Schuster, 1977b.

COX, S., ed. *Female Psychology: The Emerging Self.* California: Science Research Associates, Inc., 1976.

DALY, M. *Beyond God the Father: Toward a Philosophy of Women's Liberation.* Boston: Beacon Press, 1973.

DALY, M. *Gyn/Ecology: The Metaethics of Radical Feminism.* Boston: Beacon Press, 1978.

DAVID, D. S. and BRANNON, R. *The Forty-Nine Percent Majority: The Male Sex Role.* Reading, Massachusetts: Addison-Wesley, 1976.

DEAUX, K. *The Behavior of Women and Men.* Monterey, California: Brooks/Cole Publishing Company, 1976.

DE BEAUVOIR, S. *The Second Sex.* New York: Knopf, 1953.

DE CASTILLEJO, I. C. *Knowing Woman: A Feminine Psychology.* New York: Harper Colophon Books, 1973.

DELIA, J. G., CROCKETT, W. H., and GONYEA, A. H. "Cognitive Complexity and the Effects of Schemas on the Learning of Social Structures." *Proceedings of the Annual Convention of the APA 5* (1970): 373–374.

DEMPEWOLFF, J. A. "Feminism and Its Correlates." Doctoral dissertation, University of Cincinnati, 1972

DE RHAM, E. *The Love Fraud.* New York: Pegasus, 1965.

DINNERSTEIN, D. *The Mermaid and the Minotaur.* New York: Harper & Row, 1976.

EDINGER, E. F. *Ego and Archetype.* Baltimore, Maryland: Penguin, 1972.

ELIADE, M. *The Sacred and the Profane: The Nature of Religion.* New York: Harcourt Brace Jovanovich, Inc., 1959.

ELIADE, M. *The Two and the One.* Chicago: University of Chicago Press, 1965.

ELLMAN, M. *Thinking About Women.* New York: Harcourt Brace Jovanovich, Inc., 1968.

ERIKSON, E. H. *Childhood and Society.* New York: W. W. Norton & Company, Inc., 1963.

FALLACI, O. *Letter to a Child Never Born.* Garden City, New York: Anchor Press/Doubleday, 1978.

FARRELL, W. *The Liberated Man.* New York: Random House, 1974.

FERRO-LUZZI, G. E. "The Female Lingam: Interchangeable Symbols and Paradoxical Associations of Hindu Gods and Goddesses." *Current Anthropology 21*(1) (1980): 45–68.

FIRESTONE, S. *The Dialectic of Sex.* New York: Morrow, 1970.

FLAX, J. "The Conflict Between Nurturance and Autonomy in Mother-Daughter Relationships and Within Feminism." *Feminist Studies 4*(2) (1978): 171–189.

FRANTZ. G. "On the Meaning of Loneliness." In *From Chaos to Eros,* a collection of presentations at a C. G. Jung Institute of Los Angeles Symposium. Los Angeles: C. G. Jung Institute, 1977.

FRENKEL-BRUNSWIK, E. "Intolerance of Ambiguity as an Emotional and Perceptual Personality Variable." *Journal of Personality 18* (1949): 108–143.

FREUD, S. *Civilization and its Discontents.* London: Hogarth Press and The Institute of Psycho-analysis, [1930], 1955.

FRIDAY, N. *My Mother/My Self.* New York: Dell, 1977.

FRIEDAN, B. *The Feminine Mystique.* New York: W. W. Norton & Company, Inc., 1963.

FRIEDAN, B. *It Changed My Life.* New York: Dell, 1977.

FROMM, E. *The Forgotten Language.* New York: Grove Press, 1951.

GINN, R. O. "Psychological Androgyny and Self-Actualization." *Psychological Reports. 37* (1975): 886.

GLENNON, L. M. *Women and Dualism: A Sociology of Knowledge Analysis.* New York: Longman, 1979.

GOLDBERG, H. *The Hazards of Being Male: Surviving the Myth of Masculine Privilege.* New York: NAL, 1976.

GOLDBERG, S. and LEWIS, M. "Play Behavior in the Year-Old Infant: Early Sex Differences." *Child Development 40* (1969): 21–31.

GONEN, J. Y. and LANSKY, L. M. "Masculinity, Femininity, and Masculinity-Femininity: A Phenomenological Study of the Mf Scale of the MMPI." *Psychological Reports 23* (1968): 183–194.

GRAVES, R. *The White Goddess.* New York: Farrar, Straus, & Giroux, 1948.

GREELEY, A. M. *Unsecular Man: The Persistence of Religion.* New York: Delta, 1972.

GREER, G. *The Female Eunuch.* New York: McGraw-Hill, 1970.

GRIFFIN, S. *Woman and Nature: The Roaring Inside Her.* New York: Harper & Row, 1978.

GRODDECK, G. *The Book of the It.* New York: Mentor, 1961.

GUGGENBÜHL-CRAIG, A. *Marriage Dead or Alive.* Zurich: Spring Publications, 1977.

GUMP, J. P. "Sex-Role Attitudes and Psychological Well-Being." *Journal of Social Issues 28* (1972): 79–92.

HACKER, H. M. "Women as a Minority Group." *Social Forces 30* (1951): 60–69.

HALL, C. S. and LINDZEY, G. *Theories of Personality.* New York: John Wiley, 1978.

HALL, N. *Mothers and Daughters.* Minneapolis, Minnesota: Rusoff Books, 1976.

HALVERSON, C. F. "Interpersonal Perception: Cognitive Complexity and Trait Implication." *Journal of Consulting and Clinical Psychology 34* (1970): 86–90.

HARDING, M. E. *The Way of All Women.* New York: Harper Colophon Books, 1970.

HARDING, M. E. *Woman's Mysteries: Ancient and Modern.* New York: Harper Colophon Books, 1971.

HARFORD, T. C., WILLIS, C. H. and DEABLER, H. L. "Personality Correlates of Masculinity-Femininity." *Psychological Reports 21* (1967): 881–884.

HARRISON, J. E. *Mythology.* New York: Harcourt Brace Jovanovich, Inc., 1924.

HARTLEY, R. E. "Sex-Role Pressures in the Socialization of the Male Child." *Psychological Reports 5* (1959): 457–468.

HEILBRUN, A. B. "Sex Role Identity and Achievement Motivation." *Psychological Reports 12* (1963): 283–290.

HEILBRUN, A. B. "Sex Role, Instrumental Expressive Behavior and Psychopathology in Females." *Journal of Abnormal Psychology 13* (1968): 131–136.

HEILBRUN, C. G. *Toward a Recognition of Androgyny.* New York: Harper & Row, 1973.

HEILBRUN, C. G. *Reinventing Womanhood.* New York: W. W. Norton & Company, 1979.

HENNIG, M. and JARDIM, A. *The Managerial Woman.* New York: Pocket Books, 1976.

HILLMAN, J. *The Myth of Analysis: Three Essays in Archetypal Psychology.* New York: Harper Colophon Books, 1972.

HILLMAN, J., NEUMANN, E., STEIN, M., VITALE, A., and VON DER HEYDT, V. *Fathers and Mothers*. Zurich: Spring Publications, 1973.

HJELLE, L. A. "Self-Actualization and Sex Role Orientation in Young Women." Paper presented at Western Psychological Association convention, Seattle, Washington, April, 1977.

HORNEY, K. *Feminine Psychology*. New York: W. W. Norton & Company, Inc., 1967.

JACUBOWSKI-SPECTOR, P. "Facilitating the Growth of Women Through Assertive Training." *The Counseling Psychologist 4* (1973): 75–86.

JAFFÉ, A. *The Myth of Meaning*. New York: Penguin, 1971.

JANEWAY, E. *Man's World, Woman's Place: A Study in Social Mythology*. New York: Morrow, 1971.

JANEWAY, E. "On the Power of the Weak." *Signs: Journal of Women in Culture and Society 1*(1) (1975): 103–109.

JARVIS, L. "Letter to the Editor." *Newsweek 93* (1979): 5.

JOHNSON, A. *The Incest Symbol and Individuation*. Senior Honors Thesis, Linfield College, 1979.

JOHNSON, R. *He: Understanding Masculine Psychology*. New York: Harper & Row, 1974.

JOHNSON, R. *She: Understanding Feminine Psychology*. New York: Harper & Row, 1976.

JOURARD, S. M. *The Transparent Self*. Princeton, New Jersey: D. Van Nostrand, 1964.

JUNG, C. G. *The Collected Works of C. G. Jung*. "Symbols of Transformation," Vol. 5, 1956; "The Archetypes and the Collective Unconscious," Vol. 9, part 1, 1959; "Psychology and Religion: West and East," Vol. 11, 1958; "Alchemical Studies," Vol. 13, 1967; "Mysterium Conjunctions," Vol. 14, 1963. Princeton, New Jersey: Princeton University Press.

JUNG, C., ed. *Man and His Symbols*. Garden City, New York: Doubleday, 1964.

JUNG, C. G. "The Psychological Aspects of the Kore." In *Essays on a Science of Mythology: The Myth of the Divine Child and the Mysteries of Eleusis*, edited by C. G. Jung and C. Kerényi. Princeton, New Jersey: Princeton University Press, 1949.

JUNG, E. *Animus and Anima*. Zurich: Spring Publications, 1957.

KAGAN, J. *Personality Development*. New York: Harcourt Brace Jovanovich, 1971.

KANTER, R. M. "Women in Organizations: Sex Roles, Group Dynamics, and Change Strategies." In *Beyond Sex Roles*, edited by A. G. Sargent. New York: West Publishing Company, 1977.

KELLY, G. *A Theory of Personality: The Psychology of Personal Constructs.* New York: W. W. Norton & Company, 1963.

KERÉNYI, C. "Kore." In *Essays on a Science of Mythology: The Myth of the Divine Child and the Mysteries of Eleusis,* edited by C. G. Jung and C. Kerényi. Princeton, New Jersey: Princeton University Press, 1949.

KERÉNYI, C. *Eleusis: Archetypal Image of Mother and Daughter.* New York: Schocken, 1977.

KOESTENBAUM, P. "The Interpretation of Roles." In *The Potential of Woman,* edited by S. M. Farber and R. H. L. Wilson. New York: McGraw-Hill, 1963.

KOESTLER, A. *The Ghost in the Machine.* New York: Macmillan, 1967.

LAING, R. D. *The Politics of Experience.* New York: Ballantine, 1967.

LANDER, K. F. *The Anima.* The Guild of Pastoral Psychology, Guild Lecture No. 32, April 1962.

LANE, A. J. Introduction to *Herland,* by Charlotte Perkins Gilman. New York: Pantheon, 1979.

LANGER, S. K. *Philosophy in a New Key.* Cambridge, Massachusetts: Harvard University Press, 1942.

LASCH, C. *The Culture of Narcissism.* New York: W. W. Norton & Company, Inc., 1978.

LAYARD, J. *The Virgin Archetype.* Zurich: Spring Publications, 1972.

LEAKEY, R. E. and LEWIN, R. *Origins.* New York: Dutton, 1977.

LEGUIN, U. *A Wizard of Earthsea.* New York: Bantam, 1968.

LEGUIN, U. Introduction to *The Left Hand of Darkness.* New York: Ace Books, 1976.

LEONARD, L. "Amazon Armors." *Psychological Perspectives 10* (1979): 113–130.

LESHAN, L. *The Medium, the Mystic, and the Physicist.* New York: Ballantine, 1966.

LEWIN, K. "The Conflict Between Aristotelian and Galileian Modes of Thought in Contemporary Psychology." *Journal of General Psychology 5* (1931): 141–177.

LEWIS, M. "Culture and Gender Roles: There's No Unisex in the Nursery." *Psychology Today 5* (1972): 54–57.

LINDBERGH, A. M. *Gift from the Sea.* New York: Vintage Books, 1955.

LOEVINGER, J. "The Meaning and Measurement of Ego Development." *American Psychologist 21* (1966): 195–206.

MACCOBY, E. E. "Sex Differences in Intellectual Functioning." In *The Development of Sex Differences,* edited by E. E. Maccoby. Stanford, California: Stanford University Press, 1966.

MACCOBY, E. and JACKLIN, C. *The Psychology of Sex Differences.* Stanford, California: Stanford University Press, 1974.

MacKinnon, D. W. "The Nature and Nurture of Creative Talent." *American Psychologist 17* (1962): 484–495.

Marcuse, H. *One-Dimensional Man.* Boston: Beacon Press, 1964.

Maslow, A. H. "Self Esteem (Dominance Feeling) and Sexuality in Women." *Journal of Social Psychology 16* (1942): 259–294.

Maslow, A. H. *Toward a Psychology of Being.* Princeton, New Jersey: D. Van Nostrand Company, 1962.

Maslow, A. H. *Religions, Values, and Peak-Experiences.* New York: Viking, 1970.

Masters, R. E. L. and Houston, J. *The Varieties of Psychedelic Experience.* New York: Delta, 1966.

Masters, R. and Houston. J. *Mind Games: The Guide to Inner Space.* New York: Delta, 1972.

Masters, R. and Houston, J. *Listening to the Body.* New York: Delacorte Press, 1978.

May, R. *Love and Will.* New York: Delta, 1969.

McGlashan, A. *Savage and Beautiful Country: The Secret Life of the Mind.* New York: Hillstone, 1966.

Mead, M. *Sex and Temperament in Three Primitive Societies.* New York: Dell Pub., Co., Inc. [1935], 1969.

Mehta, G. *Karma Cola: Marketing the Mystic East.* New York: Simon and Schuster, 1979.

Miller, D. L. "Orestes: Myth and Dream as Catharsis." In *Myths, Dreams and Religion,* edited by Joseph Campbell. New York: Dutton, 1970.

Miller, J. B. *Toward a New Psychology of Women.* Boston: Beacon Press, 1976.

Money, J. and Ehrhardt, A. A. *Man and Woman, Boy and Girl.* Baltimore: John Hopkins University Press, 1972.

Morgan, E. *The Descent of Woman.* New York: Bantam, 1972.

Morris, D. *The Naked Ape.* New York: Dell Pub. Co., Inc., 1967.

Mussen, P. H. "Long-Term Consequents of Masculinity of Interests in Adolescence." *Journal of Consulting Psychology 26* (1962): 435–440.

Needleman, J. *A Sense of the Cosmos.* New York: Dutton, 1965.

Neumann, E. *The Origins and History of Consciousness.* Translated by R. F. C. Hull. Bollingen Series XLII. Princeton, New Jersey: Princeton University Press, 1954.

Neumann, E. *The Great Mother.* Princeton, New Jersey: Princeton University Press, 1955.

Neumann, E. *Amor and Psyche: The Psychic Development of the Feminine.* Princeton, New Jersey: Princeton University Press, 1956.

Neumann, E. "On the Moon and Matriarchal Consciousness." In *Fathers and Mothers,* by J. Hillman, E. Neumann, M. Stein, A. Vitale and V. von der

Heydt. Zurich: Spring Publications, 1973.

NICHOLS, J. *Men's Liberation: A New Definition of Masculinity*. New York: Penguin, 1975.

NIN, A. *A Woman Speaks*. Edited by Evelyn J. Hinz. Chicago: Swallow Press, 1975.

OCHS, C. *Behind the Sex of God*. Boston: Beacon Press, 1977.

OETZEL, R. "Annotated Bibliography." In *The Development of Sex Differences*, edited by E. E. Maccoby. Stanford, California: Stanford University Press, 1966.

OLSEN, T. "The Mother Tongue." Lecture at a symposium on women and literature: The First Word: Women, Language, Writing. Reed College, Portland, Oregon, Feb. 7-9, 1979.

ORENSTEIN, G. "Goddess Themes, Symbols, and Energies in Contemporary Art by Women." A slide presentation at the Great Goddess Re-Emerging, a conference sponsored by University of California Extension, Santa Cruz, March 31-April 2, 1978.

ORNSTEIN, R. *The Psychology of Consciousness*. San Francisco: W. H. Freeman & Company Publishers, 1972.

ORNSTEIN, R. E., ed. *The Nature of Human Consciousness*. San Francisco: W. H. Freeman & Company Publishers, 1973.

ORNSTEIN, R. E. "Eastern Psychologies: The Container Vs. the Contents." *Psychology Today 10* (1976): 36, 39, 43.

ORWELL, G. *Nineteen Eighty-Four*. New York: Harcourt Brace Jovanovich, Inc., 1949.

OTTO, W. F. *Dionysus: Myth and Cult*. Bloomington, Indiana: Indiana University Press, 1965.

PEARCE, J. C. *The Crack in the Cosmic Egg*. New York: Julian Press, 1971.

PERLS, F. S. *Gestalt Therapy Verbatim*. Lafayette, California: Real People Press, 1969.

PLECK, J. H. and SAWYER, J., eds. *Men and Masculinity*. Englewood Cliffs, New Jersey: Prentice-Hall, 1974.

POLSTER, E. and POLSTER, M. *Gestalt Therapy Integrated*. New York: Brunner/Mazel, 1973.

POSTLE, D. *Fabric of the Universe*. New York: Crown Publishers, 1976.

PUTNEY, S. and PUTNEY, G. J. *The Adjusted American: Normal Neuroses in the Individual and Society*. New York: Harper & Row, 1964.

RAM DASS. *The Only Dance There Is*. Garden City, New York: Anchor Press/Doubleday, 1974.

RAM DASS. *Grist for the Mill*. Santa Cruz, California: Unity Press, 1977.

RANK, O. *The Trauma of Birth*. New York: Harcourt Brace Jovanovich, Inc., 1929.

RICH, A. *Of Woman Born*. New York: Bantam, 1976.

Romero, J. A. "The Protestant Principle: A Woman's Eye View of Barth and Tillich." In *Religion and Sexism,* edited by R. R. Ruether. New York: Simon & Schuster, 1974.

Roszak, T. *The Making of a Counter Culture.* Garden City, New York: Anchor Books/Doubleday, 1969.

Roszak, B. and Roszak, T., eds. *Masculine/Feminine: Readings in Sexual Mythology and the Liberation of Women.* New York: Harper & Row, 1969.

Ruether, R. R. "The Personalization of Sexuality." *Christianity and Crisis 33* (1973): 59–62.

Ruether, R. R. *Mary—The Feminine Face of the Church.* Philadelphia: The Westminster Press, 1977.

Ruether, R. R. "Motherearth and the Megamachine: A Theology of Liberation in a Feminine, Somatic and Ecological Perspective." In *Womanspirit Rising: A Feminist Reader in Religion,* edited by C. P. Christ and J. Plaskow. San Francisco: Harper & Row, 1979.

Rychlak, J. F. *A Philosophy of Science for Personality Theory.* Boston: Houghton Mifflin, 1968.

Saiving, V. "The Human Situation: A Feminine View." In *Womanspirit Rising: A Feminist Reader in Religion,* edited by C. Christ and J. Plaskow. San Francisco: Harper & Row, 1979.

Sanford, J. "Healing and Wholeness in the Gospels and in Psychotherapy Today." Lecture sponsored by the Oregon Friends of C. G. Jung and the Department of Lay Ministries, Portland, Oregon, November 9, 1979.

Sarton, M. *Journal of a Solitude.* New York: W. W. Norton & Company, Inc., 1973.

Shah, I. "A Psychology of the East" and "On the Nature of Sufi Knowledge," two presentations given at the Psychologies East and West Symposium sponsored by the Institute for the Study of Human Knowledge and the University of California, San Francisco, November 13-14, 1976.

Sheehy, G. *Passages.* New York: Dutton, 1974.

Sherman, J. A. *On the Psychology of Women.* Springfield, Illinois: Charles C. Thomas, Publisher, 1971.

Shostrom, E. L. *Man, the Manipulator.* New York: Bantam, 1968.

Singer, J. *Boundaries of the Soul.* Garden City, New York: Anchor Press/Doubleday, 1973.

Singer, J. *Androgyny: Toward a New Theory of Sexuality.* Garden City, New York: Anchor Press/Doubleday, 1976.

Slater, P. *The Pursuit of Loneliness.* Boston: Beacon Press, 1970.

Slater, P. *Earthwalk.* Garden City, New York: Anchor Press/Doubleday, 1974.

Smith, B. "Ariadne: Her Thread." Tape from the C. G. Jung Institute of Los Angeles Conference, "The Feminine," October 25-26, 1975, Immaculate Heart College, Los Angeles.

SMITH, B. "The Mirror of Aphrodite." Tape from the C. G. Jung Institute of Los Angeles Conference, "The Living Dream," May 14-15, 1977, Immaculate Heart College, Los Angeles.

SMITH, B. "Myself the Twins." Seminar on the twin motif in Greek myth as part of the C. G. Jung Institute of Los Angeles Summer Session, June 20, 25, 27, 1978a.

SMITH, B. Conference on the Feminine in Mythology: The Myth of Psyche and Eros. Los Angeles, California (Lake Arrowhead), August 10-16, 1978b.

SMITH-ROSENBERG, C. "The Female World of Love and Ritual: Relations between Women in Nineteenth Century America." *Signs 1*(1) (1975): 1–29.

SONTAG, L. W., BAKER, C. T., and NELSON, V. A. "Mental Growth and Personality Development: A Longitudinal Study." *Society for Research in Child Development Monographs, 23* (1958): 68.

SPENCE, J. T., HELMREICH, R., and STAPP, J. "Ratings of Self and Peers on Sex Role Attributes and their Relation to Self-Esteem and Conceptions of Masculinity and Femininity." *Journal of Personality and Social Psychology 32* (1975): 29–39.

SPRETNAK, C. *Lost Goddesses of Early Greece.* Berkeley, California: Moon Books, 1978; Boston: Beacon Press, 1981.

STEIN, M. "The Devouring Father." In *Fathers and Mothers,* by J. Hillman, E. Neumann, M. Stein, A. Vitale, and V. von der Heydt. Zurich: Spring Publications, 1973.

STEINMANN, A. and Fox, D. J. *The Male Dilemma: How to Survive the Sexual Revolution.* New York: Jason Aronson, 1974.

STONE, M. *When God was a Woman.* New York: Dial Press, 1976.

STRAHAN, R. F. "Remarks on Bem's Measurement of Psychological Androgyny: Alternative Methods and a Supplementary Analysis." *Journal of Consulting and Clinical Psychology 43* (1975): 568–571.

SUDANO, G. R. "Exorcising the Demons of Academe." *The Chronicle of Higher Education 19* (January 28, 1980): 17.

SUZUKI, D. T. *An Introduction to Zen Buddhism.* New York: Grove Press, 1964.

TART, C. "States of Consciousness and State-Specific Sciences." In *The Nature of Human Consciousness,* edited by Robert E. Ornstein. San Francisco: W. H. Freeman & Company Publishers, 1973.

TAVRIS, C. and OFFIR, C. *The Longest War: Sex Differences in Perspective*. New York: Harcourt Brace Jovanovich, 1977.

TOBEN, B. *Space-Time and Beyond.* New York: Dutton, 1975.

TOFFLER, A. *Future Shock.* New York: Random House, 1970.

TOMKINS, S. S. "Left and Right: A Basic Dimension of Ideology and Personality." In *The Study of Lives,* edited by R. W. White. New York: Atherton

Press, 1963.

TRIBLE, P. "Eve and Adam: Genesis 2-3 Reread." In *Womanspirit Rising: A Feminist Reader in Religion,* edited by C. P. Christ and J. Plaskow. San Francisco: Harper & Row, 1979.

TRIPODI, T. and BIERI, J. "Cognitive Complexity, Perceived Conflict, and Certainty." *Journal of Personality, 34* (1966): 144–153.

TRUNGPA, C. *Meditation in Action.* Berkeley, California: Shambhala, 1969.

TRUNGPA, C. *Cutting Through Spiritual Materialism.* Berkeley, California: Shambhala, 1973.

ULANOV, A. B. *The Feminine in Jungian Psychology and in Christian Theology.* Evanston: Northwestern University Press, 1971.

VAN DER POST, L. *The Heart of the Hunter.* New York: Morrow, 1961.

VITALE, A. "The Archetype of Saturn or Transformation of the Father." In *Fathers and Mothers,* by J. Hillman, E. Neumann, M. Stein, A. Vitale, and V. von der Heydt. Zurich: Spring Publications, 1973.

VON FRANZ, M-L. *Problems of the Feminine in Fairytales.* Zurich: Spring Publications, 1972.

VON FRANZ, M-L. *Shadow and Evil in Fairytales.* Zurich: Spring Publications, 1974.

VON FRANZ, M-L. and HILLMAN, J. *Lectures on Jung's Typology.* Zurich: Spring Publications, 1971.

WARNER, M. *Alone of All Her Sex: The Myth and the Cult of the Virgin Mary.* New York: Pocket Books, 1976.

WATTS, A. *The Two Hands of God: The Myths of Polarity.* New York: Collier Books, 1963.

WATTS, A. "The Religion of No-Religion." Tape recording of lecture. Sausilito, California: MEA, 1965.

WATTS, A. *The Book: On the Taboo Against Knowing Who You Are.* New York: Collier Books, 1966.

WHITEHEAD, A. N. *Science and the Modern World.* New York: Mentor, 1925.

WILLIAMS, E. F. *Notes of a Feminist Therapist.* New York: Dell, 1976.

WOLFE, T. "The 'Me' Decade and the Third Great Awakening," *New York Magazine 9* (1976): 26–40.

WOLFE, V. *A Room of One's Own.* New York: Harcourt Brace Jovanovich, Inc., 1929.

WORELL, J. and WORELL, L. "Support and Opposition to the Women's Liberation Movement: Some Personality and Parental Correlates." *Journal of Research in Personality 11* (1977): 10–20.

ZIMMER, H. *Myths and Symbols in Indian Art and Civilization,* edited by Joseph Campbell. Princeton, New Jersey: Princeton University Press, 1946.

Index